UNSEEN FORCES

THE INTEGRATION OF
SCIENCE, REALITY & YOU

112

UNSEEN FORCES
THE INTEGRATION OF
SCIENCE, REALITY & YOU

Robert Davis, Ph.D.

Visionary Living Publishing/Visionary Living, Inc.
New Milford, Connecticut

Unseen Forces: The Integration of Science, Reality and You

By Robert Davis, Ph.D.

Copyright 2019 by Robert Davis, Ph.D.

Front cover design by April Slaughter
Back cover and interior design by Leslie McAllister

ISBN: 978-1-942157-46-5 (pbk)
ISBN: 978-1-942157-47-2 (epub)

Visionary Living Publishing/Visionary Living, Inc.
New Milford, Connecticut
www.visionarylivingpublishing.com

To my wife, Randy – My love will last till time is through.

To my children, Michelle and Scott, and grandson, Jack – You are the answer to what my life is about.

TABLE OF CONTENTS

INTRODUCTION

Overview: Although humankind as a species is about three million years old, modern civilization is only approximately 10,000 years old, and it was only about 2,000 years ago when perspectives we contemplate today were initiated from a few enlightened individuals who strove to make sense of reality. Only in the last few centuries have western societies researched the nature of reality and the relationship among the physical sciences, the spiritual, and the supernatural realms. The great divide between spirituality and the physical world did not prevent the founders of modern science, such as Galileo, Copernicus, Einstein, Kepler, and Newton, from having a deep spiritual mindset to seek truth as their writings affirm. And today, there is a resurgence of spirituality with more people having a personal spiritual, or Peak Experience (PE).

A PE is usually understood as a way of being that evolves from a profound incident of reality, known as a mystical, religious, or spiritual experience. There are numerous descriptions of one's spiritual experience in religions—a direct experience of reality that transcends the separation of mind and body, and the separation of self and reality. The essential feature of the PE is a profound sense of oneness with all—a sense of belonging to the universe as a whole. Researchers in the neurosciences, physics, and philosophy are trying to better understand the concept of one's spirituality and "sensation of the mystical" or the surreal, and how it may interact with the physical laws of nature, the brain, and "consciousness."

Throughout recorded history, people have reported PEs and other extraordinary experiences from intuition and dream insights to the paranormal and extrasensory perception. However, in today's world dictated by Newtonian physics, many of these experiences are associated with superstition and delusion and described as "woo-woo" by skeptics and scientists. The general scientific community, for instance, contends no acceptable theory can appropriately assess and validate the inexplicable anecdotal reports by those who have had a PE since they violate known scientific principles. For this reason, the PE has received very little research attention. This is unfortunate for many reasons, especially since eminent scientist Albert Einstein described the essence of this unique experience as follows: "The most beautiful and profound emotion we can experience is the sensation of the mystical. It is the fundamental emotion which stands at the cradle of true art and true science...the mystery of the eternity of life, and the inkling of the marvelous structure of reality."[1]

Even today, many truth seekers question how Einstein's "sensation of the mystical" may relate to the scientific view of many unseen forces and phenomena addressed in this book, as follows: (1) the peak experience or transcendent moment; (2) the mind-body relationship, consciousness, and the power of intention; (3) extrasensory perception (ESP); (4) interactions with unidentified aerial phenomena (UAP) and non-human entities (NHE); (5) the out of body experience (OBE) and near death experience (NDE); (6) after death communication (ADC) and death bed visions (DBV); (7) the biofield, alternative medicine, and energy healing; and (8) synchronicity.

The Soul and "I"

Ever since life crawled out of the primordial soup and evolved into self-aware, inquisitive and inventive bipedal primates, humans have wondered if one's personal identity—you, the soul or "I"—is just the physical body. A human being contemplating one's existence is like a fish contemplating water; an identifiable component that is part of a larger organism—the universe. Unlike the thinkers of the past who did not have the benefits of current technology to test their theories, the current scientific materialist viewpoint is that the brain facilitates your sense of "I," intention, and free will. Not surprisingly, therefore, science has yet to verify whether "consciousness"—a term to be used instead of "I," "soul," or "spirit"—acts independent of the brain, what it is, what it does, how it functions, where it originates, and why it even evolved.

Consequently, explaining the functioning of the brain in terms of just neuroelectrical events, while stimulating at some level, has not yet solved the mystery of why or how it *feels* like something to *be* a conscious self. By default, except for a few brain regions which appear to be loosely related to the sense of identity, science has no explanation for the mechanism that governs and regulates the profound and inexplicable anecdotal features of the PE. After all, the spiritual realm is not compatible with science. For spiritual phenomena such as souls and the PEs to be real, most of science would have to be wrong. It likely is.

It has been said that "we have too much intellect and too little soul, but too little intellect in matters of soul."[2] This is as true today as it has been throughout history. And historically, the location of the soul—an immaterial spirit of a yet to be discovered energy within the body but is also distinct from the human body. Termed "psyche" by the Greek and "anima" by the Romans, the soul is immortal—death is simply a transitional phase of life when the soul departs from the body. But if the soul is immortal, when does this entity of energy enter the body—when the sperm enters the egg or during embryonic development? Does the soul influence the body, mind and intellect? Is the soul the same thing we call consciousness? What happens to it after it leaves the body? And where, in the body, does the soul reside? If you ask a Hindu philosopher, the soul is the God within each of us. If you ask a hardcore materialist scientist, you are nothing more than your brain. If you should ask your neighbor next door, beneath the quizzical look, any and all possible scenarios based on their religious teaching, experiences, and a touch of "gut feeling" will likely come your way. So, who holds the ultimate truth? Just maybe it is deep within you.

The prominent debate of the soul revolves around two distinctly opposing issues: (1) the soul is spiritual and immortal, and (2) the soul is material and mortal. This paradox is beyond a play on words. There is no agreed upon criteria to define the "soul," spirituality, and "immortality." Another confounding variable is the indefinable nebulous task to determine whether the soul is located in a specific organ, infuses the entire body, or even resides beyond the universe.[3] For some, the quest for answers to explain the difference between the body and the soul comes from religious figures, while others look to science for answers. But answers for the soul is something science will likely never provide. To science, the answer is in the form of biochemical processes in the brain. And while that may not be the answer you seek, it cannot be disproven so it may be true.

If you ask a hardcore materialist if an immortal "immaterial spirit" resides within the body, expect the prevailing response to be "gobbledygook." To a neurosurgeon, expect an answer in the form of a complex biochemical explanation, such as, the soul exists as "the cocktail of brain soup and spark within the deep cerebrum and brainstem, whence dopamine, noradrenaline, acetylcholine are released in a fountain-like arrangement on to the more sophisticated regions of the cortex and immediate subcortical structures to produce a series of electrical and chemical events."[4] Moreover, neuroscientist V. S. Ramachandran contends that there might be a soul in the sense of "the universal spirit of the cosmos," but the "soul that occupies individual brains and that only evolved in humans is complete nonsense. Belief in that kind of soul is basically superstition."

This is the typical mantra expected from materialistic, biased viewpoints who dismiss the soul as a non-scientific idea because it is not measurable in today's world of science. Based on this mentality, unless something can be measured and analyzed by traditional scientific techniques, it must not exist. This unsubstantiated viewpoint serves only one purpose—to impede any potential progress toward a better understanding of the human condition and meaning of life. Didn't I warn you? But you can't really place all the blame on neurosurgeons since they are taught early on in their academic careers that the brainstem is the "abode of the soul."[5] So, instead of asking, "How are you today?" maybe the more precise phrasing should be "How is your brainstem today?"

Aside from debating the location of the soul, why do we even consider belief in the soul? Noted psychoanalyst Otto Rank felt that belief in the soul evolved to reassure ourselves of immortality. He said, "The collision (between our need and the fact of death) created a spark in our individual and social consciousness that through history has become both consolation and inspiration: the immortal soul, whether fact or fiction, gives comfort."[6, 7] I take some comfort in speculating about the soul and maybe that comfort alone is the purpose of the soul's concept. Is the soul just a conceptual non-material theory, or is it an immortal energy that resides in the brain, the pit of your stomach, or beyond the cosmos? Is the loving and compassionate part of you an aspect of your personality or does it come from experiences of the soul? These innate qualities have been evolving for billions of years and you are a by-product of this cycle of evolution within the universe to which you are connected. You are one and the same with the cosmos and the Earth. For this reason alone, one intuitively aches to see the balance of our planet's life decay in a sea of ecological pollution, the depleted ozone layer, and melting glaciers. If we are indeed an intellectual species, we should better understand the delicate balance between the soul of life and our physical world.

Maybe your intuition, or that aspect of you which reflects the higher capacity of mind, connects the soul with your personality of knowing right from wrong. Intuition alone may provide the best evidence for the soul's existence. Your intuitive process, in other words, reflects communication between the personality and your soul. When you make a decision, you use information from your mind, brain, and intuition or "gut-feeling," that informs your soul to act. But how and when to act is more art than science and the brain often gets in your "intuitive" way. How many times have you questioned in hindsight that you should have listened to your first intuitive impression instead of acting without acknowledging it? It is not possible to always know the right decision and resulting course of action to take and, hopefully, we learn from our mistakes. Answers that emerge from the intuitive process may challenge you to follow its direction, especially when your brain begins to rationalize the problem at hand. The brain often muddles the decision-making process, but you know the truth. You need to be secure knowing that you are far more capable than your brain in guiding you down the one of many paths most appropriate to take.

Intuitively, you may feel you have a soul or something beyond the brain that is the essence of you—the soul or "I." But intuition cannot prove the existence of the soul any more than it can prove the existence of God. But we don't need to be able to see and measure something to prove its existence as science requires. Some things are real that simply cannot be proven using pure scientific methods. You can't measure love or a broken heart, but it certainly is as real as the measurable microscopic world of atoms and cells. These particles didn't exist in the world of science until we developed the microscope which allowed us to discover and study a new world of phenomena. But they existed before the microscope. Maybe the next discovery will identify the existence of who you truly are.

We can't look to science for answers to every unseen aspect of your body, mind, and soul. You, like love, cannot be identified, observed, measured, computed, or calculated. And maybe that alone proves you are not just your physical brain. But the initial challenge toward new discovery is to question that which does not exist or, at least, is acknowledged by science.

The ability to use intuition and existing knowledge to guide us is the key. History tells us that an unseen force like gravity can exist despite our inability to see and measure it. So, will you be realized like gravity was when an apple fell from a tree on a scientist's head? Newton had to first contemplate the possible existence of gravity to connect the dots toward discovery. Today, the contemplation of an unseen force of a yet-to-be discovered energy in the form of a soul or you should not be considered nonsense or a product of superstition. The PE may be today's apple ready to fall from somewhere above.

The Peak Experience

Overview: Humankind from the beginning of its existence has asked the same questions you may have asked, "How was the world created?" "What is its nature and destiny?" and "What is the origin, purpose and meaning of life and all things?" Historically, the answers were usually found in the world of the gods. Today, we still seek answers to life in philosophy, science, and religion. But, although the answers for many questions are incomplete, poorly defined, or not adequately supported by scientific verification, some contend to have obtained the answers from their self-transcendent experience or PE.

The PE represents the broad classification of spiritual, mystical, and extraordinary experiences widely reported throughout human history and across cultures. It is characterized by various types of altered or non-ordinary states of consciousness beyond the realm of normal everyday awareness that feel more real than "real-life" experiences.[8-11] Such states may contain indescribable awareness of time, space, and physical reality—characterized by perceptions of oneness/interconnectedness with the universe, ineffable emotions, alterations of time and/or space, insight and wisdom, and visionary encounters and communication with the divine (Deity) and NHEs (angels, apparitions, the alien "greys" elves, and fairies, etc.).

The PE applies not only to the similarity of such reports but also to the feeling of one's consciousness separating from the body, telepathic communication, increase in intuitive and psychic capabilities, a sense that reality is a manifestation of one cosmic creative energy, and dramatic changes in one's personal and philosophical viewpoints—life, health, love, death, and spirituality, resulting from the PE. Those who have had a PE see themselves as more than just physical stuff and contend to be more humane, aware and alive.[12]

Over the past decade, the PE has been the focus of increasing research interest. This emphasis makes sense since the PE can have a profound effect on the psychological health of those who experience it. Subjectively, the PE represents an intense and unifying experience which many call "pure consciousness"—one in which there is no subject-object distinction. That is, there is no content but rather a transformational process that often results in remarkable change in one's attitudes about life, truth and even the nature of reality.

The PE is often believed to be the medium for access into an unseen realm by those who experience it. The realization of this indefinable realm facilitates a new perspective by which one's daily waking consciousness and experiences are perceived differently. Remarkably, the PE can serve as a central aspect of transformation in one's life.[13] A PE can have a profoundly positive effect on the human psyche—"your sense of self completely dissolves and you feel at one with the universe."[14] But whether the PE allows one to access an alternate dimension is an enduring mystery and the central theme of this book. Regardless of its cause or characteristics, however, the PE has been recognized as a fundamental aspect of human nature among all belief systems throughout humankind. But is it a normal innate tendency or an illusion created by the mind?

What is a Peak Experience?: One of the most influential psychologists of the twentieth century, Abraham Maslow, best known for defining a human's Hierarchy of Needs, starts with the basic building blocks of life (food, water, warmth) and culminates with the "highest plane" or self-actualization.[15] This state of self-actualization or PE, represents an "ego-transcending moment" accompanied by "epiphanies," and emotions such as "wonder at the oneness with the world, awe, and reverence seen only as beautiful, good, desirable, and worthwhile. It is an "awareness of ultimate truth and the unity of all things and the loss of placing in time and space" that makes one feel "eternal and in touch with God."[16] This state of self-transcendence is characterized by a shift in focus from the self to others accompanied by a change in values. This shift from selfishness and egoism to consideration of the needs of others is the core feature of self-transcendence. Those who have achieved self-transcendence no longer find themselves driven by extrinsic motivation, or external rewards and demands, but by intrinsic motivation—the reward for an activity is the activity itself.[16]

A similar description of self-actualization was provided by Walter Stace, a pioneer in the philosophical study of mysticism, who described the subjective characteristics of a PE or "mystical" experience as follows: (1) undifferentiated unity—diminished spatial and temporal awareness; (2) a sense of "oneness with the world"—dissolution of the self; (3) feeling of revelation—profound joy and peace; (4) a sense of "divinity"; (5) ineffability—the difficulty of expressing the experience in words; and (6) the transformation of the subject's "moral character from evil toward good and nobility."[17]

One example of a PE triggered by an OBE was described by my friend J.P., who wrote: "When I am in an OBE in a higher plane, or around non-human intelligent beings, my emotions are very different. I have no fear, nothing negative, it's pure bliss, and it feels right. These dimensions look very different than our typical physical surroundings. They are very beautiful, and full of nature in its purity, consisting of vibrant colors that glow."[19]

Such revelations, considered as vividly real by millions of others like J.P. are often explained by Western science as a type of dream-like, dissociative or psychotic episode—not to be interpreted literally as evidence of the "supernatural." Although this interpretation does apply in some cases, it is certainly premature to firmly conclude that all PEs are pathologic in nature. Some PEs provide one of the most memorable and subjectively significant events in life. But the nature and significance of the PE is debatable. To some, the PE is a guarantee of truth or some kind of personal guarantee of an insight the mind considers most profound. The PE is therefore a signal that states: "This is amazing, don't ignore it, and try to understand it." The PE seems to function as a path towards marked insight—something to dwell upon and do something about. But a vital component of the PE is how it changes the lives of those who experience it. The PE should not be simply a passive feeling of ecstasy and insight. Indeed, episodes of quiescent bliss and personal insight are easily confused with PEs. But what they signify is controversial.

Some people regard the PE as the way to a truly healthy, ideal human life. By this account, normal everyday life is an abnormal state during which we function at a lower level — not running on all cylinders, so to speak. Everyday life is less than human, and only during PEs are when we behave fully alert, aware, conscious, and alive. According to this notion, PEs provide a privileged insight into reality. Because they represent a higher state of consciousness, knowledge obtained in this state has greater validity than the insights of the normal, sub-optimal level of consciousness associated with everyday ordinary life.[20]

To others, the PE is a window onto a transcendental reality, a pathway to a higher evolutionary conscious state. Although individuals who report having PEs are also likely to have experiences involving intense happiness, they are even more prone to report having cognitive experiences of a transcendent and mystical nature.[21] This suggests that although the PE involves positive affect, it is primarily a transcendent and mystical consciousness-based event.

The PE has special significance. It is associated with particular circumstances, and it transforms one's personal behavior and goals. The profound subjective significance of a PE is not open to serious doubt—but the objective validity of the content of that experience is another matter. The type of PE focused on in this book, therefore, is the one that changes one's personal viewpoints from that moment forward—an extraordinary ego-transcending moment that has a profound impact on one's life and the way the world is perceived from that moment forward. As Maslow wrote, "A single glimpse of heaven is enough to confirm its existence even if it is never experienced again. Experiencing an "awareness of ultimate truth" is the "openness to finding the extraordinary in the ordinary. They give meaning to life itself."[2]

If one is familiar with the PE literature, it becomes apparent there is far more than just pure brain-based events to explain the nature and essence of a personal event that has left millions breathless and yearning for an answer to the questions: What happened to me? Why me? Am I more than a physical body? These same questions must have been asked by those who had a PE throughout time. One can only speculate if the PE contributed to ancient cultural beliefs in the existence of the supernatural. Every culture observed by anthropologists, for instance, has endorsed beliefs and practices predicated on the existence of human-like beings with non-human properties, such as beings who change shape, read minds, or control the weather and our behavior.

Even in more recent times, a 2013 Harris Poll found that in the United States alone, about 42 per cent believe in ghosts, 64 per cent in survival of the soul after death, 68 per cent in heaven, and 74 per cent in God.[23] According to Huffington Post/ YouGov and Pew Research polls, up to 65 percent of American's believe in paranormal/supernatural phenomena that include spiritual energy, premonitions and interacting with the dead.[23] Surprisingly, most scientists are not materialists. In a 2009 Pew poll on religion, only 40 percent of scientists considered themselves to be atheists, while 50 percent believed in God, a universal spirit, or a higher power.[23] And "you can bet your bottom dollar" that a large percentage of those who pray to a "higher power" on a Sunday denounce the validity of the peak experiencer (PEr) who claims to have interacted with a "Supreme Being" and/or other forms of NHEs on Monday. Their biased contradiction is annoyingly palpable. Maybe times haven't changed as much as we may think?

There are millions of individuals today who have had spiritual, mystical, and extraordinary experiences who long for an explanation of "what just happened to me?" Unsolved problems can be the greatest teachers. Maybe noted astrophysicist Carl Sagan captured it best in his remark that, "Science is not only compatible with spirituality; it is a profound source of spirituality. When we recognize our place in an immensity of light-years and the passage of ages, when we grasp the intricacy, beauty and subtlety of life, then that soaring feeling, that sense of elation and humility combined, is surely spiritual."[24] Since millions of people maintain a faith-based belief in some form of heaven, God, and the supernatural, if science has something to say about such beliefs and the PE, we should listen. But science tends to negate the validity of the PE despite the fact that it feels vividly real and has a dramatic longstanding and largely positive effect on those who experience it. Yet one thing is very clear: those who have had a PE consider it as genuine as the nose on their face. If the PE and associated phenomena are someday proven to be authentic by science, it will certainly have profound implications at the individual, societal, and religious/spiritual levels. Such ramifications are certainly a matter of speculation and awe.

Triggers of the Peak Experience

There are several types of "trigger events" that facilitate a PE. These include: the near death Experience (NDE); out of body experience (OBE); unidentified aerial phenomena (UAP); psychoactive drugs; after death communication (ADC); deathbed visions (DBV); and interactions with non-human entities (NHE) or the deceased. A brief synopsis of each PE trigger follows:

The Near Death Experience: The NDE is a life-threatening crisis characterized by dissociation from the physical body (OBE) and transcendental or mystical elements. Although NDEs have been reported for centuries, they have become more prevalent as technological medical advances in recent decades have increased the incidence of life saving measures from the brink of death and the associated NDE. An NDE typically occurs to individuals "close to death or in situations of intense physical or emotional danger."[26] It has also been reported to occur during states of meditation, severe psychological events,[27] and even in healthy individuals present during a loved one's death.[28]

The NDE has served as a primary source of evidence to support the validity of a PE and even life after death. To the experiencer, the NDE is so vivid and real that it is believed to represent the separation of one's consciousness from the brain. The most common characteristics of the NDE include: (1) an awareness of being dead; (2) an improved mood (e.g., intense feelings of pure love, euphoria, happiness, and well-being); (3) an OBE; (4) entering a tunnel-like realm; (5) a sensation of movement; (6) a perception of a heavenly or hellish landscape; (7) an encounter with deceased relatives, religious figures, or beings of light; and (8) an experience of a life review."[25]

The term "veridical perception" is used to denote accurate perceptions of events from a vantage point outside the physical body during an NDE. This incorporates the appearance of three simultaneously occurring components to test the validity that consciousness may function independently of the body. These components consist of: (1) "normal or enhanced mentation when the physical body is ostensibly unconscious; (2) seeing the physical body from a different position in space; and (3) perceiving events beyond the normal range of the physical senses."[29] For these reasons, the NDE is one of the most intriguing research topics in the physical and social sciences.

The Out of Body Experience: An OBE, or the sense of being out of one's body, is one of the key components of expanded spiritual awareness and is becoming a more common occurrence for many people. A common feature of an NDE is the OBE. As in NDEs, those who have an OBE report to have perceptions from a position outside and above their body—a feeling that they have removed their body like an old suit and have retained their own identity and a very clear consciousness.

An OBE is often very vivid and resembles everyday, waking experiences rather than dreams. Many individuals report having a second body called an "astral body" and that their consciousness is contained within this body similar to that when awake.[30] When their "astral body" travels away from their physical body, they may report that: (1) their consciousness goes with it; (2) they don't believe they left their body; and (3) their consciousness linked to this second body will persist after death. Many who report this experience do not sense leaving their body but recognize this only when they observe their body and realize that it is "me down there."

Some individuals report to have had an OBE during their daily routine in their normal waking state, but for the majority the experience occurs spontaneously during the sleep process. To explain them, it has been suggested that they stem from brain disorders and/or psychological reactions to approaching death; a type of wishful thinking in response to the perceived threat.

Unidentified Aerial Phenomena: Extraordinary phenomena not identifiable as a known object in the sky is termed an unidentified flying object (UFO); however, the term unidentified aerial phenomenon (UAP), a preferred and more neutral alternative to UFO, will be used throughout this book. Whatever the term used, the startling fact is that millions of individuals worldwide have reported to experience varying types of interactions with this phenomenon.

Belief in UAPs as extraterrestrial craft has remained high over the past several decades, especially since UAP researchers have continually asserted that: (1) NHEs in physical craft have visited our planet and abducted humans; (2) the military has retrieved crashed UAPs; and (3) the government/military continue to withhold information of UAPs from the public. Several formal military and government sponsored investigations conducted worldwide (Project Blue Book, Grudge, Sign, The Robertson Panel, Project Condign, and the COMETA report, etc.) have consistently found that approximately 90-95 percent of reported UAPs are explainable with the remaining of unknown origin.[31] Since a very small percentage cannot be reliably identified as "known" objects or events, we must accept the fact that UAPs do exist. The key question is whether any of the 5-10 percent unexplained UAP represent a physical craft governed by NHEs.

The UAP has been characterized by rapid acceleration from a stationary position, hovering for long periods of time, descending like a leaf falling as if wobbling, and changing shape. But despite frequent UAP reports, the lack of tangible, objective evidence has compromised our ability to determine if the UAP is associated with: (1) NHEs from another planet (extraterrestrial) or space-time (intra-dimensional); (2) psychological and/or cultural influences; and/or (3) atmospheric, geological, and/or meteorological phenomena, among other possibilities.

The UAP provides the foundation for explaining the alien abduction phenomenon (AAP); an individual's conscious or hypnotic induced recall of contact with UAP occupants. More specifically, the AAP entails various physical and/or non-physical interactions with a NHE that may include one or more of the following experiences: (1) sensing the presence, interacting, and/or communicating with a being; (2) biological procedures;

(3) telepathic communication; (4) altered perceptions; and (5) other physiological and psychological forms of interaction and outcomes.

Interactions with Non-Human Entities: Interactions with NHEs have been described by humans within folklore and religious texts over the centuries and across all cultures. Historically, humans believed that many types of NHEs existed as the forces at work "behind the scenes" in our natural world. The only thing that has changed is what we call them. The common visual and narrative themes throughout time, across cultures, and in Bible texts, strongly imply that all NHEs (spirits, magical beings, alien "greys," apparitions, and angels, etc.) may be one and the same manifestation, perhaps evolving as we do or just perceived through the eyes of the current times.

The NHEs our ancestors portrayed as gods, angels or spirits from the heavens, appear to be today's "extraterrestrials" or "aliens" from another planet and/or alternate dimension. They have been described to range in height from just a few inches to over 10 feet tall, and in appearance from small hairy dwarfs, to bald giants, to human-looking. Many display odd behavior and speech content and perform ghost-like feats such as walking through walls despite their solid flesh and blood impression.

Psychoactive Drugs: A psychoactive drug is a chemical that changes your state of consciousness, perception and mood. You likely take one or more of these drugs every day. They are commonly found in everyday foods and beverages, such as caffeine in chocolate, coffee, and soft drinks; and in alcohol and over-the-counter drugs, such as aspirin, Tylenol, and cold and cough medication. Psychoactive drugs are also prescribed as sleeping pills, tranquilizers, medical marijuana, and anti-anxiety medications.

Psychoactive drugs such as dimethyltryptamine (DMT), psilocybin and LSD produce hallucinogenic effects and PEs. DMT may even be produced in the pineal gland of the brain and facilitate dreaming and natural visionary states such as mystical experience, NDE, OBE, psychosis, and encounters with NHEs. Many DMT experiencers come away from these encounters convinced of alternate realities, life after death, and that there is an objective spiritual presence in the universe.[32]

After Death Communication and Deathbed Visions: After death communication (ADC) is an experience that occurs when one is contacted directly by someone who has died. A form of ADC is the deathbed vision (DBV), represented by cases in which a sick individual reports the bedside appearance of a dead relative, friend, or a being of light to guide one through the dying process. Caregivers and loved ones of the dying often report attempts by the dying individual to communicate with someone only visible to themselves. Spontaneous ADC and DBV experiences have been reported to positively impact the grieving process and to provide for a spiritually transforming experience on dying individuals and their family.[33]

The PE and its triggers may be products of imagination, but it is also possible that these experiences point to unconventional sources that deserve far greater attention than currently allocated by science. For the general scientific community, it may be prudent to consider the broader notions of extraordinary experiences in the form of the PE and its triggers that may complement conventional methods of achieving a greater understanding of unique human experiences. This is the essence of this book. Achieving an objective perspective of such experiences is required if science is to evolve toward a new paradigm shift. We still know very little about the true nature of extraordinary personal experiences, and the possible theoretical existence of alternate realities.

Seeing a Different World or Seeing this World Differently?

Human consciousness has been a focus of study in the fields of neuroscience, biology, psychology, physics, and philosophy. Scholars across these disciplines have attempted to better understand the nature and meaning of consciousness, and how our brain provides a sense of an individual "self." This objective has been approached in different ways consistent with the theoretical principles and research methods unique to each discipline. Despite these efforts, there remains no widely accepted theory of how your brain facilitates your sense of reality and what you know, self-awareness, intention, and abstract thought.

The PE is intimately associated with the nature and function of consciousness. Given our limited understanding of consciousness, several questions fundamental to the PE remain unanswered. Those who report a PE, for example, often sense their consciousness leaving their body and the ability to communicate telepathically with the deceased and NHEs. In other words, is consciousness a by-product of your brain or does it exist independently of your brain?

The reason why some people believe that consciousness is not the brain and may persist after physical death is based on experimental evidence of "nonlocality." Nonlocal intuition, a concept often associated with the PE, suggests that humans can exchange information without the use of their sensory systems. This exchange transcends space and time, and intentionally effects change in other people and physical systems at a distance.

This ability includes the broad spectrum of phenomena associated with extrasensory perception (ESP), such as: (1) telepathy (communication between minds); (2) precognition (prediction of future events); (3) clairvoyance and remote viewing (perception without the use of known physical senses); and (4) psychokinesis (manipulation of physical objects by mental influence).

While evidence to support nonlocal intuition is an important step toward understanding consciousness and the PE, it is another thing entirely to explain the mechanism which governs and regulates them. ESP and nonlocality violate established scientific laws that govern known sensory and cognitive abilities. But this fact does not completely dismiss the possibility that ESP and nonlocality are valid characteristics of human ability.

If you are a truth seeker, you may wonder with fierce determination, like I do, whether an aspect of your consciousness can separate from the body and perceive the world without your normal sensory systems, communicate telepathically with deceased relatives when near death, or interact with NHEs. Does the PE provide access to an alternate realm, or is it either a misinterpretation of explainable events or an illusory induced physiological/psychological manifestation? These possibilities, or something else we simply cannot conceive of or even explain using scientific principles at hand today, leave truth seekers, and especially PErs yearning for answers. What may be the most important concern of all is whether the characteristics of the PE provide sufficient evidence that proves you are not just a physical body. While it is certainly easy to ask these questions, it is entirely another thing to provide answers with confidence. Despite our ability to more effectively study this phenomenon than ever before, definitive answers to the many questions associated with the PE remain tenuous at best.

Discussion

The collective theories and associated compelling experimental and anecdotal evidence presented in this book are designed to demonstrate that you are indeed interconnected with reality in a nonlocal manner. What is common to all nonlocal phenomena, like ESP and the PE, is that their occurrence requires the perception of information without any physical mechanism through which this information can be communicated.[34]

For this reason, it remains a scientific challenge to discuss new hypotheses that explain the reported PE in the form of experiencing: (1) an interconnectedness with the consciousness of other persons and of deceased relatives; (2) an instantaneous and simultaneous dimension without our conventional body-linked concept of time and space, where all past, present, and future events exist; (3) a clear consciousness with memories, self-identity, and cognition of perceiving one's body from a vantage point above their body during an OBE/NDE; and (4) the retrieval of accurate information sent by another person without the use of their ordinary senses (nonlocality). For these reasons, you may be connected by an invisible yet-to-be discovered energy that science is only now beginning to realize—the biofield.

Spiritual masters have known for centuries that everything and every event in the universe is interconnected with every other thing and event in the universe. This interconnection may be allowed for by the "biofield" and justified by the Quantum Hologram Theory of Consciousness.

This invisible connection may be the mechanism that facilitates the realization that there is far more to the world than that which is seemingly known and seen in those who have had a PE. We have yet to determine if brain activity and/or this invisible connection facilitates the essence of the PE, let alone your "gut feeling," "broken heart," burning sense of revenge, and the feeling of unconditional love when you first looked into the eyes of your newborn child. Language alone fails to capture the profound essence of emotion that elevates one's awareness and purpose in life incurred from a PE, or when one must decide to sacrifice their life for another, or realizing death is imminent. But science cannot "capture" how a rubber-like mass of fat and protein consisting of some 100 billion nerve cells, with each cell capable of processing activities much more complex and faster than a computer, can facilitate such indescribable sensations.

Given this context, this book provides a foundation for you to formulate an opinion to many associated elusive questions such as, what is consciousness? (1) Is consciousness independent of your brain and does it persist after death? (2) Are the PE and associated phenomena valid? That is, can the PE be explained as an altered state of consciousness facilitated by the brain, or are humans interacting with an alternate reality and NHEs? (3) Why does the PE facilitate similar transformations in one's personal and philosophical viewpoints? (4) Can the PE be explained by principles within quantum physics and/or neuroscience? and (5) Are there invisible connections between humans that allow for nonlocal intuitive perceptions (ESP)?

Addressing these concerns in a relatively short narrative is a daunting, if not impossible, task. This task becomes all the more difficult given the lack of justification for what governs and regulates the nature of consciousness and one's interpretation of reality. Explaining the interrelated concepts of "consciousness" and "reality" becomes all the more complex when trying to explain the poorly understood altered perceptions and behavioral after-effects facilitated by the PE. But given humans' innate tendency to have more confidence in information consistent with your beliefs than that which differs from your viewpoints, it may be challenging for you to maintain an objective perspective of the many interrelated concepts and evidence in this book. So, if the validity of the PE and associated phenomena are to be evaluated without bias, it is necessary for you to find a way of bypassing the barriers of any preconceptions and wishful thinking before deciding if you should believe an alternate realm is as real as the PEr believes it to be.

The overriding concern of this book is this: Does the PE provide evidence that people are "seeing a different world, or are they seeing this world differently?" Related to this overarching concern is whether existing evidence provides clues to perceived encounters with an unseen realm and its inhabitants, that seem to permanently transform the personal and philosophical viewpoints of millions who experience these encounters. The ultimate foundation to this topic of concern is this—are you just a brain? Within this context, this book may help you develop a more informed perspective of the many controversial and intriguing issues of the PE, reality, and you. After all, the only way to truly know the answers is to study what we don't know... the unexplained. Let's begin.

CHAPTER 1

CONSCIOUSNESS, THE BRAIN, AND "YOU"

Introduction

The nature and function of consciousness must first be addressed before one accepts the existence of alternate realms and the convincing reports by those who contend to have communicated with NHEs and the deceased. After all, if one is able to access other dimensions and/or interact with NHEs and the deceased, then it should be a non-physical form of "you," not bound by space and time that, in some inexplicable way, is capable of doing so. The question of how consciousness emerges from the brain lies at the heart of this issue.

Your consciousness and/or a yet to be discovered aspect of brain activity, facilitate subjective interpretations of the physical world that give you meaning. But have you ever considered why you are conscious, or if the essence of "you" is nothing more than a jellylike mass of fat and protein consisting of some 100 billion brain neurons that resides above your shoulders? Above all, how

1

and why did the subjective sense of "I" arise from lifeless matter? The objective world of science provides only theories to explain conscious experience and the sense of "I." The answer may serve as the necessary pre-requisite to determine once and for all if consciousness creates your reality, or instead, does the physical universe create your consciousness?

An extension of these overarching concerns is whether consciousness is a form of energy that is either independent of the brain or a pure brain-based event, or did it evolve as an outcome of language? Despite the absence of a definitive answer, it seems surreal that a three-pound mass of tissue lying between my ears enables the passionate feeling of unconditional love for another, the deep, awe inspiring wonder of nature's beauty, and the ability to intend and plan for the future. Or is consciousness simply an aspect of life not to be questioned and just "is"?

The evolution of scientific discovery from Galileo's proof of a heliocentric universe and experiments paved the way for the methods of classical mechanics by Isaac Newton, the unified field theory by Einstein, to when Neil Armstrong first set foot on the moon. These accomplishments led to advanced technologies and principles that have generated extraordinary increases in our capacity to formulate and analyze information. Despite this revolution, many more questions than answers exist about the nature of our reality, and our evolving planet and expanding universe. The overarching fundamental question has remained the same. That is, is conscious experience a part of concrete reality and an intrinsic aspect of the universe?

Consciousness

Overview: Human consciousness is one of the most far-reaching ambiguities of our time. It's like asking how we think about our own thinking, or how we can become aware of our own awareness. How do you know that you are "you"? Does your sense of being aware of yourself come from an aspect of "you" that exists apart and interrelates with your body, or is it just your body that is creating it? First, we must ask, what is consciousness?

Consciousness, sometimes referred to as "qualia" or moments of experience, is what make us human. That "I am aware of being aware" represents the act of consciousness. Our personal experiences and characteristics of sensation such as pain, love, and depression, and feelings and sensations, decision-making, and free-will make you feel alive and give you a sense of purpose. Consciousness incorporates your awareness of the world. This concept alone has served as a major focus of study in the fields of neuroscience, biology, psychology, philosophy, and physics. But the search to understand the nature and meaning of consciousness and how your brain provides a sense of an individual "self," intention, and abstract thought remains a controversy. The problem is that attempts to solve the mind-brain relationship have been approached in different ways consistent with the theoretical principles and research methods unique to each field of study.

There is even considerable controversy in the use of the term "consciousness," which is often used in different ways. In biology and medicine, consciousness is studied in terms of brain mechanisms of arousal and responsiveness (alertness through disorientation, loss of communication, and depth of coma), and on identifying brain regions which mediate sensory and motor signals that induce feelings of self-location and the first-person perspective. In contrast, consciousness studies in psychology and cognitive science tend to focus on asking verbal reports of experiences and subjective states (self-awareness, subliminal messages, denial of impairment, and altered states produced by drugs and meditation).

In light of such diverse definitions and associated theories of consciousness, it is not surprising that vastly different approaches have been used to study it within the scientific community. This narrow focus ignores the importance of integrating contributions of knowledge from other disciplines. Consequently, bias is created through this filtered lens, as if searching for gold with blindfolds and stone knives.

Consciousness: An endless stream of papers written on consciousness has been generated by scholars across many disciplines over countless decades in an attempt to better understand the nature and meaning of consciousness, and how your brain provides a sense of an individual "self." But despite these efforts, there remains no widely accepted theory of how the brain facilitates self-awareness, intention, and abstract thought. This overwhelming mass of information has even failed to generate a uniformly accepted theory as to what consciousness is.

So, apparently with nothing to lose, my two-cents' worth is that consciousness may be defined by five behavioral attributes: (1) realization of one's location and relative position in space and time; (2) recognition and reaction to other people's physical and emotional behaviors; (3) recognition of one's social behavior within the context of environmental situations; (4) intuition—one's insights, feelings, and impressions to understand something without thinking or reasoning of possible future events relative to one's knowledge of situations, events, and laws governing the universe; (5) free-will or the decision of choice to decide if and how to pursue one's destiny. This is enabled through one's ability to constantly sense, interpret, and make predictions based on information received which is then acted upon to create expected future outcomes to oneself and others; and (6) ESP—nonlocal communication with other minds.

The search for neural correlates of consciousness may never explain the essence of the mind-brain relationship or the "hard problem" of consciousness (how reality comes about from the physical activity of our nervous system) or help to better understand "qualia," which has never been proven as fact. Some scientists, however, believe that the subjective attributes of consciousness will eventually be found within the nervous system. Hardcore materialists, for instance, believe that the "mind-body" concept is a misnomer because there is only the body.[2]

According to the materialist mindset, all aspects which define a specific thing (color, smell, behavior, physical attributes, etc.) are represented as bits of information in neurons which the brain synthesizes to arrive at the final neural representation. Consequently, a neural analog for everything we know and experience subjectively may provide the biological foundation that enables you to determine that this is a flower, a car, or a human, etc.

Related to this theory is the view that your conscious activity, subjective experience, and decision making processes are facilitated from the collective functioning of computational networks of correlated neurophysiological activity which incorporate all incoming sensory information among many brain regions (cortical-thalamic, brainstem and limbic networks) that is interpreted into a meaningful whole.[3,4,5] Consciousness may not emerge from a specific brain region but instead arises from the integrated output of billions of neurons which communicate with one another. Or not.

The reason "consciousness" equates with the brain in conventional science is that manifestations of consciousness, such as free will, determinism, and planning for the future are considered to be driven by neuronal impulses of the brain. Consciousness, which escapes objective measurements of its space, time, and functionality, creates your life and reality. Your conscious intention is capable of great things, such as playing a major role in your health and well-being, sharing love, modifying brain activity, and even by affecting your genes. It can be trained through meditation to improve your emotional state, cognitive abilities, and to even reduce pain. So, is it my brain telling me to meditate, or is it me telling my brain to execute the behavior of meditation to improve certain aspects of my world? Besides confusing, the question comes down to who is minding the store? Several assumptions applied in the study of these topic areas have served as a foundation to test the consciousness-brain distinction. These include:

(1) Consciousness is a by-product of brain activity. Consciousness is eliminated along with the body upon death. We are gone forever.

(2) Consciousness is not dependent on the brain and can affect physical matter outside the body. It extends beyond normal space/time.

(3) Consciousness extends beyond the brain and persists after bodily death. It suggests a mechanism and explanation for

5

the PE and associated phenomena. The mind doesn't seem to follow the rules we usually apply to the physical world.

The connection between human consciousness and the physical world is precisely why so many of the founding fathers of quantum physics were so preoccupied with learning more about consciousness, and "non-material" science in general. Eminent physicist Max Planck regarded "consciousness as fundamental" and matter as "derivative from consciousness." Eugene Wigner, another famous theoretical physicist and mathematician, also emphasized how "it was not possible to formulate the laws of quantum mechanics in a fully consistent way without reference to consciousness,"[6] and Nobel Prize-winning physicist Erwin Schrödinger believed that ESP could be explained by realizing that our consciousness is immersed in the quantum mechanics wave function which serves as a "field of consciousness" over the Earth.[7] Sir John Eccles, the physiologist who received the 1963 Nobel Prize for his work on the nervous system, also believed that "ESP and PK are weak and irregular manifestations of the same principle which allows an individual's mental volition to influence his own material brain."[8]

The expression "which comes first, the chicken or the egg?" seems to apply to the different perspectives of the PE. The Western scientific community, for instance, does not support the conclusion by those who have had a PE that they have interacted with another reality. This notion is inconsistent with their cultural background and scientific mindset, which views matter as the ultimate form of reality, and believes consciousness is a characteristic of it.

The Eastern perspective is the exact opposite, with the ultimate reality being consciousness and the physical universe a byproduct of it. In other words, science considers what is perceived with the senses to be the highest form of reality, whereas, the Eastern view considers that higher faculties of mind must be developed in order to interact with reality in a more direct way. But a paradox exists with the scientific perspective since discoveries in physics tell us that matter is profoundly different from what our senses tell us. Noted physicist David Bohm agreed that it makes "no sense to separate physical effects from spiritual effects."[9]

6

Although the conclusions by such great minds are grounded in scientific logic and were arrived at methodically, experientially, rationally, and even mathematically, the concepts that emerge of interconnectedness, consciousness, and higher intelligence are decidedly non-material. If they are correct, then consciousness may indeed be an aspect of "I" and not the brain and possibly even persist in some unseen, unknown realm of existence upon death. But if mainstream materialist scientists are correct, once the hard drive is shot, so goes memory and one's conscious perception of reality—it's all "dust to dust and ashes to ashes." While the general scientific community considers consciousness an aspect of brain function, there exists anecdotal, theoretical, and experimental evidence to suggest that consciousness may be independent of the physical body and somehow capable of transcending the physical world. This concept is a dilemma that ultimately rests with you.

You may regard this indefinable, unproven, and intangible thing called "consciousness" as irrelevant and not worth discussing since it may represent wishful thinking, religious and/or cultural indoctrination, scientific, emotional, and/or intuitive reasons or possibly even a touch of your "gut feeling." The brain obeys all the physical laws of the universe. It's not anything special. Yet, it's the most special thing in the universe. That's the paradox.

Is the Universe Conscious? Is consciousness a basic feature of the universe? It is according to the Integrated Information Theory (IIT) theory proposed by neuroscientist Giulio Tononi.[10] The IIT, the most popular neuroscience theory on consciousness today, provides the foundation for a mathematical formalization of both the quantity and quality of conscious experience. The IIT considers that a "central network of brain regions" with high capacity for information integration enables consciousness.

The IIT applies not only to the human brain but also to all physical matter. That is, every particle in existence has a form of consciousness, and if the information contained within the structure is sufficiently "integrated," it will allow for more complex forms of consciousness, such as humans' subjective experiences. The IIT essentially tells us that the "more possible links between

7

cells, the more possible combinations there are and therefore a greater number of thoughts are possible."[11] Consciousness is informationally very rich and depends on physical matter but is not regulated by it. Your experience of seeing and hearing a bird in flight is networked to your brain but is different from your brain. The bird's color and sound are an integrated part of your experience which cannot be subdivided. A computer analogy may explain this elusive concept. When you have a family picture up on your computer screen, the machine doesn't know that the boy and girl are your children. To your computer, the children represent a meaningless random cascade of 0s and 1s. But the picture obviously has meaning to you because your memories and feelings are uniquely integrated with your children's picture.

Not to purposely confuse you more than you already may be, just about everyone in consciousness studies is now adopting the view that consciousness is a universal feature of all things. This represents an extension of the IIT called "panpsychism." Guess what, "panpsychism" says that consciousness exists in molecules and atoms, perhaps as some kind of quantum mechanics effect that somehow represents a well-designed explanation for your subjective experience. Even neuroscientist Christof Koch, considers that IIT offers a "scientific, constructive, predictive and mathematically precise form of panpsychism for the 21st century" and a "gigantic step in the final resolution of the ancient mind-body problem."[12]

Does this view imply that the universe may be self-aware? It has even been proposed that the "quantum vacuum, which is thought to contain all the information of our history—from the Big Bang to now—is also consciousness. Everything in the universe, therefore, has consciousness; from a pebble to a tree, to a cloud, to a person." Now, try to wrap your head around the notion that these informational fields of consciousness, called the zero-point-field or Akashic Field, contain all knowledge, wisdom, and unconditional love. Language alone just doesn't do it.

Maybe the evolving field of IIT and "panpsychism" will eventually provide an answer to the subjective experience and associated questions in the form of the existence of a higher consciousness, divine consciousness, or cosmic consciousness.[13]

No one can say for sure, despite statements made with certainty by so many in the absence of supporting evidence. What we do have is anecdotal evidence to support theories of "interconnectedness," "unconditional love," and "cosmic consciousness" from those who have had a PE triggered by a NDE. One individual NDE account that illustrates this notion is as follows: "My mind and spirit felt as if they might burst with all my new-found knowledge. At once, I was taken up into a brilliant light. An energy and vibration, deep and profound, shook me like thunder in my bones. A booming voice spoke..."I AM"...and I knew immediately who was with me. The spirit of God surrounded me, and His light permeated every part of me, filling me to overflowing. As His radiant love soaked into me, every question I ever had was answered. Every wondering and pondering were put to rest with knowledge from this higher source. Answers from the universe were downloaded into my DNA. I didn't have to try to remember or retain the information; it became part of me. As questions came to mind, the answers were immediately there. All my past hurts were reframed by the bright shining love of God that surrounded me."[14]

Similar to the reported accounts by NDErs, this perceptual description is certainly inconsistent with the view of mainstream science. Nevertheless, there are many highly respected scientists who contend that the universe is, in fact, conscious. If it is indeed true that each subatomic particle exists as a tiny conscious entity, then maybe consciousness represents the missing link from Einstein's Unified Field Theory—consciousness will be on par with electromagnetic, gravitational, and the nuclear forces that describe universal reality.

Many scholars of our time consider that "fields of consciousness are stored in a dimension without our concept of time and space," with non-local and universal interconnectedness in the "quantum vacuum, with a holographic cosmic memory by interference patterns of scalar wave fields."[15-17] It is hard, if not impossible, to fathom that "the interconnectedness with these informative fields of consciousness explains enhanced intuition, prognostic dreams and visions—seeing apparitions at the moment of death and in the period following death, like being in contact with the consciousness of dying persons on a distance, or of deceased relatives, the so-called peri- and post-mortal experiences or after-death communication."[18]

If consciousness is nonlocal, then why don't we sense it routinely as part of our normal waking experience? If nonlocality is a core feature of consciousness, as it is in ESP, then what prevents you from using it? Must it be cultivated through awareness and teachings from childhood before it becomes vestigial like your appendix? Nonlocality, along with meditation, would seem to be much more productive to the well-being of the individual if such teachings began early in life to cultivate the mind-brain potential. Such educational pursuits would seem to be more important than the established fruitless and non-productive practice of forcing young kids to remember the dates of historic events, and debating who discovered America, among other useless information that serves no beneficial and creative purpose.

Are You the Brain?

Overview: Think about this: The brain makes you human. It helps to facilitate art, music, language, ethics, rational and abstract thought, and how you sense and interpret the world. But making sense of the brain's mind-boggling complexity isn't easy. It is incomprehensible to think that all this comes from a jellylike mass of fat and protein consisting of some 100 billion neurons and associated 100 trillion synapses where substantial local and long-range simultaneous communication appear to be involved in very complex decision-making tasks. But this does not still provide evidence to explain the elusive "subjective experience." Science simply has yet to identify the neurological substrate which facilitates many aspects of our extraordinary brain's behaviors.

The Brain: The book you are reading right now may be a hallucination. You, the part of you that's conscious, that makes decisions, is on the very front tip of the brain. The rest of the brain, those automated systems that do all this wonderful stuff for you, are creating the reality around you. But you are the captain of the ship and steer the brain to filter the most important aspects of physical reality you wish to experience, process, interpret, and react to.

Neural processes may explain functions such as how sensory input is represented as a motor output, and certain cognitive activities like working memory, but how and why these functions are accompanied by conscious experiences remains unknown. The question is: how do your personal experiences, emotions, actions, and free will emerge from this three-pound sophisticated biological learning machine that constantly learns by re-wiring its neural networks over time to life events? The sheer complexity of your brain's interrelated network alone requires the application of mathematical and neurobiological models to attempt to understand how it functions. It is impossible to fully comprehend. Given its extraordinary complexity, it is not surprising that no one knows exactly how information is coded through this system and how it facilitates consciousness.

To understand the basics of brain function, we need to know the current state of the billions of neurons and their 100 trillion interconnections in terms of their output intensity, frequency and phase of these connections, and the state of more than 1,000 proteins that exist at each synapse. On top of all that, how do we account for the distinct differences of each brain brought about by the uniqueness of each person's life history?

Neurologists and neurosurgeons are constantly dealing with matters of life and death in patients who have fallen into the deep hole of unconsciousness. Inevitably, many ponder spirituality and the soul's domain to consider an afterlife. Neurosurgeons often attempt restoration of the brain using deep brain stimulation or ablation and some operations are even executed on awake patients. These procedures can provide clues to the functions of the mind in relation to the brain.

For example, when an electrical current stimulates certain brain regions, the person can have a vivid lifelike experience, and when brain chemicals are disturbed, they can alter one's perception, personality, and cognition.[19] Chemicals within the nervous system, such as adrenaline, serotonin, dopamine, and the endorphins, allow for and modify the many functions of your brain, mind, and body we take for granted. "Our personalities, the entities that make us both unique and predictable as individuals, emerge out of these patterns of chemical release."[20]

By studying brain abnormalities, we have learned that emotion and thought are correlated with brain regions. When brain tissue dies, a part of the mind can disappear. One may lose the ability to name common objects, recognize people, anticipate outcomes, empathize with others, or accurately identify their location in space. The left and right hemispheres, for example, are characterized by qualitatively different modes of cognitive processing—the left being basically analytic and sequential, the right spatial, nonverbal, non-mathematical and non-sequential in nature. Now, new technologies can literally read a person's mind and tell a cognitive neuroscientist whether the person is imagining a face or a place. Neuroscientists can even delete a gene in a mouse that prevents the mouse from learning or insert extra genes to facilitate faster learning.[21]

Studies on patients who have suffered brain injury provide clues on the mind-brain relationship. Damaged frontal lobes, for instance, lose their inhibitory influences on the limbic system, which results in aggressive behaviors, and abnormalities to a specific area in the dominant cerebrum results in expressive and/or receptive language disorders. Damage near the base of the left temporal lobe abolishes the capacity to understand spoken language. Speech continues to be heard but the meaning is lost.[22] This tells us that word comprehension resides in the left hemisphere. A few examples of specific areas of the brain linked to characteristics attributed to the mind include the relation between the volume of grey matter in the frontal lobes and intelligence; the inferior parietal lobules and spatial reasoning and intuitions on numbers, and the third interstitial nucleus in the anterior thalamus and homosexuality. Despite your brain's ability to organize your experience of "self" and the world into a seamless unity, the loss of brain activity in damaged regions can have dramatic effects on the whole person.[23-25]

Moreover, electrical stimulation of certain areas of the brain trigger vivid memories of past events. According to neurosurgeon William Penfield: "This is a startling discovery. It brings psychical phenomena into the field of physiology. It should have profound significance also in the field of psychology provided we can interpret the facts properly. We have to explain how it comes about that when electrical impulses are applied steadily to the cortex it can cause a ganglionic complex to recreate a steadily unfolding phenomenon, a psychical phenomenon."[26,27] When activated, it reproduces the thoughts and emotions experienced during the original experience.

Nobel Laureate Roger Sperry's concepts of the mind were shaped, in part, by his observations made after splitting the corpus callosum and thus, the two brain hemispheres.[28] His experiments showed that the cat with divided corpus callosum now had two minds either of which was capable of learning on its own, and of responding intelligently to changes in the world around it on its own. Such experiments led Sperry and others to conclude that each of the separated hemispheres has its own sensations, perceptions, thoughts, feelings, and memories. They constitute two separate minds, two separate spheres of consciousness: "splitting the brain amounts to nothing less than splitting the self."[29, 30] According to Sperry, "The more we learn, the more complex becomes the picture for predictions regarding any one individual and the more it seems to reinforce the conclusion that the kind of unique individuality in our brain networks makes that of fingerprints or facial features appear gross and simple by comparison."[31]

Moreover, neuroscientist R. Carter, who described techniques for mapping the brain and mind stated: "It is now possible to locate and observe the mechanics of rage, violence and misperception and even to detect the physical signs of complex qualities of the mind like kindness, humor, heartlessness, gregariousness, altruism, mother-love and self-awareness."[32] Carter pointed out the on-going debated implications of such findings by concluding: "whilst the optimist might wish for a complete understanding of human nature and experience from such studies, others may insist that a map of the brain can tell us no more about the mind than a terrestrial globe speak of Heaven and Hell."[33, 34]

13

The brain is able to convert incoming stimuli to action in particular ways. But the manner in which its neurons and infinite connections that result in chemical and electrical reactions within it and its unimaginable complexity of structure and function remain poorly understood. So, the question remains whether the brain and/or mind are interrelated components which give rise to you and your sentient life. It even seems strange that science often equates the brain with a lifeless computer.

Neuroscientist E. Krishnamoorthy used an analogy based on computers to explain this concept of the mind: "The mind is a virtual entity, one that reflects the workings of the neural networks, chemical and hormonal systems in our brain. The mind cannot be localized to particular areas within the brain, though the entire cerebral cortex and deep grey matter form important components. Consciousness, perception, behavior, intelligence, language, motivation, drive, the urge to excel and reasoning of the most complex kind are the product of the extensive and complex linkages between the different parts of the brain."[35]

The highest level of consciousness, in other words, is thought to depend on the integrity of the brain's prefrontal activity. Many scientists consider your "self" as a manifestation of this activity—it enables you to become aware of individual experience in a way that gives a "sense of an inner life."[36]

The Mind-Brain Relationship: Millennia ago, we embarked on a mission to understand the human condition. The organ that puzzled most throughout time was the human brain. We are now aware of nerve cells, their connections and their modes of communication amongst themselves and with a variety of other structures. Abnormalities of the brain provide crucial insights on the role of its different parts. Modern technology such as computerized tomography and magnetic resonance now allow us to localize function within the structure of the brain and correlate abnormalities of its structure and function. Even so, two entities remain enigmatic: the mind and the soul. Are they located within the brain? Modern technology cannot tell us yet, if ever.

The brain is the most complex of complex adaptive systems in which the whole is greater than the sum of its parts.

14

And its emergent property called the "mind" or subjective sense of self, is different qualitatively from the billions of interconnecting neurons and synapses which form its parts. This is true for any complex adaptive system that exists in our world; financial markets, flocking birds, herd migration, traffic flows, cities, the internet, ecosystems, and climates. Each system, which produces a network of many interacting variables between their component parts, change and self-organize in response to their changing environment and generate an emergent phenomena. Before evolution itself, a complex adaptive system within the organization of atoms in the primordial soup likely served a key role in the initial origin of life, even before evolution forces took over in driving increasing complexity. Life, therefore, was a by-product or emergent phenomenon of this soup, and the mind or consciousness emerged from the brain's complex adaptive system through evolution.

What we have left from the endless stream of papers written on consciousness and the mind-brain relationship are only different theories to digest. So, we continue to wonder what region(s) and processes in the brain, if any, facilitate the conscious experience and the mind-brain relationship, which philosopher D. Chalmers termed "The Hard Problem."[37] But Nobel Laureate Francis Crick, the co-discoverer of the molecular structure of DNA, doesn't consider consciousness a "hard problem." He stated, "You, your joys and your sorrows, your memories and your ambitions, your sense of personality and free will, are no more than the behavior of a vast assembly of nerve cells and their associated molecules."[38]

While not all scientific researchers studying consciousness today have this same physical reductionist view, it's probably safe to say that a great many do. But of course, not even the most avid materialists live their lives as if the mind is not real. That's why, when they kiss their children goodnight, they say, "I love you," not "My brain loves you."[39]

Not all great minds share the materialistic view. Residing on the opposite end of the theoretical spectrum are philosophers such as Kant, Berkeley, and Hegel, who contend there is no mind-

15

independent reality; the mental realm is the only realm and everything in the world is your mental construct. This is called "Idealism." The list of theories doesn't end here. Those who ascribe to "substance dualism" claim there is no direct correspondence between mental and physical states; they are independent of each other. The mind-brain relationship has even been explained using mathematical models.[40]

For decades, scholars on human behavior have also been telling us that the brain operates like a computer. This concept is a version of materialism, called "functionalism," which suggests the mind-body interaction behaves like a computer in terms of their functional interaction as input, process, and outcome. In some ways, it does. Computers process, store, and retrieve information, without exception, by algorithms. Humans, on the other hand, do not. No matter how hard neuroscientists try, I doubt they will ever find a copy of Shakespeare's tragedy, *Romeo and Juliet*, in the brain.

To remain objective, scientists have tried to suppress the innate feeling that you are not your brain, and their discoveries have been remarkable. Regardless, they have lost sight of the big picture, that the "impossible" may be possible. I challenge the materialistic mantra that the brain functions like a computer and that you are your brain. If this is true, then why are any two of us changed the same way by the same experience? If you and I watch *Romeo and Juliet*, for example, the changes that occur in my brain will be completely different from the changes that occur in your brain. Those changes are built upon a foundation of existing neurological representations developed over a lifetime of unique experiences. This is why 10 people at the scene of the same crime will tell 10 different stories to the jury. Recitations of the same story diverge more and more. More and more, the evidence suggests you are not your brain.

Symbiosis: The Brain and You

Overview: The hard problem of consciousness is knowing how reality comes about from the physical activity of our nervous system and realizing how you become aware of and experience reality (qualia). Today, science has no definitive answer to this problem. Many of us, regardless of our religious beliefs, feel intuitively that our consciousness exists apart from the brain. Human cultures throughout history have adopted this same important principle, that you survive bodily death and exist eternally as an individual spirit.

My answer, for what it's worth, is that "you" and "your" brain are likely separate entities that are interdependent but symbiotic. Your sense of reality is nothing more than the response by your central nervous system's ability to convert external forms of energy (light, sound, pressure, etc.) to a form of neuro-electrical energy the brain can process for you to realize, process, and interpret, in an appropriate manner that drives your experiences, current circumstances, and memory. Your brain's physical interpretation of incoming energy allows you to act accordingly to the information received using free-will and intention—the brain is essential in helping you react accordingly to the world at large. You depend on a normal functioning brain to allow you to perceive and react to all reality and associated circumstances presented within that reality.

Our nervous system enables us to have different sensory experiences and an ability to reason. Although humans are thinking creatures that feel, biologically we are emotional beings that think. Experimental findings in the form of "neural correlates of consciousness," cognitive science, and effects of brain injury on consciousness using brain imaging technology, have allowed us to better understand how the brain converts energy to a form of energy which enables us to realize and act upon.

A brief and simplistic explanation is as follows: All incoming physical energy (light, acoustic, and tactile, etc.), which is initially processed in each sensory system, is composed of a complex cascade of neurons that process and transmit neural activity almost instantaneously to appropriate areas in the brain. This neurological code of information is then integrated with sensations about movement and position, memory, and emotion to facilitate a decision to act, as appropriate. Any disruption of this integrated process can influence an aspect of consciousness.

17

Behavior is modifiable, and it is controlled by the anticipation of pain or pleasure, punishment or reward. The anticipation of pain or pleasure is coded in the brain—emotions have biochemical correlates located primarily in the limbic system below the cortex, the old mammalian brain. Remember the experiments in which rats were given the chance to self-stimulate different parts of the limbic system by pushing a lever? They stimulated the pleasure center in the brain until they fell from exhaustion. Well, it turned out that the electrical stimulation caused the release of brain chemicals associated with pain or pleasure. Endorphins are very pleasurable and serve as a motivating influence for runners who seek that so-called "runner's high"—the release of endorphins.

For this complex delicate process between you and the brain to be successful, a symbiotic relationship exists which requires a great deal of balance. We see evidence of symbiotic relationships in many forms of living processes and systems that are the product of millions of years of co-evolution. Mutualism is a form of a symbiotic relationship in which both species benefit. Parasitism, for example, where one microbe is harmed, is balanced so that the host lives long enough to allow the parasite to spread and reproduce. Another example of mutualism involves goby fish and shrimp. The nearly blind shrimp maintains a burrow in the sand in which both the fish and shrimp live. When a predator arrives, the fish touches the shrimp with its tail as a warning to enable them to retreat to the burrow to avoid the predator and to allow a safe environment for the fish to lay its eggs.

The question, of course, is whether you and the brain maintain a type of mutual symbiotic relationship whereby you maintain a healthy brain (diet, exercise, meditation) to allow the brain to provide you with an accurate interpretation of the physical world to manage in as appropriate a manner as possible. You need the brain and the brain needs you. That is, you interact with your brain.

What we see depends to a large extent upon what you anticipate seeing. The activity of neurons in the primary visual cortex is affected by brain regions involved in prediction and planning. When the brain can predict what you see, it readies areas in the primary visual cortex and other regions to enable you to interpret visual stimuli more quickly. If you stop to interpret all the sounds, smells, touches, tastes, and sights right now, you realize that this moment is continuous with every other moment leading to this one. It does not stand alone. Instead, every one of the moments in your life is not separate from all moments to come—perception is based solely on subjectivity. You interpret reality based on the accumulation of your personal experiences. You can't isolate yourself from your experiences or view the world outside of yourself from a non-judgmental standpoint. We try to be objective to view reality in a non-judgmental sense.

In practice, objectivity facilitates a type of aberration of consciousness that leads many people to be extremely judgmental of others because they think their points of view are absolute. They refuse to acknowledge the existence of any other reality paradigms than their own because they are not willing to see their own biases as being biased in the first place. This borders on illogic insanity, and most scientists who ascribe to materialism fit this mindset. This is one reason why science is slow to even just consider the possibility that the PE and its triggers allow one to experience an alternate reality.

Our Unconscious Feedback Loop: We tend to reconstruct the traumas in our life in the world around us. Think about it. Don't the same horrible events happen to you repeatedly, as if your mind contains a neural feedback loop that you can't control? The same patterns play out along with the same adverse consequences. Why do we often engage in the same kinds of destructive behaviors— we drink and eat too much, argue with and criticize others too often, and/or keep making bad financial decisions—despite trying so hard to change? What are we, insane?

Albert Einstein once said insanity is, "doing the same thing over and over again and expecting different results." If this is insanity, then we all must be insane. Despite our best intentions to change our counterproductive behaviors, we find ourselves thinking, acting, and feeling the same way every day for months and years on end. The founder of psychoanalysis, Sigmund

Freud, may have discovered the reason for this behavior—the unconscious mind. Freud thought there was something significant below your state of awareness responsible for this unwilling impulse to repeat your anxieties and misfortunes—even when you are trying to do otherwise. What motivates you, concerns you, and impedes your objectives resides in your unconscious mind. Since you often unconsciously assign meaning to events, whether they are inherently meaningful or not, coincidences can create meaningful synchronicity.[41]

When you have an expected outcome in mind, it changes the outcome of the event. Experiences perceived as coincidences may not be chance; they may represent an aspect of what psychologist Carl Jung called the "collective unconscious," a governing foundation of human experience that incorporates history, social, emotional, psychological, and spiritual experiences.[42] Like the blueprint of your home, the "collective unconscious" is the unseen mind humans share. And this shared "unconscious" may be part of the reason why we repeatedly behave in a neurotic manner.[43]

Perceived threats are stored in the unconscious. Freud called this defense mechanism "repression." Repressed or not, these threats exert great influence on your behavior. The problem is that you are not even aware of them. The only proof of their existence is how you unconsciously impede the changes you want to make and believing you are a victim of the action of others, your environment, or life itself. Unless you realize your repetitious behavior is facilitated by an unsolved emotional issue from the past, you will continue to act the same, only for repressed thoughts to be reflected in your behavior. The problem resides beneath your awareness in the unconscious mind, which governs most of our behavioral actions and reactions to important matters in life—we usually act without conscious thought. Like the PE, they are an unseen force, and it may be that the PE is also governed and expressed by the unconscious mind.

Most of us never stop following the habitual and conditioned nature of our unconscious mind, and this is why we suffer. Our unconscious ego continues to criticize, analyze, process and argue. Ego is habitual. It is a conditioned, psychological, reflexive, unseen force. Yet, most of us fully identify with this force without judgment because we are not aware that this drive arises from one's self. But we are never satisfied because this force exists without awareness and thus drives both our good and bad actions and decisions. To be immune from this negative force, you must realize that your destructive behaviors and thoughts are governed by that which may not be in your best interests. This is what psychologists charge plenty of money for—to help tap the unconscious through conscious awareness and interpretation to break this negative feedback loop. As Freud stated, "You can look at the events and think about the emotional tone and content and figure out what your own unconscious is processing at any given time."[44]

Freud tells us we are held hostage by our unconscious mind. If you can somehow learn to master the interrelated characteristics of synchronicity, intuition, and precognition, you may be able to evolve to the next level of high order thinking—to take better control over your actions and reactions that are, all too often, governed by your painful memories. Recognizing your synchronistic events can help reveal negative feedback loops of your unconscious mind. It is certainly easier said than done, but it achieves better results in the long term than suppressing the unconscious mind with frequently prescribed pills and/or therapy which often don't suffice.

Can You Affect Your Body? You can intentionally change processes in your body that are under voluntary control. You can improve your cognitive ability by learning to control the electrical activity of your brain using neurofeedback. You can exercise your mind through meditation and yoga to change the structure of your brain to enhance brain activity and to improve psychological well-being and attention. Meditation has been associated with decreases in stress, depression, anxiety, pain and insomnia, and an increased quality of life. Maybe that is one reason why there is growing interest in meditation in the United States. A 2017 government survey, for example, found 14 percent of adults said they had recently meditated, up from 4 percent from a similar survey five years earlier.

21

At one level, I hold great admiration for scholars who attempt to better understand the mind-brain relationship, but on another level, I wish they would apply more of their mind instead of just their brain toward this analysis. To most of them, the mind doesn't exist. The brain is it and nothing more. The brain, of course, enables the body to work efficiently without any conscious contribution from "you." But definitive conclusions regarding the mind-brain relationship must be interpreted with caution since the interrelated concepts of the "self," "consciousness," and the brain are poorly defined phenomena.

What we do know, which has been largely ignored from mind-brain theories, is that your intentions and feelings are vital to your well-being. You steer the ship. You tell your brain what to do to keep your body healthy, and your psychological state can even affect genetic behavior. Stress can turn genes "on" or "off" making you more or less susceptible to illness. And this causal relationship between stressful life events and the manifestation of disease has been a common clinical observation and the focus of much research.

Stress-related health problems are responsible for up to 80 percent of medical related visits and account for the third highest health care expenditures. But less than 5 percent of doctors discuss how to reduce stress with patients. This is a paradox to the extreme, especially since the medical community largely ignores this mind-body relationship, despite the fact that several techniques have been shown to have many health benefits, including improving heart health and helping relieve depression and anxiety. Preliminary research on the effects of meditation and yoga, for example, can even improve psychological well-being and have a positive effect on the structure and function of the brain—it reduces the body's stress response by strengthening your relaxation response and lowering stress hormones like cortisol. And you thought your doctor knows how to treat diseases? Think again.

Several studies have clearly established the link between stress in the year prior to the onset of symptoms and a number of diseases that affect many biological systems, such as endocrine, cardiovascular, respiratory, gastrointestinal, autoimmune, and skin.[45] Stress has also been shown to induce inflammation in the body through the mediation of a variety of neurotransmitters, pro-inflammatory cytokines, and hormones.[46] This outcome has been implicated in the pathophysiology of cancer and cardiovascular disease.[47-49] Psychiatric illness is also strongly associated with physical diseases. Depression increases your susceptibility to illness, characterized by an increased concentration of inflammatory markers which increase the risk for cardiovascular and neoplastic disease. But while stress can have adverse biological consequences, several studies have suggested that positive emotions can have a beneficial influence on the course of disease.[50, 51] Individuals with high psychological well-being have a reduced gene expression to adversity, suggesting a potential protective role of psychological well-being in a number of medical disorders.[52, 53] Some "psychosomatic medicine" researchers are telling us that by understanding the mind-brain relationship, an overdue reappraisal of medicine is forthcoming. One major obstacle to overcome is that since psychosomatic medicine goes hand-in-hand with the mind-brain relationship, it is not accepted as medical reality. Medical training largely ignores this, and as a result, appropriate health care is questionable in many cases.[54]

Such existing medical ignorance is compounded by studies that clearly demonstrate the beneficial effects of complimentary alternative medicine such as yoga, Reiki, and meditation interventions on depression, stress, and anxiety. A review and meta-analysis of 47 clinical trials with 3,515 participants conducted by researchers at The Johns Hopkins University Department of Medicine, for example, found that meditation significantly reduced stress with outcomes relating to depression, anxiety, and attention, eating and sleeping habits, pain, and weight. Seven studies on the effect of Reiki for pain and anxiety yielded statistically significant results either for pain or anxiety or both.[55] Research also suggests that yoga increases parasympathetic nervous system activity (responsible for sexual arousal, salivation, lacrimation, urination, digestion and defecation), and GABA (neurotransmitter that regulates communication between brain cells) levels in the thalamus and that these increases are correlated with improved mood.[56, 57]

Why doesn't medicine incorporate routine, simple ways to help mitigate a variety of illnesses? Well, they do, but in a far less than acceptable manner in the form of anti-depressant and anxiety medication. While pills may be appropriate in some cases, alternative mind-body training techniques should be recommended to patients on a formal, routine basis by the medical community. One exception is the Veterans Administration which employs meditation, yoga, and similar mind-body training techniques to supplement traditional therapy in many of the 400,000 veterans who have been diagnosed with post-traumatic stress disorder (PTSD). This practice was supported in a recent study by the Department of Defense which showed that meditation (repeating a mantra to calm the mind) worked as well as traditional therapy for military veterans with PTSD. More specifically, researchers measured symptoms in about 200 veterans who were randomly assigned to one of three groups: 1) meditation training, 2) traditional behavioral therapy, and 3) attending classes on nutrition and exercise. After three months, 61 percent of the meditation group improved on a standard PTSD assessment, compared to 42 percent of those who received behavioral therapy, and 32 percent of those who went to classes on nutrition and exercise.[82]

Additional evidence to support health related mind-body techniques was demonstrated in a study by neuroscientist Sara Lazar, who found that in comparison to a non-meditator control group, those who participated in a mindfulness-based stress reduction program had larger brain volume in specific key regions. This included the: (1) posterior cingulate—involved in mind wandering, and self-relevance; (2) left hippocampus—assists in learning, cognition, memory and emotional regulation; (3) temporal-parietal junction—associated with perspective taking, empathy, and compassion; and (4) amygdala—the fight or flight part of the brain which regulates anxiety, fear and stress in general.[83]

All of these regions increased in volume except the amygdala. This area got smaller in the group that went through the mindfulness-based stress reduction program which is a positive outcome since the amygdala was also correlated to a reduction in stress levels. Lazar also found that long-term meditators have an increased amount of grey matter in the insula and sensory regions, the auditory and sensory cortex. This makes sense, because "when you're mindful, you're paying attention to your breathing, to sounds, to the present moment experience, and shutting cognition down—your senses become enhanced."[84] But despite a wealth of scientific data showing that certain emotional states can lead to chronic illness, many who work in mainstream medicine remain entirely ignorant of these concepts. Even physicians who are aware of the effect of stress on health often don't take advantage of them to the benefit of the patient. One example is the placebo effect.

The Placebo Effect: The mind can be a powerful healing tool when given the chance. This is clearly illustrated in the placebo effect which has generated increasing attention by academics around the world. The placebo effect is the idea that you can convince your body that a fake treatment is the real thing, and thus stimulate healing. In most cases, even though placebos contain no real treatment, they can produce a variety of both positive physical and psychological effects. The interaction of our thoughts with the physical material world can be just as valuable as traditional treatments, and studies have found that placebo treatments can stimulate everything from changes in heart rate to blood pressure and even chemical activity in the brain.

A placebo is a substance with no known medical effects, such as sterile water, saline solution, or a sugar pill. The placebo is designed to seem exactly like the real treatment, so people receiving it believe that they are the recipients of the real treatment. This belief alone can have positive outcomes and has been demonstrated experimentally in many different physical conditions such as: migraine headaches, allergies, fever, the common cold, asthma, various kinds of pain, nausea and seasickness, ulcers, depression and anxiety, and arthritis, to name a few. Placebo-related research reveals that your state of mind produces physiological effects. The cognitive influences of conditioning and expectation act to become the two main drivers of placebo responses, each influencing different biological pathways.[58] The placebo effect has been extensively researched and on average 35 percent of all people who receive a given placebo will experience a significant effect.

One of the most studied and strongest placebo effects is in the reduction of pain. According to some estimates, approximately 30 to 60 percent of people feel that their pain has diminished after taking a placebo pill. One major review of more than 200 studies involving the use of placebos found that the placebo had no major clinical effects on illness. Instead, the placebo effect had an influence on patient-reported outcomes, particularly of perceptions of nausea and pain.[59-61] Placebos often work because people don't know they are getting one. But what happens if you know you are getting a placebo? One study explored this by testing how people reacted to migraine pain medication.[62] One group took a migraine drug labeled with the drug's name, another took a placebo labeled "placebo," and a third group took nothing. The researchers discovered that the placebo was 50 percent as effective as the real drug to reduce pain after a migraine attack. This finding showed that: "people associate the ritual of taking medicine as a positive healing effect. Even if they know it's not medicine, the action itself can stimulate the brain into thinking the body is being healed."[63]

One study even demonstrated the power of the placebo effect in surgical outcomes for patients with severe and debilitating knee pain. The patients were divided into three groups. The surgeon shaved the damaged cartilage in the knee of one group, and flushed out the knee joint, removing all the material believed to be causing inflammation in the second group. The third group received a "fake" surgery; the patients were only sedated and made to believe they had knee surgery— the surgeon simply made the incisions and splashed salt water on the knee as they would in normal surgery. All three groups went through the same rehabilitation process, and incredibly, the placebo group improved just as much as the other two groups who had surgery.[64] The surgeon involved in the study concluded that his "skill as a surgeon had no benefit on these patients," and that "the entire benefit of surgery for osteoarthritis of the knee was the placebo effect."[65]

Another example of the power of the placebo effect was demonstrated in a 1999 report by the United States Department of Health and Human Services. This report documented that half of severely depressed patients taking drugs improved compared to the 32 percent taking a placebo.[66] This finding was further reinforced in a study published in the American Psychological Association's journal, *Prevention & Treatment*, which showed that 80 percent of the effect of antidepressants in clinical trials is attributed to the placebo effect.[67] The brain is a marvelous tool indeed.

The Quantum Brain

You know that different parts of your brain interpret different types of incoming physical energy from your world remarkably fast, and that this complex neurological process culminates in a unified experience called consciousness. This activity occurs more quickly than can be explained by our current understanding of neural transmissions in the brain. Because of this, some scholars, such as neuroscientist Karl Pribram, consider brain activity and memory to be facilitated by encoding incoming energy in a holographic manner.[68] Our brain may operate like a 3D holographic matrix which influences our experiences. Each brain fragment, in other words, translates information of the whole that enables aspects of your consciousness to be connected among different areas of stored information.

Look at it this way: the brain is like a mirror. If you break the mirror into thousands of pieces, each piece still captures the whole image. You can comb your hair using the reflection from just one tiny piece of the mirror in the same way you use the full-size mirror. Similarly, each brain fragment may behave like each piece of the broken mirror since each piece represents the whole. This holographic concept may explain the brain's ability to operate in accordance with principles in quantum mechanics (QM). Consciousness may even be explained in this way. The neurons in your brain may behave as "quantum computers" which interact nonlocally with other neurons to facilitate a "conscious event"—conscious moments manifest as quantum computations in microtubules (protein polymers which form the cytoskeleton in neurons which govern neuronal) inside brain neurons. [69]

Consider this: to accomplish the same task that just one of the hundred billion neurons in the brain completes, a modern-day computer the size of the United States would be required. For this reason alone, many scientists support a model of quantum consciousness—the "orchestrated objective reduction" (Orch-OR)—to explain your brain's ability to facilitate consciousness and process information.[70]

Based on the brain's apparent ability to retain quantum states, S. Hameroff and R. Penrose, co-founders of the Orch-OR, contend that microtubules serve as carriers of quantum properties inside the brain.[71] Consciousness, therefore, may be facilitated by the rules of QM and holographic principles within the microscopic spaces between neurons in the brain. This yet to be realized network may facilitate nonlocal communication and integration of purposeful information at the neuronal and DNA level for memory and learning.[72]

If you disagree that your self-awareness emerges from the "quantum space-time micro-wormhole network" within the brain, what do you think of the idea proposed by esteemed physicist Bernard Haisch, who declared that, "quantum fields permeate all of empty space (the so-called "quantum vacuum") which produce and transmit consciousness."[73]

Like you, I admit I am somewhat confused too. Yet, it is difficult to completely ignore the ideas proposed by leading respected scholars that this is indeed true. But how do we know they are correct? Well, no one does—that's why it's called a "theory." If such theories are proven valid, these poorly understood self-organizing systems in your brain may have significant implications toward understanding the PE, consciousness, and even reality itself. Although this thought is an admitted stretch, the Orch-OR theory may serve as the foundation for consciousness. If true, consciousness may then "exist apart from the brain and body, perhaps indefinitely, as a soul."[74] This model of microtubule

28

consciousness may explain the PE and associated altered perceptions of time and space.[75] According to S. Hameroff and R. Penrose, "the quantum information within the microtubules is not destroyed—it can't be destroyed. It just distributes and dissipates to the universe at large."

They further speculate that "quantum information can exist outside the body, perhaps indefinitely as a soul" and may explain the NDE and OBE. One of several physicists who share this perspective is my former colleague, physicist Claude Swanson, who stated, "Some of the weird phenomena we have called "paranormal" might really be just quantum mechanics working its strange magic on the large scale of everyday life."[77] Leading physicist W. Tiller also advanced the idea that the holographic properties of space are key to understanding the effects of consciousness and how ESP can take place in single living cells.[78]

Summary: What scientists seem to be telling us is that like both the wave and particle aspects of light, your consciousness may also have an aspect of interacting waves and particles. The implication is that both the subjective (conscious) and corresponding objective physical properties are two different aspects of the same one underlying deeper reality.[79] The more profound implication of this deeper reality may be that during a PE trigger (NDE or OBE), and upon death, the "wave aspect of our consciousness in phase-space will no longer have an aspect of particles, but only an eternal aspect of waves."[80] Thus, we may be immortal.

Discussion

What we observe every moment in time are photons (light energy) emanating from the Big Bang some 14 billion years ago that are just now bouncing off physical objects and entering your visual system where your eye and brain help to convert this energy into a form of energy (electrophysiological and chemical) the brain can understand. Your reality, in other words, is literally created by photons from the Big Bang. I can't, however, firmly accept this as true reality. Look at it this way. The brain initially filters out information coming in from the senses and then takes trillions of bits of information and constructs the reality that you're experiencing right now. Then, based on your thoughts, emotions, and intentions, the brain determines what patterns are of most interest to you. It filters the important and meaningful information you desire by sensing and then presenting those for you. But your amazing brain shows you only the patterns it thinks are most relevant to what you want to see.

So, in a real sense, "you create your own reality" by crafting the neurological representation that is of most interest to you each moment in time. You don't create the external reality that the senses are reporting on but instead direct the brain to help you experience what you decide to experience. That's how you purposefully give rise to the physical universe. So, does consciousness create reality?

If Nobel Prize winning father of quantum mechanics, Niels Bohr, is correct in his statement that: "Everything we call real is made of things that cannot be regarded as real,"[81] then "physical reality" is non-existent—reality is a non-localized energy and empty space. If we extrapolate this notion to the subjective experience, then your thoughts and the sensory information the brain interprets should also have these same characteristics. Since your thoughts are also part of the physical world, then your free will and intentions may occur within the same quantum realm prior to manifesting in physical reality. Consciousness and reality are not only interrelated—they may be one and the same. You and the universe are a cosmic connection.

CHAPTER 2

THE PEAK EXPERIENCE
ENCOUNTERS WITH AN UNSEEN REALM

Introduction

The PE represents a specific type of altered state of consciousness (ASC)—the subjective perception and recognition that one's own experience has changed. The ASC is a state in which the neurocognitive mechanisms of consciousness produce alterations of reality, such as hallucinations, delusions, and memory distortions. An ASC may also be a misrepresentation of the actual relationships between one's consciousness and reality, such as dreaming, psychotic episodes, psychedelic drug experiences, epileptic seizures, and hypnosis in highly hypnotizable subjects. By association the PE is generally viewed as abnormal in nature, and detrimental or unwanted. This "abnormal" classification, however, may not be accurate, especially since scientists, psychologists, philosophers, and theologians often interpret ASC differently.

From a scientific and psychological point of view, the PE is simply either a pathological hallucination—sensations in the absence of a relevant external stimulus—or a delusional disorder—a fixed belief despite being presented with conflicting evidence. The testimonies of mystics and meditators who claim that their ability to enter an ASC has brought them enlightenment or transcendence, therefore, are generally regarded with great skepticism among scientists in Western society. Philosophers and theologians, on the other hand, who are generally more open to alternative explanations, do not necessarily consider a PE an abnormality of the mind in all cases. The controversial nature of the ASC and PE is compounded by the existing debate of the nature and definition of "consciousness" itself. Consequently, the only thing that can be said with certainty is that PEs cannot be easily rationalized and scientifically validated but are perceived as "real" by those who experience them.

Encounters with an Unseen Realm

Peak experiences have been elicited through meditation,[1] under conditions of sensory isolation,[2] with psychedelics,[3] NDEs and OBEs, from exposure to awe-inspiring situations such as interactions with UAP and NHEs,[4] and from non-invasive cortical stimulation and brain injuries.[5,6] Personal encounters with an unseen realm (PE) induced by anomalous experiences, meditation, OBEs, and NDEs are as follows:

(1) A PE from anomalous experiences: "I have had a lifetime of anomalous experiences of beings, of other worlds, a connection and a communication that reveals itself in purity and total transparency. The stars are within us, and they are ours. I am me, in this here and now, but I am also there in what is unseen. We are multidimensional beings, a consciousness of nonlocality, our minds are beyond our physical bodies, enabling us to experience other realms. The universe creates life. That is its purpose. Whether this life is in our own "dense" reality or in realms we cannot see, it is there, and it is real. It is within us to

explore it, as it reaches out for us. All we need to do is reach out and grab it."[7]

(2) A PE during meditation: "I remember at that time I was really into meditation and I remember sitting downstairs meditating and what I can describe as "waves of bliss" coming over me. They were really intense and felt like it was coming from outside of me and I remember a voice repeating, "All is One." I remember feeling a sense of oneness with everything and things seemed clear, and absolutely beautiful. It was a very meaningful experience, very liberating and beautiful, I felt inspired, strong, full of life, and in awe, and I miss it."[8]

(3) A PE during an OBE: "During OBEs I feel an awareness that is even greater than my awakened reality. Emotions are intensified. Colors are brighter, and living things glow with an internal light. There is such a huge input of sensory data that my attention becomes overloaded. I call this 'Astral ADHD.' I want to look at and feel everything, and it seems my experiences move at such a fast speed as I try to take everything in. Then I stop and tell myself to slow down. I lie down on my stomach, and look at one blade of grass, and it's as if I see the whole universe in that blade of grass."[9]

(4) A PE during an OBE: "When I am in an OBE in a higher plane, or around non-human entities, my emotions are very different. I have no fear, nothing negative, its pure bliss, and it feels right. These dimensions look very different than our typical physical surroundings. They are very beautiful, and full of nature in its purity, consisting of vibrant colors that glow. Earthly time has no meaning in the spirit realm. There is no concept of before or after. Past, present, and future exists simultaneously."[10]

(5) A PE during an NDE: "I spent some time alone in a dark and endless void. Then, a bold spirit came to me. Her hair, a brilliant orange-red, looked as though she wore a crown of fire. She was striking and larger than life. It took a moment before I realized it was my maternal grandmother. I wept as she held and comforted me. I had so many questions and as I thought them, the answers came telepathically from her spirit to mine. You aren't dead. There is no death, except that the body becomes useless

and is cast away. You've heard it said that energy isn't created or destroyed, it just changes form. This is true on the earthly realm and in the spirit realm. You haven't died, dear one, you've simply changed forms."[11]

(6) A PE during an NDE: "I was amazed to find that my consciousness endured without aid of my body or brain. The spirits on this other side of reality had profound resonance; each one different from the other, but all connected. It was as if I was connected to every spirit that had ever been created, both on the spirit side and in the earthly realm. I knew each of them, and felt their joys, hopes and sorrows. I understood that everything I'd ever thought, said, or done, had impacted every other spirit in the universe."[12]

Collectively, such indefinable accounts fail to provide an understanding of the essence of a PE. It must be experienced to understood. Even PErs frequently report having difficulty putting an "other-worldly" experience into worldly terms. It seems as if their ego melts away and a new way of being emerges. They report an expanded awareness, or an awakening, similar to other cultures and spiritual traditions who use the word "enlightened"— the ability to sense moods and states of consciousness of others; a sudden dramatic sense of "oneness" or a feeling of unity with the universe; as if consciousness exists everywhere and they are connected to everything.

Incidence of a Peak Experience: The incidence of PEs is surprising high. Survey research has reported that about one-third of Americans have had intense spiritual experiences,[13] and about 10-15 percent of the general population has had a PE in the form of an OBE[14] or NDE,[15] with an estimated 200,000 people in the United States and millions worldwide having reported an NDE annually.[16] Even more astonishing is the remarkable similarity of detailed PE accounts by millions worldwide who contend to have had no communication with those who had the same experience. But while national sample surveys show that approximately 30 to 50 percent of Americans claim to have had a PE in the form of a "mystical experience" or "religious awakening,"[17] few empirical studies have investigated the specific causes and conditions that might elicit them. This limited research attention is unfortunate but not surprising. After all, science focuses on "nature"—an area subject to empirical investigation, and not the "supernatural"—an area whose existence is indeterminate.

While there is little doubt that individuals believe their PEs to be "real" in nature, one's sense of realness can be altered by different psychological conditions.[18] Most ASCs, though seemingly real while they occur, are often described as less real in hindsight. Thus, for those convinced their PE felt unmistakably real, the question remains as to whether their perceptual experiences represent a true aspect of physical reality. That is, is the PE a real, tangible event, or an illusion induced by a psychological (psychosis and dissociation disorder) or neurobiological (brain and neurochemical dysfunction, memory disturbances, and sleep pathology, etc.) abnormality?

Consciousness and the Peak Experience: Most scholars who adopt the materialistic viewpoint that consciousness is an outcome of brain activity are skeptical of PE evidence and associated theories that explain it. The expression "which comes first, the chicken or the egg?" applies to this concern—is consciousness a by-product of the physical world, or does consciousness give rise to the physical world?

The Western scientific community does not support the conclusion that PErs interacted with another reality and/or NHEs, and the spiritual belief that consciousness is not the brain. This notion does not fit with their cultural background and scientific mindset, which views matter as the ultimate form of reality, and consciousness as a characteristic of it; that is, consciousness and the brain are one and the same. The Eastern perspective is the reverse—consciousness is the ultimate reality and the physical universe is a byproduct of it. They consider consciousness distinct from the brain and that it continues in some post-mortem realm of existence after death. Western science considers your perceptions as the highest form of reality, whereas the Eastern view considers that higher capacities of mind must be developed to interact with reality in a more direct way.

Mainstream science fails to consider the transcendent reality of consciousness and the core beliefs (life after death, heaven, God, and the PE) shared by millions, if not billions, of people worldwide today. By default, science does not research the PE, especially since it appears to be an aspect of the poorly understood concept of consciousness. For this reason alone, no acceptable theory exists to explain the incomprehensible PEs consistently reported by millions throughout time who yearn for answers to the questions: "Why me?" "What does it mean?" "Am I going insane?" Unfortunately, adequate reassuring answers cannot be provided. The only conclusive answer from the medical and scientific communities is that the PEr suffered an illusion requiring counseling, medication, or both, to resolve.

But how can we prove the validity and actual nature of the PE without firsthand experience? Similar to the many elusive answers to the workings of the universe, your brain and consciousness, science cannot prove people are interacting with another reality and NHEs via a PE. It is, nevertheless, unreasonable to ignore those who fiercely contend that their consciousness, somehow, and in some way, accessed another unseen realm. To them, it was "real," but to the medical and scientific communities, it really wasn't. So, who do you believe?

Paradoxically, although science views the PE as science fiction or an aberrant disorder, what is now considered science fiction may eventually become scientific fact; at least, that is what history tells us. Maybe the time has come for science to begin thinking less materialistically and more outside the box, devoid of preconceived and biased notions. But there are a few bold "outside-the-box" leading thinkers who do not share the narrow view of scientific materialism. These scholars realize that everything about the PE and its triggers (NDE, OBE, psychoactive drugs, meditation, and the UAP, etc.) may not be pathological. To them, the PE may represent the nature of an alternate reality unlike the 3D existence of our everyday waking experience. These "outside-the-box" scholars buck conventional science. They contend that consciousness is a form of energy not bound by established concepts of space and time. Nobel Prize winner

Werner Heisenberg, for example, considered all matter an "indivisible and unseen realm, from which objects spring into existence when observed by an intelligent observer."[19]

Similarly, physicist David Bohm, a pioneer in the study of quantum physics, concluded that all reality is "inseparably interconnected" and that "it makes no sense to separate physical effects from spiritual effects."[20] Astronaut and scientist Edgar Mitchell, who founded the Institute for Noetic Sciences, thoroughly captured this paradox by stating: "There are no unnatural or supernatural phenomena, only very large gaps in our knowledge of what is natural."[21]

This "gap in knowledge" is revealed when trying to explain the description of a NDE by my friend, who wrote: "My near-death experience definitively convinced me that consciousness is not held in the brain, like some sort of component, but rather, is accessible via the brain. My work as a nurse further solidified my belief that consciousness is indeed non-local. As patients neared death, it was clear to me they were communicating with and accessing other realms."[22] For these reasons, her personal and philosophical viewpoints changed from that moment forward.

Transformative Outcomes of a Peak Experience

Overview: A PE can change one's perception of the world permanently, changes that seem positive, empowering, and deeply spiritual. Their experience, real or not, often has a pronounced effect on one's life from that moment forward and can foster the belief that reality harbors a hidden spiritual structure with unseen connections among people and events.

The PE facilitates largely positive transformative after-effects, and most consider it to be among the most important experiences in their lives.[23,24] Several studies have indicated that the majority of PErs who had an OBE reported remarkably similar positive after-effects that changed their life in the following ways: (1) increased interest in spirituality and psychic phenomena;[25] (2) more love and understanding of others; and (3) realized the benefit of a "greater awareness of reality."[26] My colleague, who alleges to have had thousands of OBEs, captured the essence of transformative PE outcomes by stating: "They express a profound inner wisdom based on personal spiritual experience. Many contend to be connected to something greater than themselves, connected to the very source of life—a powerful feeling of breaking through a dense barrier of ignorance, fear, and limitation."[27]

A PE facilitates intuitive feelings of a strong personal connection with others and a new global-like consciousness. Many PErs become more sensitive to Earth's ecology, more compassionate and sensitive to the needs of other people and animals, and have answers to life's questions such as: "Why are we here? How does it all relate? Why does it matter?" Documented statements from PErs include the following: (1) it's all homework; (2) it's not the experience but how we respond to it; (3) we manifest our own disasters; and (4) in order to appreciate life more, we must experience loss.[28] Their new knowledge influences them to turn devotion and consideration away from the "self" toward a newfound, awe-inspiring connection to humanity.[29] This is represented in common expressions such as: "I just communed with the universal knowing and being, as if I were the universe. I mean, the conviction was absolute. I know everything that is in the universe," and "There's nothing that I don't know. And I was it."[30]

Experimental Results: Studies have shown that PE triggers (OBE, NDE, psychoactive drugs, and interactions with UAP and NHEs, etc.) facilitate similar positive changes in psychological well-being and related outcomes. The reason for this may be that the shock of experiencing themselves "independent of their physical body gives them a more expansive vision of themselves, awakening new levels of personal growth."[31]

They also "recognize for the first time that they are the creative center of their physical existence; that they are completely responsible for all their actions, both thoughts and deeds."[32] For these reasons, several studies have associated the PE with positive outcomes that include: greater concern for others, reductions in distress associated with the prospect of dying, increased appreciation for nature, reduced interest in social status and possessions, and increased self-worth.[33, 34] As one

PEr related: "My NDE was the best experience of my life, and absolutely shaped me in a profound way—everything in reverse, so to speak. I cannot 'evaluate' in terms of good, bad or neutral. I can only say it is 'real' reality."[35]

To determine the positive outcomes of an OBE on psychological well-being, one study analyzed the descriptive content of the PE and noted frequent expressions of similar emotions. This included a sense of the ineffable; feeling of oneness with God, nature, or the universe; changed perceptions of time and surroundings; and a feeling of "knowing" coupled with a reordering of life priorities.[36]

Following an OBE, many people report an inner awakening of their spiritual identity; they feel more aware and alive and view themselves as more than just physical matter. A large majority of the 700 subjects in one study, for instance, described their PE as being "more real than their usual sense of reality," as if, "all is one," and that there is an "inherent goodness" of the world.[37] These viewpoints were associated with positive self-reported transformative impacts on one's life, represented by a greater sense of purpose, an increase in spirituality, and a reduced fear of death. Such outcomes likely contributed to the result in one study which demonstrated that over 75 percent of 339 OBE respondents wanted to have the OBE again, especially since most felt it was "very pleasant," and to be of "lasting benefit."[38]

A prospective study on cognitive processes in cardiac arrest NDErs (N = 344) also revealed similar outcomes in social functioning and psychological well-being two years after their NDE.[39] One intriguing result was that 24 percent of the subjects claimed to have watched events during their resuscitation despite their unconscious state. One patient correctly identified the nurse who removed his dentures during emergency revival efforts and where she placed them. Many survivors and medical professionals have also reported similar experiences that are likely underreported due to fear of stigmatization.[40]

One common outcome of the NDE is the realization that consciousness continues after death. Several studies have clearly demonstrated that nearly all NDErs lose their fear of death, they strongly believe in an afterlife, and their "insight in what is important in life had changed—love and compassion for oneself, for others, and for nature" is now what matters most of all.[41] This was evidenced in one study which found that 84 percent of 51 subjects who reported a fear of death before their NDE declined to only 2 percent after their NDE.[42] One subject stated that: "It is outside my domain to discuss something that can only be proven by death. The experience was decisive in convincing me that consciousness lives on beyond the grave. Death was not death, but another form of life."[43]

Curiously, interactions with NHEs associated with the UAP and alien abduction phenomena (AAP) also have similar behavioral after-effects with the OBE and NDE induced PE triggers. The most comprehensive study of the AAP was addressed in a survey study of physical, psychological, perceptual, and paranormal aspects of contact experience in 3,256 individuals who had conscious recall of their UAP encounter by the Dr. Edgar Mitchell Foundation for Research into Extraterrestrial and Extraordinary Experiences (FREE).[44] The FREE analyzed their reported interactions with UAP and NHEs to assess a diverse range of physical, psychological, perceptual, and paranormal aspects of reported non-hypnotic based recall of both physical and/or non-physical interactions associated with this contact experience. The UAP interaction experience was specifically selected for study since it appears to contain a number of PE triggers that give rise to an altered state of consciousness, similar to that reported by those who have an OBE, NDE, among other triggers that facilitate a PE. The study results were obtained from two comprehensive quantitative surveys totaling 554 questions. The most significant results of the FREE study[45] are as follows:

(1) Approximately three-quarters of the subjects (N = 655) reported an altered sense of reality—senses were "more vivid"; a distorted sense of time and body awareness; the perception of an "unearthly world"; and a feeling of "harmony with the universe."

(2) Approximately one-third reported seeing a bright light; encountering a "mystical being" or hearing an unidentifiable voice; seeing deceased or religious spirits; and the feeling of "peace or pleasantness."

(3) About 80 percent claimed that their consciousness was separated from their body and 72 percent felt a sense of "expanded consciousness" in the presence of NHEs associated with or without the UAP.

(4) Approximately 85 percent of 1,919 subjects reported that they "did not want their contact experience to end.

(5) Perceptions of alternate realities/dimensions, an OBE, and past life experiences during a "contactee" (non-physically abduction) interaction, were more frequent in occurrence than in those "abducted" (physically taken to a UAP craft).

(6) The majority (71 percent of 455 subjects) of those having "conscious recall of being on board a UAP craft" claimed that their UAP-NHE interaction changed their life in a "positive way." Only 15 percent reported a "negative" impact.[45]

The FREE results were consistent with the survey findings by Kenneth Ring (1992) in those who reported an interaction with UAP (N = 97) and NHEs, and in NDErs (N = 74).[46] Both groups manifested similar positive change in their personal and philosophical viewpoints. Moreover, the similar findings by each study were reinforced by the recent Mutual UFO Network (MUFON) Experiencer Research Team UAP abduction and contact experiencer survey study.[47] This study indicated that a significant percentage of the 516 subjects who reported to have been either "abducted" or "contacted," benefited from their interaction with "benevolent entities."[48] The majority of those reporting positive behavioral after-effects from their UAP experience claimed to have become more "spiritual, empathic, psychic or intuitive, and less oriented toward aggression, negativity, and the acquisition of material goods."[49]

Collectively, the similar positive behavioral outcomes in the majority of subjects in these three studies suggest that an aspect of consciousness may serve as the unifying characteristic of interactions with UAP and NHE, the OBE, and NDE induced PE triggers. This possibility was explained by noted psychiatrist and UAP researcher John Mack, who stated: "This awakening, the heightened awareness that grows out of the ego shattering impact of the encounters, carries with it quite consistently certain interrelated psycho-spiritual changes. The cosmos that is revealed by this opening of consciousness, far from being an empty place of dead matter and energy, appears to be filled with beings, creatures, spirits, intelligences, and God."[50] The profound realization that: "we live in a multidimensional universe populated by beings or life forms that are less densely embodied than we are, or perhaps not embodied at all," may have facilitated the behavioral outcomes in those who interact (abducted or "contactee") with the UAP and NHEs.

Within this context, the conclusions by leading UAP researchers that an apparent intelligence or force of some type seems to take control of the individual and induces altered patterns of consciousness and behavior, telepathic communication, and/or perceptions of space and time, among other complex symptoms associated with the AAP, are consistent with the OBE and NDE study results.[51] While subject to debate, the only thing that can be said with certainty is that the reported positive psycho-spiritual behavioral outcomes cannot be easily rationalized and scientifically validated. Despite this limitation, however, their PE is perceived as "real" and has a positive transformative impact on those who experience it. And that is what matters most of all.

Similar to the study results in those who report an OBE, NDE and UAP, the PE trigger facilitated by psychoactive drugs can also facilitate positive behavioral outcomes. The psychoactive drug psilocybin, for example, has been shown to promote positive social attitudes/behaviors and psychological well-being. One study, for instance, noted significant positive changes on measures of interpersonal closeness, gratitude, life meaning/purpose, forgiveness, death transcendence, and daily spiritual experiences, six months after subjects had a drug induced PE. Similar benefits attributed to PE induced psychoactive substances like DMT and LSD include reduced death anxiety,[52] pro-ecological behavior,[53] significant clinical improvements in depressed patients[54] and recovering addicts,[55] and lasting improvements in psychological well-being in healthy populations.[56]

Love is the Answer: Perhaps the most common takeaway from those reporting a PE is to love everyone unconditionally. As a 62-year-old businessman who had an NDE stated: "One thing I learned was that we are all part of one big, living universe. If we think we can hurt another person or another living thing without hurting ourselves we are sadly mistaken. I look at a forest or a flower or a bird now, and say, 'That is me, part of me.' We are connected with all things and if we send love along those connections, then we are happy."[57] John Lennon nailed this concept beautifully with the verse in his song, *Mind Games:* "Love is the answer and you know that for sure. Love is a flower. You got to let it grow."

Love is certainly "the answer" for many PErs. Even children who have had a NDE realize the importance of love. One little boy, for example, who after being hit by a car was guided into the world beyond by two people in "very white" robes, said: "What I learned there is that the most important thing is loving while you are alive."[58] I can't help but be reminded of the expression: "Out of the mouths of babes."

Transformation: The integration of one's newly formed perspective is "an inner process, a fundamental work of reorganization, and a reorientation of priorities."[59] This "inner process" is represented in the research by pioneer on near-death states PMH Atwater, whose work established that the PE is characterized by a "transformation of consciousness." This elusive concept is depicted in selected excerpts from her extensive collection of behaviorally transformative after-effects in nearly 7,000 PErs, as follows:[60]

"All I was taught in my life became irrelevant. I was transformed. I was forced to grow and that has made me a better person, still not with all the answers, but inquisitive about the unknown."

"Because of these experiences, I am a much more open-minded person. I have such a broader perspective on life."

"Happier, more open-minded, a belief in the oneness of all things."

"I think differently and view everything with a new perspective. My worldview changed everything, as if a veil was lifted in understanding the nature of everything as a whole."

"I was able to shed many fears and outdated beliefs as I began to emerge from my experiences."

"My entire frame of mind has changed ever since this contact happened. I see things more clearly as far as philosophically and religiously. I am more aware of a greater power."

"These experiences have helped me to expand my consciousness, to think more clearly about the world and about humans, and to wake up to the different realities and dimensions."

"I no longer fear death as I know now that is just a continuation from this reality...This life is basically just a play on the stage."

"I now understand myself to be part of universal consciousness that is linked not only to every being in the universe but also to the entire universe itself."

"Within 24 hours of my experience, I learned that we are eternal spiritual beings living a physical life, and that we learn through the process of reincarnation until we "graduate" to the next stage of our conscious evolution. I am now very spiritual and practice meditation daily."

"My entire frame of mind has changed ever since this happened. I see things more clearly. I am more aware of a greater power, and I found myself being separated from others. I don't think anyone would understand what I've experienced unless they've been through it themselves."

"All my attachments to life have vanished. My "self" identification to life has gone. I am no longer the seeker in this life, I am now the experiencer; the observer of life which is what we truly are, experiencing life for life. It's only until the 'self' starts to seek, desire, and think, that suffering starts."

"I can feel people's energy, I can see people's lessons in life, their directions, and each day this awesome understanding grows and grows. Life comes and it goes. Everything is always moving."

Overall, the personal accounts of transformation from a PE make it apparent that the reality they once accepted without question has been irrevocably changed, and once they firmly believe that they are having these experiences, the world as they knew it ceases to be. This is represented by several newly adopted behavioral outcomes which include, but are not limited to, the following: (1) gaining a better understanding of themselves (self-realization, confidence); (2) attaining greater confidence in determining answers to life's questions and achieving a more complete and confident perspective of life's purpose (self-realization); and (3) manifesting a heightened sensitivity of compassion and empathy toward others. These outcomes are not opinion but fact to those who have experienced a PE.

The similar psycho-spiritual outcomes facilitated by PE triggers raise an important question. That is, what common feature shared among these states may be responsible for mediating the apparent psychological benefits that follow them? The answer may be the experience of unity—a symptom of ego-dissolution or a compromised sense of "self."[61] This so-called "unitive experience" was originally identified as the core component of the mystical experience by its most influential scholar, Walter Stace,[62] and in descriptions of the PE introduced by noted psychologist A. Maslow.[63] Ego-dissolution and the unitive experience that accompanies it, may be the unifying attribute responsible for the psychological benefits associated with the each PE trigger.[64]

Conclusion: A PE may result in the experiencer finding less value in impressing others or adhering to hierarchies or routines.

45

More importance may be placed on family, health, and the environment and spirituality, rather than focusing on money or fame. Destruction of the environment may be especially painful and a cause for activism. Emphasis is also placed on positively influencing people with deeper, more spiritual values. It can also alter some or all of an individual's prior held spiritual or religious beliefs; atheists may report complete conversions to spirituality or religion, and some report leaving their religious communities for a more spiritual, individual approach to life and spirit. Some find confirmation and strengthening of their pre-existing spiritual or religious beliefs in their experiences and may begin a journey of seeking out a faith that is consistent with their experience. Experiencers may devote increasing amounts of time and energy into families, caring for children, animals, the sick or dying, or volunteering for nonprofit causes.[65]

For some, the PE is considered a psychopathology. For others, it represents an evolution toward psychological health and enhanced psycho-social effectiveness. The only definitive answer is that "the transcendent experience may be regarded as among the most important in a person's life."[66] Limited research in this important arena, however, begs for more research on the psycho-spiritual outcomes on the relationship of each PE trigger among diverse cultural populations. It remains a unique mystery in need of dire attention by the scientific and psychological communities. The PE may be the key to understanding the concept of fierce debate—the nature and meaning of consciousness.

The Overview Effect

One type of PE termed the "Overview Effect" (OE) may best be understood as a state of awe with self-transcendent qualities, precipitated by a particularly striking visual stimulus. It incorporates a noetic quality and a feeling of "appreciation and perception of beauty."[67] Astronauts have been describing such a transcendent experience evoked by the overpowering impact from viewing Earth in a tin can while circling the globe. This sight from space has been described as "visions of the possibilities of a world without boundaries," an "overwhelming emotion," and as an increased sense of "connection to other people and the Earth as a whole."[68]

One can only imagine the profound sense of emotion viewing and contemplating Earth from a distance. Astronaut Edgar Mitchell on his return trip from walking on the surface of the moon in Apollo 14 expressed it as a "universe of consciousness," an "explosion of awareness," an "overwhelming sense of oneness and connectedness accompanied by an ecstasy...an epiphany."[69] Mitchell's emotional reaction was so deeply moving that he stated: "I had to know what in the world it was. I got in touch with scholars to help me try and find some of the answers. They came back to me a few weeks later with an experience described out of the Sanskrit of India called savikalpa samadhi that described the same thing. A perception of unity accompanied by ecstasy; exactly what I had been feeling."[70]

In Hindu and yogic philosophy, savikalpa samadhi is one of several levels of samadhi – a state of "bliss when one comes to realize the nature of the higher Self."[71] This higher state of consciousness, an intimate merging between you and all around you, is a unification with your consciousness and the universe. This state may very well be the unifying characteristic among all different types of PEs. It is, in other words, all about "consciousness"! And Mitchell realized this during his PE in Apollo 14. His OE sparked more than his sense of wonderment and curiosity. He became convinced that the human mind was even more important to explore than the moon that he walked on. It took less than two years after his expedition to found the Institute of Noetic Sciences, an organization dedicated to "supporting individual and collective transformation through consciousness research."[72] Like Mitchell, many astronauts came to see themselves and their world differently upon their return to Earth. One astronaut said it was "one of the deepest, most emotional experiences I have ever had,"[73] and another stated that, "when you go around the Earth in an hour and a half, you begin to recognize that your identity is with that whole thing."[74]

The OE appears to expand one's perspective and approach to life. One way is that it removes national boundaries. The Earth is viewed as the home of people not separated by borders but as a world common to all and to be equally shared. It seems that the more humane perspective induced by the OE is just the needed prescription for inhabitants of our planet. If only we could build a large enough spacecraft to transport a few billion people in orbit around our pale blue dot in space.

Spiritual Emergency

The profound aftereffects of a PE can be catalysts for permanent positive transformations. But it requires a period of adjustment to be incorporated into one's life and can be a challenge to live with. For some, a PE elicits a "spiritual emergency."[75] A spiritual emergency can cause many negative feelings—depression, confusion, and feelings of insanity and loneliness are common. And for some, their "spiritual emergency" is considered a psychopathology to be treated with medication and/or psychotherapy.[76]

The integration process resulting from a PE may evolve over many years. During this time, the individual reflects upon the meaning and values gained by the experience, which presents great challenges. But once the experience and its accompanying challenges have been fully integrated, the following attributes may become part of the person's life: changes in values; a greater sense of well-being and a more positive outlook on life; a greater desire to learn and an increased sense of purpose; increased creativity and psychic abilities; loss of fear of death; and improved behavior and attitude toward others (unconditional love, empathy and compassion, etc.). A unique realization from a PE, especially in those who have had a NDE, is that death is a transition to one's next life.[77]

But a PE can certainly bring friction in life. It can adversely affect relationships with others, careers, money, religion, and spirituality. It is also very common for PErs to report an enhanced sensitivity to strong emotions and negative behaviors. While some PErs report no problems adjusting to "life as always," the majority find that they must face and deal with some very difficult issues.[78] Such consequences are reflected in these ensuing comments by PErs: (1) "I had to be alone with my senses a lot. This caused a problem with my relationships"; (2) "It's hard for other people to understand why I am so sensitive. I feel other people's pain"; (3) "I would pick up on people's anxiety and get stomach problems"; and (4) "I walk out of places that feel evil."[79]

One of the greatest challenges of a PEr is the impact of their experience on family members who struggle to understand their loved one's experience, who question its validity, and are perplexed by the "stranger" their loved one has become. This is especially true for one who has a NDE. In NDErs, for instance, separation is common and approximately 75 percent divorce within 7-10 years.[80] Although the behavioral effects of an NDE typically produce "positive changes in attitudes, beliefs, and values, it can also lead to interpersonal and intrapsychic problems."[81] Spouses, for instance, often report they no longer know or understand their loved one. Family members also report difficulty in accepting the NDErs expressions of love toward others and regard the perception of social connections in behavior as "silly," and the person's new interest in the paranormal as "unusual." The most common complaints from spouses are: "I don't know this person anymore," or, "This unconditional love nonsense is just an excuse to insult me by flirting with others." For the PEr, a common attitude is that "since I no longer fit in, I'll move on."[82] For these reasons, "the general mindset is that significant others become convinced that the experiencer was out-of-touch with reality, while the experiencer becomes convinced that significant others were slow to move forward and were not interested in making changes. It is as if the two speak different languages and no longer communicate effectively."[83]

One example of the effect that a PE had on a couple's relationship is highlighted as follows: "Consider the case of a woman who was married to a fundamentalist preacher. The two had been married for many years and had three children and a busy lifestyle. Since her NDE, it had become increasingly difficult for her to attend her husband's church services. As she put it: "He's wrong. I know now deep in my heart he's wrong. What he's preaching, that's not the way it is. I feel like he's telling everyone a lie and I don't know what to do about it. I love my husband and I love our children. I don't want to upset him or anyone else. I don't want a divorce or anything like that. But I can't listen anymore. I try to pretend I'm too busy to come.'"[84]

The search for validation and integration of the PE can be a daunting process. This is depicted by one who conveyed the following experience: "My relationship with my fiancé of four years became increasingly strained. The more I searched for answers and meaning to help me assimilate my experience, the further apart he and I became. It felt like there was no one I could talk to. No one understood what I'd been through and how terribly homesick I was for Heaven. I longed to go back to the light of God. I tried talking to my doctor and was met with a blank stare and his advice was that I should just forget about what had happened to me."[85] For this reason alone, these individuals deserve the opportunity to meet with a qualified therapist who is familiar with the PErs "spiritual emergency" and unique concerns. But the problem is that there are too few qualified to do so.

Discussion

The anecdotal and experimental PE evidence suggests that your consciousness may be separate from the physical body. And for those convinced that their PE felt unmistakably real, the burning question is whether their experience enabled them to become aware of another reality. The meaning of the PE, and its different triggers and associated anomalous perceptions are not well understood. But the validity of individual reports of a greater knowledge of one's self and life that accompany a PE may be more suited for philosophers and psychologists rather than scientists to solve. Regardless of who holds the possible solutions, however, the feeling of "realness" of the experience is generally associated with self-reported positive impacts across multiple life domains. Even if the PE is just an illusion that is, nevertheless, considered "very real," the fact that the subsequent personal transformations are largely positive are what matters most of all.

Regardless of whether the PE is facilitated by either a pure brain-based event or from a true interaction with an alternate realm, a matter of most importance to the individual and family members is trying to effectively manage and integrate the experience for all concerned. And, despite its elusive meaning, the nature of the PE's positive transformational character should somehow be added to every bottle of soda, beer, and water worldwide. If only it can! New paradigms for studying consciousness, an essential component of the PE and its triggers, may somehow determine if one does "see a different world" or is, instead, "seeing this world differently."

CHAPTER 3

INTERACTIONS WITH NON-HUMAN ENTITIES

Introduction

In ancient times, indigenous populations practiced complex physical, mental, and spiritual exercises aimed at providing them access to alternate realms. For them it was not a question of whether it was real. It was their practice and a living reality. Today's accounts of accessing other realms via a PE may be one and the same. Although science will typically view this notion as culturally loaded imaginative events, many millions contend this alternate realm exists. Why? Because they believe they pierced its veil and experienced it!

Over the centuries, people have accepted stories in religious texts as literal accounts of actual events. These stories have been a source of inspiration. They tell us that God chose Moses, Mary encountered the angel Gabriel, and powerful supernatural beings were considered as gods. Despite the allegorical and controversial nature of such writings, a large portion of most societies today believe the stories to be true. The unique similarities of these narratives with those described by modern day PErs, suggest that ancient versions of NHE interactions may be the same as those reported today.

Cultures throughout the world have numerous legends about heavenly beings appearing to them from the skies. Maybe such encounters helped transition them from primitive lifestyles to more civilized human beings. Anthropologist A.P. Elkin, for example, obtained data from more than 80 tribes of aboriginals from Australia about their 60,000 year tradition of crystal-insertion operations done on them by "sky people."[1] They tell of how the "sky people" come down from the heavens and take humans to the "sky world," cut them open and insert quartz crystals or other magical substances into their bodies. Afterward, that person becomes a medicine man or shaman and is said to have the "clairvoyant Strong Eye," can perform "healing or killing," and has the ability to appear in more than one place simultaneously. They have supernatural abilities that allow them to interact with spirits, and travel between our physical world and the dream world, the spirit world, and the world of the dead and safely back again.[2]

The belief and reports of NHEs, such as spirits, ghosts, and the afterlife are generally considered an irrational byproduct of religious texts and culture practices. Interactions with NHE in humankind's past could well have been the basis for our religious beliefs today. Today's knowledge provides no better answers than thousands of years ago. Even today, reported NHE interactions are quite common among individuals of all educational levels, religious backgrounds, and cultural upbringing. Comparison of ancient accounts and traditions to our modern day UAP abductions and alien experiments are strikingly similar.

It is certainly premature to firmly conclude that NHEs are conscious beings and possess some kind of non-physical body (resurrection body, subtle body, astral body, etc.), and who may interact with our body and/or consciousness and influence our thoughts and experiences. Still, it is more than just my gut feeling that tells me the PE may be responsible, in part, for the many unexplained experiences reported by millions across cultures to the present day. This kind of larger reality thinking suggests the possibility that beings, spirits, or anything at all could "crossover" from the unseen or "other" world into our material reality. "This crossover seems to be regarded as a regular occurrence in many if not most indigenous cultures, but in our Western or scientific/materialist society, the domains of spirit and matter have been kept separate and distinct, and the possibility of traffic between them is looked upon as doubtful if not altogether impossible."[3]

Interactions with Non-Human Entities

Overview: The PE covers a huge landscape. It includes virtually all forms of anomalous contact with NHEs—aliens, angels, Djinn, fairies, ghosts, supreme beings, and the deceased. They may all be the same spokes of a wheel, but providing meaning to the experience is difficult, especially since most physicians consider the PEr just another "lunatic" in need of psychiatric attention. This may be true in some cases, but certainly not all. Well-balanced individuals have and will continue to experience such interactions, and the reason(s) cannot be entirely dismissed as a pure aberrant neurological brain event. Short circuits don't induce interactions with NHEs that transform people. Rather, the PE does. Contact experience with NHEs, for instance, has been reported in those who have had a NDE and OBE,[14-16] while remote viewing,[17,18] during hallucinogenic experiences,[19, 20] and in UAP abductees/contactees.[21,22]

Archetypes of Non-Human Entities: In centuries past, "little men" were often seen as dwellers of the "underworld," and today, these beings may very well be the so-called alien "greys" often associated with UAP. Eminent psychiatrist Carl Jung, who founded analytical psychology, termed these beings "archetypes" —a form of symbolic reality of images and dreams that interact with humans on a subconscious level (archetypes "connect" all humans).[4]

55

Archetypal images or "imprinted inherited experiences of all mankind," connect our world to the spirit. They are the same for all cultures, common to all people, and correspond to the evolutionary development of humankind.[5] In other words, human behavior is "conditioned by the aims and aspirations of the individual" and by his or her own "history of the species trapped in the experience."[6] Dreams may even represent archetypal guidance facilitated from the wisdom of our ancestors, and NHEs may represent an archetype from an alternate reality. If Jung's concept that this archetype exists in another realm and is capable of influencing us, then maybe NHEs influenced humans throughout time?

Archetypes are imprinted on our psyche, and they connect us with our ancestors. The UAP and their associated NHEs may represent a "symbolical event ushering in great changes."[7] In this sense, the UAP may be modern symbols for the ancient gods which assisted humans in time of need. The psychological and archetypal component of the UAP inspired Jung to propose that "flying saucers" were a product of the collective human unconscious and a "modern myth in the making"[8]—the physical manifestations of archetypal elements evolved from the "needs" of the human, called the "psychoid."[9, 10]

Jung's concepts raise an obvious question. That is, are archetypes the same phenomena that change their appearance to suit the culture and time period in which they manifest? He wrote, "The absurd behavior of UFO entities is the same as the mischievous behavior of elves and fairies in Celtic legends, the Norse gods, and the trickster figures among the Native Americans."[11] These entities appear intelligent, timeless, and quite possibly the phenomenon or "archetype" on which all myths are based. Like Jung, astrophysicist and noted UAP investigator Jacques Vallee considered the UAP an old phenomenon in a new guise—modern accounts of UAP resemble various folkloric traditions.[12] But are they truly one of the same phenomena experienced throughout humankind?

Unidentified Aerial Phenomena

Overview: There are more stars in the visible universe than all the grains of sand on all the beaches on our pale blue dot in space. The universe is designed for life, and the fact that you are reading this here and now should be visibly convincing that life thrives throughout the infinite universe. The question is not whether life exists beyond Earth, but rather whether non-human life forms are interacting with humans. I even wrote a book on the subject: *The UFO Phenomenon: Should I Believe?*[36]

One clue may be found in the similarity between modern accounts of interaction with NHEs and the alien abduction phenomenon and the ancient narratives described in various contexts throughout history. Even eminent astronomer Carl Sagan theorized that such stories of contact are common throughout history and share remarkable similarities with the "alien abduction experience."[37] Sagan was right. In fact, this concern was reinforced by the recent study results using a large population database (N = 3,526) which addressed the physical and psychological effects of the UAP experience on those who interact with it. In this study, which I co-authored in a 2018 publication in the *Journal of Scientific Exploration*, titled: "A Study on Reported Contact with Non-Human Intelligence Associated with Unidentified Aerial Phenomena," my colleagues and I concluded that "contact and interaction in the form of sensing, visualizing, and/or communicating with NHE occur frequently but only occasionally in connection with a UAP sighting."[38]

This research granted me the unique opportunity to critically review and analyze firsthand accounts of thousands of individuals who claimed to have interacted with NHEs—both with and without the presence of the UAP. Surprisingly, the results indicated that the vast majority of those who reported to have interacted with a NHE claimed that their contact experience was "largely non-physical and could occur via telepathy, during an OBE, being floated into a 'matrix-like' reality, as well as through physical interaction on board a craft."[39] For this reason, there appears to be many different anomalous aspects of the

UAP which incorporate the components of consciousness and holographic-like perceptions of a PE. These attributes were represented in this study as follows: (1) 67 percent reported that their "consciousness separated from their body" at the time of their contact experience, and (2) 70 percent believed to have felt a "sense of expanded consciousness" in the presence of NHEs.[40] Alterations in perception, emotion, and viewpoints were also a common outcome of the subject's interaction(s) with UAP-NHE.

Of significant importance is that the reported perceptual characteristics of the UAP were uniquely similar to that documented in other studies associated with other types of PE triggers: the NDE, OBE, meditation, and psychoactive drugs, noted prior. In other words, despite different triggers that give rise to a PE, each seems to facilitate a similar non-provable experience that can only be validated by the experiencer. Taking their word for it just doesn't cut it in our scientific materialistic paradigm. So, how can their experiences be proven?

Consciousness and the Evolution of UAP: There exists an undeniable link between consciousness and the UAP—"affairs here on earth have consistently colored our perceptions of what is going on over our heads."[41] Historical examples illustrate that many of the characteristics of the UAP are associated with an aspect of consciousness; it combines modern mythology, literary narrative, popular culture, and human psychology. It also seems likely that this explanatory approach can be generalized and applied to the so-called paranormal.[42] More specifically, there exists convincing evidence of ESP and other psychic ability as part of a UAP experience, but whether actual telepathy or psychic abilities are fully substantiated is a debatable issue. That is, are UAP experiencers interpreting their perceptions and telepathic communication as true reality? If so, how can this be appropriately measured, analyzed, and proven? It can't. At least not with current scientific principles and experimental approaches and analysis, especially since the UAP simply does not conform to our 3D reality as we know it. Science is way behind the curve on this issue.

Many features of a UAP sighting and subsequent alien abduction accounts include "missing time," and memories being "recovered" through dreams and hypnotic regression. Consciousness, therefore, may be the key to unlocking this mystery. One very curious and important aspect of UAP and NHE descriptions is how their appearance has changed as aviation technology evolved over time. The NHEs have transitioned in form from hairy dwarves, to giant insects, to today's small "greys" with oversized heads and eyes. One key hint to the nature of UAP is that both perception and memory affect the observer's pre-existing beliefs and expectations. They use their personal experiences and knowledge of world events to make sense of the UAP.[43]

The UAP evolved from descriptions of elves and gnomes in European countries, to medieval accounts of angels, to the supernatural beings described in Native American legends. It seems ancient accounts now include modern day UAP and NHE characteristics such as abductions, surgical operations, sexual intercourse with entities, and mysterious marks and scars left on the body of the experiencers.[13] Stories of NHE interactions throughout history share remarkable similarities with the "alien abduction experience" of individuals who report to have been physically taken and relocated on board a UAP craft by NHE. For these reasons, the NHE may be a recent variation on the ancient traditions of encounters with non-human forms. We can see this in the similar content of historical UAP and NHE narratives with modern-day accounts by those who have had an OBE and NDE, among other PE triggers.

The anecdotal UAP evidence typically portrays NHEs ("the greys") of short stature (three to four feet) with abnormally large, bald heads having two large round and bulging black eyes that are wide apart. Other features include a protruding forehead, wrinkled skin, absent nose except for nostrils, a horizontal slit for a mouth, and long arms. Non-grey "human-looking" NHEs have also been described as Caucasian, similar in height to humans, with shoulder-length blonde hair, oriental shaped eyes and human-like noses and ears. Some act like saints, others like demons.

The strange things humans perceive have changed over time. From the flying vehicles and NHEs in Stone Age cave paintings, to the elves, fairies, and prophetic visions of the Middle Ages, to the modern-day shaman and extraterrestrial aliens.

For this reason, many contend that UAP and NHEs have been interacting with humans for thousands of years. Evidence of their presence is found in religious texts, on cave walls, and archaeological monuments such as the Great Pyramid and ancient geoglyphs in the Nazca Desert of Peru. This controversial idea emerged decades ago by those who referred to them as "ancient astronauts."

Spectacles such as comets and meteors were rationalized within a religious or supernatural context as acts of gods and interpreted as divine communications. Accounts of UAP are rooted in culture and religious texts. One example is the story of Jacob's Ladder: it revolves around his dream of "angels of God" who were "ascending and descending" upon a "stairway resting on the Earth, with its top reaching into Heaven." As Jacob watched the angels, he heard a voice and saw "the Lord" above him in the sky.[23] The description of the Exodus and the Burning Bush story have also been interpreted as interventions by non-humans. Upon the Israelites' arrival at Mount Sinai, Moses is told to come to the top of the mountain to meet the Lord and receive the stone plaques of the Ten Commandments, an encounter that many interpret as an interaction between human beings and NHE to help guide humanity.[24] Moreover, the famous story of Elijah being taken by the Lord "up to heaven" in a "chariot of fire" may represent today's UAP and alien abduction scenario. The "fire" reference may have been in response to seeing propulsion upon its ascent into "heaven."[25]

Furthermore, in the opening verses of Zechariah 5, a description of a flying object as a "flying scroll"—"the length thereof is twenty cubits and the breadth thereof ten cubits"—suggests a UAP sighting.[26] The account of Ezekiel's wheel in the Book of Ezekiel, which describes a metallic object in the sky, has also been interpreted as a UAP event. The first verse, for example, states that "the heavens were opened, and I saw visions of God." Verse 16 speaks of a description of a gleaming object that appeared to be "a wheel within a wheel."[27] Reports of modern day UAP described as a craft made of circles spinning, sometimes in opposite directions to each other, may have also been interpreted as "a wheel within a wheel" long ago.

Moreover, the Hebrew Book of Enoch describes "evil spirits" or "fallen angels" that watch us and collect the souls of evil people.[28] These creatures have the appearance of small gray-colored children. Sound familiar? The "small gray colored children" may be today's "little "grey beings" often reported with UAP. The Bible story of the birth of Jesus Christ may also be analogous to contemporary UAP encounters. Mary, for example, discovering she is miraculously pregnant has been viewed as an alien abduction, with the implanting of a fetus in Mary's womb and instructions given to her under the guise of "God."[29]

Even in the Stone Age, as depicted on cave walls, spirits took shamans on magical trips that included surgical-like procedures with spears/arrows being stuck into them. Also painted were the half-men/half-beast-like figures, magical animals, and strange, large-headed humanoids. Similarly, the elves, fairies, little people, and women in white took people into other realms, seemingly experimented on them, and tried to create "hybrids." These humanoids varied widely in appearance; height alone ranged from a few inches to many feet. They possessed supernatural powers and sometimes kidnapped adults and children. These unpredictable creatures, considered to be of a "middle nature between man and angels," were so feared that it was considered foolish to mention their name.[30]

Fast forward to the late 1800s when giant airships similar to "blimps" of the time served as their UAP. Also, the airships themselves conformed to nineteenth-century fiction and their cultural antecedents with flapping wings and bulbous fuselages, rather than the form real aircraft eventually took. The airship fever of the late 1800s contained many of the features of the modern UFO story, including credible witnesses, media hype driving sightings, contact and even abduction, and alleged physical evidence.

Then during World War II, combat pilots reported strange objects called "foo fighters" who followed them so closely as to seem almost magnetized to their craft. In the 1940s and 1950s the UAP represented the science fiction of the time. The contactees of the 1950s described contacts with glowing humans from Venus,

Moonmen, and Martians. Sightings of drone-like objects drew concern from military and intelligence officials about possible security threats, especially since the UAP was often seen around nuclear installations around the world.[44, 45] Eventually the little grey alien became the modern myth of the time with the Betty and Barney Hill alleged abduction in 1966. The image of the little greys resonated with human consciousness and became solidified as the standard alien icon. Once certain details become a standard part of the mythology, they are often then retrofitted into older stories. The famous Roswell Incident, for example, existed for almost 30 years, from 1947 until the 1970s, without any mention of alien bodies. It was only after the little greys emerged that testimony arose of witnesses seeing similar aliens in Roswell in 1947. Consciousness, therefore, may be the key to the UAP.[46]

Conclusion: We can see from the similarities between paintings on prehistoric caves and engravings of Middle Age magical beings with today's accounts of UAP "aliens" that a common origin for these beings exists. As in the past, modern day NHE accounts involve invasive procedures, interbreeding, and UAP that defy laws of physics (mitigate inertia and gravity, appear and disappear instantaneously, and change shape). Similar to historical narratives and drawings, the modern day UAP occupant "greys" have large, pear-shaped heads and eyes, they communicate knowledge to us using telepathy, change shape, move through solid objects, and instantaneously appear and disappear. Like our ancestors, the UAP and NHE were associated with a strong indication of the supernatural.

Even noted researcher of consciousness studies and OBEs, Robert Monroe, concluded that NHEs are "totally solicitous as to the well-being of the human beings with whom they are associated. Perceiving our thoughts is absurdly easy for them, and "the entire history of humankind and earth is available to them in minute detail."[31] Likewise, eminent writer and paranormal researcher, Brad Steiger, reported that approximately 90 percent of over 40,000 respondents to his questionnaire on mystical and paranormal experiences believed they interacted with a guardian angel or spirit guide, and almost 80 percent experienced an encounter with a benevolent being of light.[32] "Manifestations of light often accompany the benevolent beings, which adds to the grandeur of their appearance and the feelings of profound reverence that suffuses those who encounter them."[33] But are both ancient and present reports of NHE and UAP caused by a brain pathology, archetypes, PEs, or real vehicles and entities interacting with humans through time? Or are they a psychic phenomenon?

Critical to better understanding the complex aspects of the apparent physical and non-physical characteristics of the UAP and their associated impact on human behavior, is research with those who interact with this phenomenon using different approaches unique to several fields of study (psychology, physics, sociology, and biology, etc.). Critical to this endeavor is to test hypotheses on the role that altered perceptions, consciousness, and changes in viewpoints and values play in those who experience a PE. This approach is essential towards understanding poorly understood and complex phenomena; the UAP and consciousness. But there exists one major limitation in the form of a confounding variable that impedes this successful analysis—current scientific principles, methodology, analysis, and the criteria for "proof" or validation of the UAP and the PE. They don't apply or even exist.

Paranormal UAP Activity: Psychic phenomena are common mysterious characteristics often associated with the UAP. These include a distortion of time and an overwhelming feeling of isolation, but once the UAP leaves, these feelings disappear. For this reason, the UAP may be creating a different local state of space-time experienced by the witness. If true, it may account for the altered state of consciousness reported by those who closely interact with UAP. That is, normal space and time end as they experience the altered time-space of the UAP.

This effect may explain why environmental sound disappears and time slows. This may be one reason why UAP events have been considered as much "psychic" as "physical" in nature, and either "very clever deception or very advanced physical principles… The manifestations of UAPs are not spacecraft in the ordinary 'nuts and bolts' sense. The UAPs are physical manifestations that cannot be understood apart from their psychic and symbolic reality. What we see in effect here is a control system which acts on humans and uses humans."[34]

This control system parallels that of the world's leading authority on the UAP, astrophysicist J. Allen Hynek, who acted as scientific advisor to UAP studies undertaken by the U.S. Air Force (Project Sign, Grudge, and Blue Book). Hynek's extensive research led him to conclude that other dimensions or parallel universes may serve as possible origins of UAPs. He stated: "I hold it entirely possible that a technology exists which encompasses both the physical and the psychic, the material and the mental. The UAP is "so strange and foreign to our daily terrestrial mode of thought... we must consider the various factors that indicate a link or at least a parallel with episodes of paranormal nature very clearly." [35, 36]

Decades later, Hynek's perspective is just now gaining acceptance by others who are moving away from the pure "nuts and bolts" aspect of the phenomena. The UAP indeed indicates the existence of some kind of intelligence that alters consciousness in those who interact with the phenomenon.

The UAP-NHEs appear to create a story of extraterrestrial visitation from a human subconscious perspective. For instance, "the Phoenician amulets, the close encounters with 'occupants' in our time, the ancient beam from heaven, and the focused light from UAPs seem to imply a technology capable of both physical manifestation and psychic effects, a technology that strikes deep at the collective consciousness, confusing us, molding us—as perhaps it confused and molded human civilization at the end of antiquity."[43] This concept was supported in a study which showed that 88 percent of 43 UAP experiencers reported paranormal activity in their homes (light orbs that dart or float through the air, poltergeist activity such as household items flying through the air, and pictures flying off walls, etc.).[44, 45] Other studies have also noted paranormal activity with UAP which include a sense of a strange figure present, ghosts, missing time, and unexplained scars on the body of the contact experiencer.[46, 47]

Many aspects of modern UAP and humanoid encounters appear analogous to ancient folklore and religious visions. A large segment of the UAP literature, for instance, is associated with the occult and the metaphysical, such as invisible beings, demons, and ghosts, and many UAP incidents are similar to demonic possession and psychic phenomena. Such evidence was popularized by John Keel in his book *Operation Trojan Horse*: "Ufology is just another name for demonology. The objects and apparitions do not necessarily originate on another planet and may not even exist as permanent constructions of matter. It is more likely that we see what we want to see and interpret such visions according to our contemporary beliefs."[37]

Keel used the term "ultraterrestrials" to describe these "shape-changing, non-human" UAP occupants. A close UAP experience, for example, often begins with a sudden flash of light which changes color, or a humming/buzzing sound followed by a type of paralysis associated with hallucinations and lost time for up to several hours. An apparent physical object also begins to form, such as an unusual flying machine or an entity of some kind.[38] The paranormal nature of UAP and their occupants is detailed in the following documented cases:

(1) "Thousands of residents in Voronezh, Russia observed UAPs over a six-day period in September 1989. In one incident, a 45-foot-wide red light descended from the sky and hovered over a park. Suddenly, a door opened and a 10-foot-tall being with no neck and three eyes, wearing a silver outfit and bronze-colored boots appeared. The door then closed and the craft landed. The being verbalized and a rectangular object suddenly appeared on the ground. When one 16-year-old boy cried out in fear, the being's eyes discharged a light at the child causing temporary paralysis. The craft disappeared but then reappeared a few minutes later. The being now held a long tube at its side which he pointed at the boy who became invisible. The being then reentered the sphere, and as the object flew away, the boy reappeared. After taking off, the craft instantaneously disappeared in the sky. An investigation revealed that the radioactivity level at the landing site was double the background level. Traces were also found where the craft's legs stood along with an area of flattened grass and soil."[39]

(2) The Skinwalker Ranch, located in the Uinta County in Utah, has been the site of many strange events witnessed by

hundreds of people over the past 50 years. This includes not only UAP sightings but also animal mutilations and disappearances; poltergeist events; sightings of Bigfoot-like creatures; crop circles; glowing orbs; and physical effects on plants, soil, and humans. More specifically, incidents at the ranch include: (1) glowing blue orbs that causes fear; (2) cattle slaughtered with precision—the removal of an ear, excision of genitals, and removal of the anus; (3) UAPs in the form of black triangles, and a large refrigerator-shaped object that hovers and disappears; (4) reptilian creatures and humanoids that exit UAPs; (5) balls of light that enter and exit a lake; (6) humanoids that exit a lighted portal; and (7) voices that speak from the air in an unintelligible language. One scientist who investigated the phenomena stated: "It isn't as simple as saying that ET's or flying saucers are doing it. It's some kind of consciousness, but it's always something new and different, something non-repeatable. It's reactive to people and equipment, and we set up the ranch to be a proving ground for the scientific method, but science doesn't seem amenable to the solution of these kinds of problems."[40]

(3) In 1965, an incident in France included landing traces, effects on vegetation and humans, and descriptions of beings associated with UAP. Near the village of Valensole, farmer Maurice Masse observed an object descend from the sky and land in a field 200 feet away. He described it as an oval-shaped structure resting on four legs with two beings in front of it who looked like "small boys" about four feet tall wearing tight, gray-green clothes. Masse portrayed them as having oversized heads with sharp chins, large and slanted eyes, and making a "grumbling" noise. Curiously, one of the beings pointed a small device at Masse, paralyzing him, and then entered the craft and flew away. Masse required 20 minutes to recover his mobility. The object left a deep hole and a moist area that soon hardened like concrete.[41]

(4) Another strange incident involved the crew and passengers of a Russian Aeroflot flight in 1984. They reported seeing an enormous "yellow star" which projected a beam of light toward the ground and then into the aircraft cabin, forming

a "green cloud." The object paralleled the plane and discharged several different colored lights and changed shape as if to mimic the plane. The crew reported it became a "wingless cloud-aircraft with a pointed tail." The "cloud" continued to escort the plane for over an hour until it began to descend to land. Strangely, ground radar had picked up two blips trailing behind the aircraft, and while these targets were reported to be "solid," the radar reflection of the aircraft kept fading in and out. As another plane approached the UAP, the object emitted a light that struck the two pilots. Several days later, one of them was taken to hospital where he later died from a type of blood cancer. A similar disease reportedly caused the other pilot to be disabled his entire life.[42]

These few UAP cases, combined with thousands of similar documented events, raise an important question: Are we dealing with something more than a projection of Jung's archetypal images, like a "psychic technology" that produces paranormal activity? Many believe we are. And if so, for what purpose? Is it to awaken human potential to accelerate our own evolution? The Distortion Theory proposed by ufologist Jose Antonio Caravaca seems to address the core aspects of this concern more than most, if not all, UAP theories. This hypothesis holds that an "unknown foreign agent uses the psyche of the witness...for the manufacture of the contents and elements that come together in close encounters with the UAP. The symbiosis or communication of the mind of the observer and this undefined operator is capable of emitting a complex type of "holographic projection" that can sometimes be tangible enough to leave footprints and marks on the ground."[43] It is common, for example, for UAP experiencers to report NHEs emitting light rays that immobilize them; study the terrain; repair their spaceship, or convey non-verbal thoughts asking where they are, for water, or other mundane or absurd questions.

Conclusion: Given this historical context, is it possible that paranormal activity associated with UAP provides evidence of its nature and origin? It is impossible to know for sure, but at the very least, we can see that a paradox exists with the UAP and associated paranormal evidence. One possible explanation is that we may be dealing with a phenomenon capable of producing paranormal events in the minds of those who interact with it. Although it would be a giant leap to claim to know the nature of the UAP-NHE relationship, the answer will likely evolve from research on paranormal activity and the altered states of consciousness associated with them.

Ayahuasca and Non-Human Entities

Overview: The altered state of consciousness associated with ayahuasca or dimethyltryptamine (DMT), a naturally occurring hallucinogenic chemical found in many plants, has been associated with induced visions of NHEs.[48] The DMT experience is novel in intensity and quality that is difficult to understand unless experienced. Commonly described features include a feeling of transcending one's body and entering into an alternative "realm," a perception of a high pitched sound, perceiving and communicating with "presences" or "entities," and considerations on death and the after-life.[49-53] More specifically, the DMT experience is characterized as: (1) an interior flow of energy/consciousness; (2) vivid two-dimensional geometric visual patterns; (3) passage through an entrance into another world; and (4) a three- or higher-dimensional space environment where interaction and communication with entities take place.[54, 55]

DMT Entities: While research on this phenomenon is limited, evidence of DMT entities has been obtained in clinical research,[56] survey studies,[57] ontology,[58] and cultural history. Perhaps one of the most significant and common aspects of the DMT experience is that of perceiving alternate realities often inhabited by discarnate NHEs. These entities are frequently described as "beings," "aliens," "guides," or "helpers," and supremely powerful, wise, and loving angels, spirits, or gods—more real than anything previously experienced and capable of interaction.[59] The DMT entities have been categorized as: (1) mythological gnomes, elves, fairies, and monsters of all kinds; (2) chimeras or hybrids: typically half-human, half-animal, or shapeshifting beings, from human to puma, to tiger, to wolf; (3) extraterrestrials: these are particularly common for some and may be accompanied by spacecraft; (4) angels and celestial beings: usually winged, humanlike beings that may be transparent or composed of light; (5) semi-divine beings: Jesus, Buddha, or pre-Columbian deities; and (6) demons, monsters and beings of death.[60, 61]

To some, these findings suggest DMT can reliably induce a perceived encounter with an alternate realm inhabited by NHEs. Sentient, independently existing entities, for example, were described in half of 19 DMT subjects in one study,[62] and in 67 percent of 340 DMT subject reports analyzed in another.[63] The NHEs in these studies covered a wide range, from teachers to archons, elves to mantids, and shapeshifting humanoids to tree spirits.[64] In one study, the diverse "ultradimensionals" appeared to be motivated by a spectrum of purposes, from visitations by "machine elves of hyperspace" to entities similar to those from alien abduction reports.[65, 66]

There exists a range of theories for DMT entities, from hallucinations to truly autonomous sentient beings from another dimension, to complex archetypal expressions.[67, 68] A common theme of DMT users, for example, is of "entering other realities" and having what the user described as "real encounters with sentient beings."[69] One significant characteristic of subjects' reports were of entities conveying "insightful information about themselves and the universe" that they inhabited, similar to the sentient beings encountered in NDEs.[70] This experience is a common occurrence for those entering these realms. Here is an exemplary report:

"They were everywhere jabbering in indecipherable tongues, juggling incandescent neon micro-worlds of dancing beings, and morphing with a Zen-like, diaphanous fluidity that remains a primal miracle no matter how often you lay your all-too-human eyes on it. The primordial intelligence being manifest before me was palpable, undeniable, transcendently amazing—it shook me to my core in a more-than-real, gleeful profundity. All I could do was sit there in divine liquid awe, my soul gaping wide open, and stare at the incalculable proportions of bizarreness and the downright weird that lay before me."[71]

Several other anecdotal accounts by DMT experiencers are as follows:

(1) "I was transported to that extremely alien-like realm that I had been to so many times before. I felt like I was being schooled on existence. A teacher entity that seemed to have some sort of almost condescending power over me was trying to convince me that 'they' constructed our reality completely and tried to get me to agree that this reality was not under our control; it was being constructed and predetermined by an outside force completely."[72]

(2) "A black field. I am ensconced but know of nothing other than vision. I see black. Then, and I am sure, for this happened several times (so similar, but never identical), the most adorable, invitingly furry, bipedal creature that I had ever seen walks from right to left. (From a post titled "You're Just as Adorable as a Muppet to DMT.")[73]

(3) "I find myself looking down from great height on a house at night. Soon I find myself looking at the house I grew up in, from a vantage point of 10 feet from the property line and 15 feet up. The music swells to a dynamic peak and I think, 'I'm home!' I feel a sense of homecoming like nothing I've ever felt before, like when you return to a beloved childhood haunt years after your last visit but magnified ten times."[74]

(4) "I continued floating around in the three-dimensional DMT space without anything too significant happening, when I was found by a very advanced extraterrestrial being. His kind liked humanity and they enjoyed helping humans evolve at a very fast rate. I could feel this being empowering me and showing me advanced things. He helped direct my awareness to different things, all of which were helpful to my evolution. Anytime my awareness shifted to something of no use, especially things that would enable fear, he would give me a nudge to not pay attention to it but to focus on the useful things that were good for me. He also could sense weaknesses in me as I brought them up from my consciousness and helped me overcome them. At the same time this being was learning from his interaction with me. It was a positive experience."[75]

(5) "I'm in a room. There are two adults, female and male. I sense their glorious power, it flows off them like the sun radiates light. I am a child here, ignorant, frightened and confused. I only see them from their waist down to their feet, I don't even try to look up to them for I am not worthy. There is a table/box full of toys and there is a young child exploring them. My God, this is so intense, I don't know if I like it. Panic grips my body once again, everything is so alien and terrifying. Wait, I'm here! I'm right here, right now! I've dreamed of being here, I've fantasized about meeting these beings, I've prayed for conclusive answers possibly arising from a 'breakthrough' experience, and here I am."[76]

Similarities of DMT and PE Trigger Experiences: Similar to all PE triggers (NDE, OBE, UAP, and meditation, etc.), the DMT experience facilitates psychological phenomena in the form of "spontaneous mystical experiences, and non-human entity contact" that can have a lasting, and generally positive, life-altering effect on one's personal viewpoints.[77] For DMT experiencers, the trance may be disturbing or it may be exhilarating, give cause for alarm, induce a state of grace, challenge one's belief system, inspire re-evaluation of one's motives, or incite a sense of responsibility.[78]

Other intriguing similarities of NHE encounters occur in those who have either a DMT[79-81] or UAP experience.[82-84] These include: (1) the probing and testing of one's mind and body; (2) the beings communicating through gestures, telepathy or visual imagery; and (3) the sensation of floating in a tunnel of light leading to the center of the galaxy or to an angelic realm, and a complete loss of ego. Like the alien abduction phenomena, DMT experiencers report experimental procedures by NHEs. Picture these accounts by DMT experiencers:

(1) "There were four distinct beings looking down on me, like I was on an operating-room table. I opened my eyes to see if it was you and Josette, but it wasn't. They had done something and were observing the results. They are vastly advanced scientifically and technologically."[85]

(2) "I felt like I was in an alien laboratory, in a hospital bed like this, but it was over there. A sort of landing bay, or recovery area. There were beings. I was trying to get a handle on what was going on. I was being carted around. It didn't look alien, but their

sense of purpose was. It was a three-dimensional space...They had a space ready for me. They weren't as surprised as I was. It was incredibly unpsychedelic. I was able to pay attention to detail. There was one main creature, and he seemed to be behind it all, overseeing everything. The others were orderlies, or disorderlies."[86, 87]

The varieties of the DMT experience, like all other PE triggers, are felt to be "more real than real and not dream-like."[88] Similarities between subjective accounts of the DMT experience and NDE have been observed with the former report emphasizing noetic quality and ineffability and the latter with the appearance of discarnate entities. Researchers, for instance, have independently reported that DMT is the main cause for producing all mystical experience and NDEs.[89] Such attributes include the subjective feeling of transcending one's body, entering an alternative realm described as "realer than real," perceiving NHEs, and themes related to death and dying.[90-92] Moreover, the DMT, NDE and UAP experiences cause similar behavioral aftereffects in one's personal viewpoints (e.g., loss of the fear of death, and an increase in spirituality, etc.). Not unlike those having an NDE event, the DMT experiencer is "embraced by something much greater than themselves, or anything they previously could have imagined: the "source of all existence; an indescribably loving and powerful white light that emanates from the divine, holy, and sacred." Those who attain this experience "emerge with a greater appreciation for life, less fear of death, and a reorientation of their priorities to less material and more spiritual pursuits."[93]

The parallels among these PE triggers have led researchers to determine the extent to which DMT could induce a near-death type experience. In one novel study, for example, a validated measure of NDEs (Greyson Scale) compared 13 subjects given intravenous DMT with individuals who claimed to have had "actual" NDEs. The results showed a "comparable profile" with "few discernable differences between the experiences of the actual NDE cases and those induced by DMT."[94] Comparable psychological relationships between the NDE and DMT in the form of "ego-dissolution and mystical-type experiences," and trait "absorption" and "delusional ideation," suggest that "delusional thinking" and "personality trait absorption" may mediate the intensity and quality of the DMT experience and NDE.[95-97]

Theories proposed to explain the DMT experience include the obvious in the form of hallucinations induced by neurological and psychological factors. One controversial theory considers the DMT experience as evidence of an actual encounter with alternate dimensions and their inhabitants. The rationale for this controversial theory evolved from the similarities of NHE reports among different PE triggers.[98-103] Research findings, for instance, indicate that NHEs serve as the foundation of the DMT and alien abduction phenomena, and both may enable one's consciousness to interact and communicate with beings of other realities.[104, 105] Noted DMT researcher Rick Strassman and psychiatrist and leading UAP abduction researcher John Mack once met to discuss their research results, and according to Strassman, they were "blown away" by the similarity of reported experiences in Mack's UAP abductees and his DMT subjects.[106] These similarities are likely more than just mere coincidence.

In fact, Mack thought that another existing dimension of space-time may intrude into one's consciousness under certain conditions, and that this alternate reality could "violate the strict separation between the subjective, psychological world inside our mind, and the objective, physical world out there."[138] This logic was the only way he could explain how clients with no psychological disorders could believe they interacted with UAP and NHEs in another realm of existence. Interestingly, Mack's conclusion is similar to Vallee's belief of a "third zone" that violates the boundaries between the subjective world of mind and the objective world of matter out there." Further, Vallee contends that "ontological shock" is actually the means by which the UAP facilitates an enhancement of one's perception of reality towards a worldview where prior absurd notions become meaningful.[139] While subject to interpretation and debate, it is tempting to speculate that the PEr's dramatic change in personal and philosophical viewpoints may support Vallee's hypothesis that the UAP experiencer's new transformative outlook on life may contribute to what he called a "new cosmic behavior" or belief system facilitated by some form of intelligence to influence our society (i.e., altering old belief systems and enacting new ones). This concept, however, cannot be either firmly dismissed or supported since we have yet to determine the individual's own contribution to their overall experience of a unique constellation of physical and non-physical phenomena.

In light of the similarities between aliens and elves induced by DMT and UAP, noted researcher and author Graham Hancock considered that the historic-folkloric legends and testimonies of elves parallel the UAP encounter/abduction experiences.[107] DMT entities have also been interpreted as "intelligent" beings that manifest as "extraterrestrial or even extradimensional alien species, spirits of the dead or time travelers from the future," who provide access to a "true alternate dimension."[108] These entities may even be real "tricksters" who are deceptive and provide false information that exceed the experiencer's knowledge.[109] In contrast to such notions, however, a materialistic perspective is that these entities are "unfamiliar aspects of ourselves" that rise from our reptilian brain or our cells, molecules or sub-atomic particles into conscious awareness.[110]

Conclusion: The DMT experiencer is frequently exposed to encounters with NHEs who convey important information that is subject to interpretation. It is as if the DMT user encounters the alien character of the self that is vital to the experience and of great significance to the user. While the nature of this alien self or NHE beings may be disputed, the experience is consistent with other PE triggers which seem to facilitate self-realization and growth. But despite the significance and explanation of DMT entities,[111-114] the nature, purpose, and validity of such entities remain poorly understood. The answer is of critical importance to those who experience it and to the world at large.

The Trickster Archetype: Are We Being Deceived?

Overview: The NHE trickster archetype is dominant in many religious beliefs, although Western science rejects any hint of the supernatural. Trickster mythology, laced with sexuality and filled with the supernatural, has been largely ignored by the academic community. Even many anthropologists have found the material too embarrassing and irrational to consider seriously. Their position, like most physicists, however, is inconsistent with the fact that they acknowledge ethereal theories such as hidden dimensions, wormholes, and dark energy, yet firmly denounce those who report to have experienced the supernatural world and interacted with NHEs. This contradiction is absurdly palpable.

The hidden "tricksters," or "Djinn," depicted in early Arabian and later Islamic mythology and theology have been referred to as genies (stories such as Aladdin) and present themselves in different forms, including humanoid, shadowy figures, and animal. Some of them are physical and may represent today's "extraterrestrials," and "ultraterrestrials." The numerous similarities between the Muslim Djinn, fairies of Celtic folklore, and "interdimensional" creatures in other cultures around the world, are uniquely similar to the modern UAP alien abductors.

The Trickster: Folklore informs us that the Djinn live in a parallel world in societies similar to ours—some are good and some are evil. It is said that the Djinn resent having to give up this world to humans and strive to take back their home. The Djinn have been reported to be both physical and non-physical in nature. They appear to be three to four feet in height, appear and disappear immediately, abduct humans and transport them across great distances in a matter of seconds, violate laws of physics as we know them (e.g., change shape and pass through solid matter), communicate telepathically, appear in any form, deceive, and seek pleasure in enticing humans into sexual intercourse. The Djinn may even represent an archetype: a universal image shared by humanity. Jung, for instance, characterized Djinn as "God, man and animal all at once. He is both subhuman and superhuman, a bestial and divine being...both superior and inferior to man."[115] Jung even noted the similarity of trickster acts to the evil traits and absurd "communications" of poltergeists.[116]

The Djinn somehow adapt to those susceptible to take advantage of humans. Leading metaphysical researcher and author Rosemary Ellen Guiley, for instance, believes the Djinn are involved with many paranormal experiences, including hauntings, NHE contacts, UAP, and alien abduction experiences—the Djinn's "agenda concerning humans are self-serving at the least, hostile at worst" and that it is the "hostile ones who strike out against people to haunt, harass, possess, abduct, and cause problems."[117]

The reported physical and non-physical attributes and associated behaviors of the Djinn appear to mimic reports by those who interact with the UAP and associated NHEs. This is not a mere coincidence. The nature and implication of these unique similarities suggest a strong interrelationship among the Djinn and other types of paranormal activity. What we find in the literature is that the so-called fairies, extraterrestrials, spirits, mythological gods, DMT entities, and UAP occupants, may not be separate phenomena but rather different manifestations of the same recurrent phenomena throughout history. The "trolls" of Scandinavia, "elves" of Germany's Black Forest, the "Stick Indians," the "Trickster" of the Southwest Pueblo culture, and the "fairies" of Ireland, who paralyzed individuals, and "distorted their reality in 'magical ways,'" may have been part of the same phenomenon.[118] The atypical transcendental experience associated with these entities itself seems to be evolving. This historical narrative raises an obvious question: Do the Djinn co-habit the earth with humans, influencing us in the past as well as now?

The Djinn and UAP: The Djinn and modern day UAP occupants may be one and the same—a modern space age manifestation of a phenomenon which assumes different guises in different historical contexts. Whatever the source of this phenomenon may be, it appears to induce perceptual distortions of reality which manifest in both physical (sensory disturbances, space and time alterations) and non-physical ways (telepathic communication, physic phenomena).

Consistent with the eyewitness reports of UAP occupants, tricksters are shapeshifters who teleport effortlessly between the earth and the heavens. They have the ability to dematerialize, communicate both profound wisdom and total nonsense, and abduct people at will. The Djinn cause people to have mysterious lapses of time, which is hauntingly similar to the "missing time" episodes reported by modern UAP abductees. Moreover, trickster legend is filled with disturbing hoaxes such as stealing and gutting animals (modern day "cattle mutilations") and creating circular patterns or nests in crops and vegetation (modern day "crop circles"). If the trickster is truly behind this, then researchers are missing vital clues to the nature of the UAP.[119]

The main role of the trickster may be to provide novelty within the culture or sub-culture, and to upset the status quo. The trickster utilizes this design to ensure we remain its "plaything," to be used, tormented, taunted and even taught; sometimes for the better and, perhaps, sometimes not.[120] In doing precisely that, the trickster allows culture to advance, instead of being firmly trapped in one control system. Maybe that's the whole point of the trickster, and the reason why it plays such manipulative games with us: for good or bad, its actions provoke and nurture new paradigms. The result is that it often succeeds in altering consciousness on a personal and societal level. The UAP and NHE imagery, therefore, may be one of the trickster's many tools of changing the status quo.[121]

Like the Djinn, UAP entities do not behave in a predictable manner. Their nature can fluctuate from acts of hostility to good will towards humanity.[122] When an individual encounter is initiated by a NHE, it appears biased and shaped by previous encounters with other beings in similar role relationships (teachers, guides, mentors, parents, etc.)—a process known in psychotherapy as transference. If the being wished to intensify this effect for purposes of placing the individual into a receptive frame of mind, they could use hypnotic suggestion, a virtual reality technology, or simply a costume to project a suitable form or identity.[123]

For example, if I'm going to hypnotize someone quickly on stage, I might wear a black cape and hood and makeup that makes me look like a demonic Bela Lugosi. These trappings place the subject in a receptive state and elicit reflexive role expectations and "scripts" which guide the interaction in the direction one wishes it to proceed or in a manner consistent with what the person believes. We would certainly expect any being who wishes to initiate contact and influence a subject to utilize whatever religious, spiritual, scientific, or science fictional trappings or symbolisms that will achieve the desired effect on the individual. Consequently, this kind of "packaging" of the trickster or NHE encounter is likely to be a mix of unconscious perceptual filtering by the individual, in combination with the intentional manipulation for effect by the being.[124]

Alternate Dimensions and the Multiverse

Overview: If you believe NHEs have visited Earth from another solar system, then you must explain how interstellar travel is possible. While some theories such as the faster-than-light, wormholes, multiverse, and superstring offer potential solutions for overcoming incomprehensible distances and associated travel time, they exist only as concepts in quantum physics. Such theories serve as an initial required step in an evolving process to better understand the laws governing the universe, which if successfully applied, may eventually provide the means to easily travel between different parts of the universe in the blink of an eye.

Although the extraterrestrial hypothesis (ETH) has re-mained the predominant explanation for UAP, some have abandoned it in favor of the intradimensional hypothesis (IH)—the UAP represents visitations from other "realities" or "dimensions" that accompany our own. This hypothesis, which evolved from the bizarre behavior of UAP, is thought to have a paranormal and dimensional aspect that can't be ignored. Could one possible "strange" hypothesis include parallel universes, or other time-like dimensions beyond the space-time reality we ascribe to? Or could the strangeness of UAP behavior be explained on the basis of differences between the time-space continuum of this phenomenon and us?

PE Triggers and the Extraterrestrial and Intradimensional Hypotheses: It is virtually impossible to substantiate the many anecdotal reports of PE-induced interactions with NHEs of various kinds. If some NHEs come from another galaxy light years away, an alternate dimension, or even emerge from the unconscious mind (archetypes), plausible theories must be considered to explain their source of origination, nature, purpose and, most important of all, their validity. One theory that serves as the most likely explanation is the IH. Though theoretical in nature, the IH has been proposed by a number of leading physicists, such as Claude Swanson, Michio Kaku, and Stephen Hawking. Such an exotic theory would seem to make sense to explain the personal accounts of time and space distortions—reports of "no space or time" and "missing time," psychic phenomena (ESP) in the presence of NHEs, paranormal events (light orbs that dart or float through the air), and poltergeist activity (household items flying through the air, etc.) preceding one's UAP "abduction" experience,[125-128] among other forms of "high strangeness."

The IH circumvents the debatable issue pertaining to the necessary use of propulsion since it holds that UAPs are devices that travel between different realities or parallel universes. This notion serves as the leading argument against the ETH—it is just too far to travel here. For example, traveling at the speed of light of about 186,000 miles per second, would still take about four years to reach our closet star, Proxima Centauri, 4.24 light years distant or 26 trillion miles away. If beings on a planet wanted to come here traveling 600,000 mph or 200 miles per second, it would take over 4,000 years![129] Despite this impeding factor, the ETH remains one of the most popular theories to explain the origin of UAPs.

Alternative theories, however, such as wormholes, the multiverse, and superstring, have been proposed to explain interstellar travel.[130] But despite theories to explain the origin of NHEs, scientist and astronaut Edgar Mitchell, the sixth man to walk on the moon, provided persuasive anecdotal evidence that NHEs have visited Earth. There is little doubt he turned many heads in his statement that: "Yes, there have been ET visitations. There have been crashed craft. There have been material and bodies recovered."[131] Based on such anecdotal testimony, and the UAPs' ability to defy laws of gravity and inertia, many quantum theorists believe that different scientific methods and principles may be required to determine what governs and regulates this phenomenon.

Within the abstract field of quantum physics, the branch of physics dealing with physical phenomena at microscopic levels, the controversial existence of alternate realities has been promoted as a possible explanation for UAP and NHE. The IH proposes that other "realities" or "dimensions" co-exist separately with ours, and if valid, this implies the UAP and NHEs are real but do not exist in our dimension and do not travel from another planet to interact with humans. In other words, NHE phenomena likely arise from the alternate space and time of higher dimensions that in some way can be realized in one's mind as physical events. NHE visitations may, therefore, originate from other "realities" or "dimensions" that accompany our own.

This notion may explain why NHEs and UAP have been reported throughout recorded history, appear to manipulate space and time, materialize and dematerialize, and produce psychic effects in people. A few physicists, for instance, have speculated that the reported shapeshifting UAP and NHE may represent the energy change occurring around them as they "move between dimensions."[132] A three-dimensional cross section of a four-dimensional tube, for example, would appear as a different shape (spherical) in our three-dimensional space as it moved.

One theoretical approach concerns the possibility of "wormholes" that may provide a shortcut through space-time. This theory proposes that the universe can be explained in terms of very small strings that vibrate in invisible dimensions that would allow travel very quickly from one part of the universe to another part of that same or different universe. According to principles in theoretical physics, for instance, a parallel universe or different dimension can be manifested via traversable wormholes that connect two different universes, having two different locations, times, and dimensions. In other words, an alternate reality may coexist with our own.[133] For this reason, PE triggers may be explainable by quantum mechanics.

Quantum mechanics and associated theories proposed by theoretical physicists tell us that there are many dimensions that we can't see and normally don't have access to. But they're there, nevertheless, at least according to physicist Stephen Hawking, who proposed that one can have different "universes" in one ultimate existence, a "multiverse."[134] Hawking explained the controversial existence of multiple universes in his statement that, "down at the smallest of scales, smaller even than molecules, smaller than atoms, we get to a place called the quantum foam. This is where wormholes exist. Tiny tunnels or shortcuts through space and time constantly form, disappear, and reform within this quantum world. And they link two separate places and two different times."[135] Physicist Brian Greene expressed a similar viewpoint in his statement that "there are a couple of multiverses that come out of our study of string theory; i.e., there are many entities allowed for by the theory."[136] This implies that we may be "living in one dimension while other surfaces with other beings on it exist out in space."[137] If Hawking and Greene are correct, the "multiverse" may explain everything in the universe from particle physics to the physical laws that govern our universe.

First described in 2017 by *The New York Times* and the *Washington Post*,[137] the Department of Defense funded research on wormholes, invisibility cloaking, and "the manipulation of extra dimensions" under its Advanced Aerospace Threat Identification Program. This program, confirmed by official documents obtained under the Freedom of Information Act, may be an example of how science fiction usually becomes fact. At least that is what history tells us. Consequently, it is not a stretch of the imagination to accept modern-day accounts by PErs of experiencing another dimension as fact—not one's fictitious interpretation of reality; a hallucination triggered by a variety of neuro-psychological abnormalities. That is, the multiverse may have been accessed by PErs who claim to have interacted, either physically or non-physically (nonlocal communication), with another realm of existence. Since the Department of Defense has been conducting research on "extra-dimensions," it would stand to reason that subjective PEr accounts should be incorporated within their comprehensive program of investigation.

Discussion

There are no definitive explanations to account for the NHEs encountered during DMT induced psychedelic experiences, NDEs and OBEs, and by those who report interactions with UAP. They may manifest as a psychic projection or as Jung would contend, a manifestation of a disturbance in the collective unconscious of the human species. Despite this archetypal characteristic, many consider NHEs a form of intelligence and not a psychic projection; an intelligence of incredible complexity who use symbolism to communicate with us. One cannot, however, completely dismiss the possibility that an endogenous biochemical, brain-based hallucinatory experience alone may account for many, if not all, characteristics of experience reported by those who sense and interact with NHEs. This notion, however, becomes all the more confusing since the PE supports specific elements within religious ideology, such as belief in a deity, an immediate judgment after death, and/or the existence of intermediate spiritual entities and alternate dimensions.

There are numerous questions for researchers to consider within the realm of consciousness and associated unexplained phenomena of the PE. The unique similarities among individual accounts of NHEs throughout history suggest that current versions of NHE interactions may be related to historical narratives of unexplainable encounters. No one sees "flying scrolls," "angels," "God," or "chariots of fire" in contemporary society; the primitive Stone Age dwellers, those from biblical times, and the Middle Ages peasants did not see aliens, but they may be the same beings, despite the different names used to describe them. Although ancient and medieval records are filled with stories of strange shapes and figures in the sky, little in these accounts elicit visions of UAP as we understand them today. Many unusual aerial phenomena of the past may simply have been meteors, comets, and other atmospheric and cosmological displays. Or not.

Currently, the validity of NHEs is interpreted with intense skepticism. It is regarded as a poorly understood manifestation that is likely facilitated from within human consciousness itself. But if there may be truth to their presence, and not an aspect of consciousness responsible for this complex phenomenon, the scientific and medical communities must regard NHEs as a significant finding worthy of serious study. Its revelation, regardless of what the cause may be, will shock humanity at its very core. Maybe it already has to a select few within the Department of Defense, CIA, and/or an Unacknowledged Special Access Program. After all, we know history repeats itself. The validity of one experiencing an alternate reality or extra-dimension, regarded as fiction by mainstream science, may be just another example of how once seemingly out-of-this world concepts (flying machines, walking on the moon, and the iPhone, etc.) eventually become science fact.

CHAPTER 4

COMMUNICATING WITH THE DECEASED

Introduction

Humankind's long held belief that some aspect of our consciousness may survive bodily death is intimately linked to experiences that offer evidence for a form of life after death. Ever since we stopped crawling out of the primordial soup and evolved into inquisitive and inventive complex language-based bipedal primates, people have wondered if upon death we diminish into a void of nonexistence, persist in an alternate realm of existence, or revive in a cycle of reincarnation. If death is just a phase on the natural continuation of life, it cannot be appropriately rationalized by science since such an outcome is not considered a part of the natural world.

As humans, we experience different perceptions and emotions, which from a strictly scientific point of view, are explained as a result of nothing more than the complex and poorly understood neurochemical processes within our central nervous system. Thus, those who believe that once these processes stop, so does consciousness and our life. This materialistic viewpoint is challenged, however, by evidence of communication with NHE and the deceased in the form of after death communication (ADC) and deathbed visions (DBV); OBEs and NDEs, DMT-induced visions, apparitions, mediumship communications, hearing words, or merely seeing or sensing the presence of a deceased loved one.

After Death Communication and Deathbed Visions

Overview: Phenomena such as ADCs and NDEs have become more prevalent as advanced biomedical technology has allowed us to bring people back from the brink of death. ADC is not uncommon and comes in many forms. One form is the DBV, represented by cases in which a terminally ill individual reports the bedside appearance of a dead relative, friend, or a being of light to guide one through the dying process. The DBV can be visual, auditory or kinesthetic in nature, and it is common for family members and hospital personnel to claim that a dying person reports seeing or hearing the deceased or other beings. In some rare occurrences, testimonies from more than one witness have been reportedly verified, and correct details of the exact date and hour of their death were provided.[1]

Hospice nurses consider ADCs and DBVs are so common that they are used as a sign of impending death. According to hospice worker and researcher D. Arcangel, "I never sat with a dying patient who was not in the presence of an apparition,"[2] and psychologist J. Assante specified that it is not unusual to hear the dying say, "Yes, dear, I'm coming" or "I'm coming, just give me a few seconds" and then die immediately afterward.[3]

The ADC and DBV are different from a NDE, in that they happen generally when a person is undergoing an extended dying process known as terminal lucidity—the unexpected return of mental clarity and memory shortly before death in patients suffering from severe physiological disorders. Such near-death-state experiences have the potential to facilitate study into human consciousness and the brain, and may even provide evidence for post-mortem survival.[4] Despite these possibilities, ADC, DBV, and terminal lucidity have received very little attention by the medical and scientific communities, who regard them as hallucinations generated by terminal disease processes or medications, especially since these events typically occur just weeks prior to death.[5]

Medical science acknowledges that ADC and DBVs occur with great frequency worldwide. In a cross-cultural survey of medical professionals in the United States and India, for instance, a stratified random sample of 1,708 physicians and nurses in both countries reported that 81 percent of 714 DBV occurred not only to individuals who were aware they were dying but also to individuals who were not aware or had not been told they were going to die.[6, 7]

The Shared and Empathic Death Experience

An emotional and experiential connection between the dying and the living occurs in rare types of similar NDEs termed the "shared death experience" (SDE) and "empathic death experience" (EDE). The SDE occurs when a person participates simultaneously in the subjective experience of a loved one dying in their presence. Alternatively, the EDE occurs when a person suddenly senses the feelings of a loved one on the verge of death miles away.[66]

The SDE and EDE provide compelling anecdotal evidence of a type of veridical perception, in which a person acquires verifiable information, like the death of a loved one, which they could not have obtained by any natural means. The validity of an experience where people become emotionally overwhelmed at the same time of their loved one's death becomes all the more persuasive when one who is emotionally close to a dying person experiences many of the same characteristics of the NDE along with the dying person; leaving their bodies, meeting beings of light, and seeing the life review of the dying person.[67] Healthy individuals who share the experience of the dying person contradicts the materialistic theory that NDEs are caused by hallucinations of a dying brain. A few examples of a SDE and

EDE from the Out of Body Experience Research Foundation are as follows:

1) "While I was standing next to Dad, with my hand on the bed next to his hand, space changed around me and I felt a love coming into my numb body. It grew very strong, extremely blissful and beautiful. The love expanded out into the room. I was this love and I became the furniture and everything in the room. I did not go thru the walls. My mind was repeatedly saying, 'What is happening' over and over again. I was outside my body, I was observing in a detached way inside my body and I was everything. There was no time. I felt I knew everything (knowledge) but was unable to pick out a thought. There was no sequence. I saw a light. I then started coming down and my thoughts were very clear. And when this experience ended, I then realized my Dad had just died."[68]

2) "They said to me (the body below me) that they were sorry they could not save me. I "think-talked" to them, feeling so peaceful, that it was ok. Next, a wonderful green-yellow-white light drew me to it while I was still floating in the hospital room. I couldn't resist the light and entered into it. There was an immense beautiful lawn, and a tree with a man gardening under it. I moved toward the man (who was somewhat ephemeral) and it was my grandfather (my grandmother's deceased husband). He began to welcome me. Then the phone in the bedroom rang and rang...my husband awoke, answered the phone, and called me to it. It was my dad on the phone, telling me my grandmother had passed away, approximately a two-hour drive from my home."[69]

3) "I was asleep in my bed in north London, England, and my father was over 80 miles distant, in a dementia nursing home on the south coast. I was jolted awake at around 1:30 AM and I sat up in the darkness. A tremendous and intense rushing energy had filled the room. I couldn't see it, but I could sense it, and it was indescribable but 'sparkling.' 'Dad!' I exclaimed. I just knew it was him. And I knew that he was dying, and that he had come to me to help him push over. And somehow, I knew what he needed and what I had to do. I concentrated for all my worth and wished him all the peace and love and energy that I had in

me—and forgiveness—and it felt both personal and universal. The following morning, I awoke early and immediately phoned the nursing home. After a pause the nurse came to the phone and informed me that Dad had died. I asked when he had died, and she replied that they had checked on him at 1:00 AM and he was alive, but that when they checked on him at 2:00 AM he had passed over. I firmly believe that I was sharing my father's death experience. I am not religious, but what I experienced that night has profoundly affected my thinking. I shared my father's death, helping him push over."[70]

Conclusion: Documented cases of accurate information of the death of a person before the percipient knows it occurred, concomitant with the apparent endless stream of similar shared and empathic death experience found in the literature, provide convincing evidence that ADCs are genuine contacts by deceased loved ones. Although ADC provides strong evidence of what happens at the time of permanent, irreversible death, the acquisition of verifiable information still requires corroboration from several independent, large-scale research studies to assess the validity of such unique experiences. This validity, however, is unlikely to be established by science, but the truth of contact with the deceased rests in the minds of those who experience it. And that is what matters most of all.

Mediumship: Communication with the Deceased?

Overview: The concept of an existence after bodily death cannot be appropriately evaluated without considering the mediums who claim to communicate with the deceased. For over a century, the objective of mediumship research has involved the analysis of anomalous information reception (AIR); the reporting of accurate and specific information without prior knowledge, fraud, and in the absence of "normal" sensory input conveyed by mediums from supposed deceased persons to the living (i.e., sitters), and from the living using AIR. Despite claims to the contrary, there exists a certain degree of compelling evidence to support the notion that some individuals are capable of communicating with the deceased, especially since research has confirmed that mediumship is not associated with conventional dissociative experiences, psychosis, or over-active imaginations.[71, 72] Mediumship is controversial and any evidence that supports one's ability to communicate with the deceased certainly provokes debate.

There are two types of mediumship: mental and physical. Communication with the deceased is experienced through some type of knowing (internal vision or hearing), or through discarnate beings controlling the person's body. In mental mediumship, an individual communicates information from the deceased to others. This may be achieved during a meditative or trance-like state to allow an unknown aspect of the deceased to utilize the medium for this purpose. In physical mediumship, the communication proceeds through paranormal physical events in the medium's vicinity, represented by reports of unexplained voices and sounds, and movement of objects in the environment.[73]

Mediumship Research: Mediumship studies provide unique evidence central to consciousness science; the relationship between the mind/consciousness and the brain. Such research has addressed the validity of mental and physical mediumship to determine if one's consciousness can indeed interact with the living and physical world and persist after physical death. A vital aspect of this research is to incorporate appropriate experimental control over one's access of information about the deceased and sitters prior to the reading. This is required to help determine if AIR by mediums is achieved by nonlocal means; perceptual ability extends beyond space and time constraints of sensory systems. Mediumship research has resulted in both positive and negative outcomes.[74-82]

Experimental Outcomes: Although some mediumistic communications contain vague messages that might apply to anyone, or that seem to originate in the imaginations of the clients and the mediums, several well-controlled studies conducted at the Windbridge Institute for Applied Research in Human Potential suggest that some mediums are capable of producing accurate detailed messages from discarnate beings. In other words, AIR may indeed be a genuine trait in some individuals.[83, 84]

90

According to lead researcher Dr. Julie Beischel, a "nonlocal source (however controversial) remains the most likely explanation for the accuracy and specificity of their statements."[85]

In one of their most well-controlled, triple-blind studies that removed any possible source of bias or fraud, AIR on individuals not present at the reading (i.e., proxy sitter) were evaluated in eight mediums. The mediums were presented with two or more alternatives and were able to produce significantly positive readings 81 percent of the time. Based on this and other studies conducted at the Windbridge Institute, the data collected under blind conditions indicates that some mediums can demonstrate anomalous information reception. That is, "they have the ability to report accurate and detailed information about a deceased person without any prior knowledge of that person, or about the sitter."[86, 87]

Additional supportive evidence was demonstrated by AIR results of nine mediums from 40 proxy sitters who blindly rated their own and five control readings. The recipient group, for example, accepted significantly more of the messages as appropriate to themselves than did individuals in the non-recipient group.[88] The odds against this result occurring by chance were on the "order of a million to one"! A similar result from another study showed that over 80 percent of statements from five mediums were rated correct by the sitter as opposed to only 36 percent for the control group. This positive AIR outcome, which represented odds of 10 million to one that the correct readings occurred by chance, suggests that the "accurate personal AIR by mediums provide compelling evidence that the deceased are capable of communicating with the living."[89, 90]

Theories to explain the positive AIR outcomes by mediums must be considered, however, before firmly concluding when one is capable of receiving information telepathically from the sitter of the deceased and/or directly from the deceased. One predominant theory advanced to address this concern is the Super-Psi. This theory contends that the reported authenticity of communication by the medium with the deceased is based on telepathy or clairvoyance from living people by the medium.[91]

Since the survival hypothesis (continuation of consciousness following death) requires an aspect of ESP to facilitate information between the deceased and living, for instance, the medium may acquire knowledge of the deceased by either telepathy, and/or the deceased telepathically sending information to the medium.[92] To some, the associated positive AIR outcomes in mediums represent "the best explanation for the survival evidence that some interaction with discarnate souls is involved," and that ESP of the living "serves as the basis of mediumship information."[93]

Conclusion: It is difficult to conclude with certainty that positive AIR outcomes in mediums provide convincing evidence that some people are capable of communicating with the deceased. Despite the significant results from several studies, questions remain regarding their validity due to methodological problems. A daunting, if not impossible task for researchers, therefore, is to resolve whether accurate AIR by mediums is obtained from the deceased and/or the living, or from other possible sources, such as confirmation bias, deception, and/or fraud.[94] While it is one thing to possibly demonstrate accurate AIR by mediums, it is another thing entirely to conclude that such information represents irrefutable evidence of communication from the deceased. The search for the ideal protocol to test whether some people are really communicating with the deceased continues.

Apparitions

Overview: Deceased persons who physically materialize as apparitions have been represented in stories from the Bible to the present day as ghosts, angels, and even the Virgin Mary. An apparitional figure is generally considered to be a form of energy of someone who either does not realize their death or who is strongly emotionally connected to their prior earthly existence. Like mediumship research, anecdotal apparitional experiences have also been advanced to support the continuation of one's consciousness after death.[95]

Many people believe in ghosts because of either a personal experience, for a sense of comfort that our deceased loved ones exist, and/or for religious or cultural reasons. These reasons contribute to the high incidence in the belief of ghosts among the general population. A 2005 Gallup poll, for example, found that 37 percent of Americans believe in haunted houses, and according to a 2013 HuffPost/YouGov poll, 45 percent believe in ghosts.[96] Several surveys in Great Britain and the United States have also reported that between 10-27 percent of the general population believe they have had a sensory perception of an apparition, and about 50 percent of those who lost a spouse report a form of contact with him/her.[97]

The Phenomenology of Apparitions: Collectively, reported characteristics and observed experiences from survey and interview studies have identified several common attributes of the phenomenology of apparitions: (1) the apparition appears real, solid, may cast a shadow, occlude objects, and be perceived in a mirror; (2) it is unusual for an apparition to communicate with the observer and any communication usually contains just a few words; (3) about 80 percent of apparitional experiences are visual and last less than a few minutes; (4) approximately 25 percent of apparitional experiences are witnessed by more than one person at the same time; (5) the apparition's head may turn to follow one's movements; has been reported to leave through a door and make appropriate noises (clothing, walking); and often materializes and dematerializes instantly with no physical evidence manifested other than photographs; and (6) about 70 percent of apparitions are those the experiencer knew to be dead.[98]

Apparitional Experiences: Research approaches designed to document the validity of an apparition experience include case studies, surveys, and the application of instrumentation techniques (e.g., Geiger counters, electromagnetic field and ion detectors, infrared cameras, and audio recording devices). If apparitions exist as physical energy, one would expect objective, tangible evidence to support their presence, but no such unequivocal evidence exists. For this reason, numerous anecdotal and experimental studies on the nature and validity of apparitional experiences have served as a source of considerable controversy. Nevertheless, many apparitional experiences are difficult to comprehend and ignore.[99] One such intriguing apparitional experience is as follows: "It crossed my bedroom one night when I was half asleep; a stocky golden entity carved out of pure, solid love, a love so powerful, certain, and condensed, so compacted, there was no room for the more vulnerable aspects of human love, like compassion. An entity of this caliber is so far beyond human capacity that we cannot really form a conception of it, let alone describe it."[100]

Apparitions have been traditionally categorized by the nature and type of sighting experienced. These include collective, crisis, and postmortem cases. Collective sightings, where more than one person reports the same apparition simultaneously, lend some degree of validity to the phenomenon. There exist over 100 cases in the literature of apparitions being perceived by two or more people. One such shared encounter was had by a woman named Lois:

"Two days after the death of her husband, Ray, Lois just happened to pass by her bedroom where she saw her son Jesse sitting on the side of her bed. He was eight at the time and was unable to deal with his father's death. Right next to him was Ray, who had his arm around his son and was talking to him in a calm voice. Ray looked up and smiled at his wife, then gestured for her to go away. She moved off to give them privacy, and after a fifteen-minute wait, Jesse came out to tell her what his father had said: 'Daddy told me that he has gone and won't be coming back and not to worry about him. Everything will be all right.' The experience marked the boy's turning point for healing."[101]

Similar to a shared death experience, a crisis sighting is characterized by one who reports a lifelike apparition of a friend or relative at a time the person was dying or in a serious accident. This incident tends to occur less than 12 hours before or after the crisis, and the person experiencing the apparition is unaware of this event. What is especially intriguing is that the experiencer is often not thinking of the dying person at the time when the apparition is perceived as a real person.[102] An example of a documented crisis sighting of a woman who was unaware that her brother was killed during World War II is illustrated as follows:

94

"On the day of the incident, she had a strong feeling to turn around; on doing so she was amazed to see her brother. Assuming that he had been visiting, she placed her child in bed, and then went to greet her brother only to find him not there. When no trace of her brother was found, she suspected he was dead. Surprisingly, the loss of her brother in combat on the same day she saw his apparition was confirmed weeks later."[103]

In contrast to crisis sightings, a postmortem sighting involves the appearance of an apparition of a person who has been dead for at least 12 hours. Interestingly, this type of sighting is analogous to reports of ADC and DBVs. Several studies, for example, have revealed that about two-thirds of recognized apparitions are of the deceased and that a common feature of such cases involves the attempt by the apparition to communicate specific information that is unknown to the experiencer.[104] The following case represents a postmortem sighting from a woman whose word, according to psychologist H. Irwin, "I have no reason to doubt":

"When I was a teenager, one of my friends, a young girl, was diagnosed with cancer. She lost her arm, but the operation did not stop the spread of the disease, and she died shortly afterward. In life, she had always been particularly close to my brother, and one day when I entered his room shortly after her death, I saw her sitting there in the chair she always occupied when she came to see him. She and I talked together for some time—just about ordinary things, very matter-of-fact."[105]

An individual whom H. Irwin considered to be "very objective and clear-headed" expressed this postmortem sighting:

"I was on a residential yoga retreat with other members of our yoga group, and one day when we were taking a walk, in single file and in silence through the woods, Brian, one of the founder members of our group who had recently died, was suddenly walking next to me. He was as tall as in life, a big smile on his face, but not quite solid. I would describe him as semi-transparent. He placed his left hand on my shoulder, and we walked together through the woods. I was struck by the fact that he still had the two deformed fingers on his hand that were a birth defect, and I said to him, "Oh, Brian, I thought we were mended when we get to heaven." We walked together for about a minute and then he disappeared just before I left the woods. Later I realized that he materialized with the two deformed fingers as clear proof of identity."[106]

A highly credible witness from the German Max Planck Society reported the following postmortem sighting:

"I awoke one night and in the twilight was able to see a young man with curly black hair. I was terrified and told the alleged neighbor that he had the wrong room. He simply cried and looked at me with great sadness in his eyes. When I turned on the light, the apparition had disappeared. Since I was one hundred percent sure it had not been a dream, I told the housemaster about the strange encounter the next morning. I gave her a detailed description of the young man. She suddenly paled. She looked through the archives and showed me a photo. I immediately recognized the young man who had visited me in my room the evening before. When I asked her who he was, she replied with a quivering voice that it was the previous renter. She then added that my room had become available because he had taken his life shortly before."[107]

Apparitional Theories: Theories to explain the nature of apparitions vary widely. Some characteristics suggest they are physical while other features indicate a possible subjective or psychic explanation. Apparitions have been considered physical since they are reported to hide objects, form shadows, make noise, produce a reflection, and are sometimes experienced by more than one person. A psychological and/or psychic rationale, on the other hand, is supported by testimony that objects perceived to move do not, there is no remaining physical evidence, and that during a group experience only some may perceive them. An alternative explanation is that an apparition is a misinterpretation of explainable events or a hallucination facilitated by altered brain activity induced by atmospheric/geomagnetic activity, environmental factors (electromagnetic fields, infrasound), stress, and/or oxygen deprivation (carbon monoxide, mold, and formaldehyde).[108] Some even consider that, "Ghosts are not all there, literally speaking. A ghost is only a portion of the core self. It is an electromagnetic imprint created by a human and is perceptible (to some) under certain atmospheric and emotional conditions."[109]

The Super-Psi theory applied to explain mediumship ability is also used as an explanation for apparitional experiences. That is, contact with the deceased may be explainable in terms of telepathy or clairvoyance from living people. In apparitional cases, however, the experiencer is thought to acquire information from the living and to then induce the apparitional experience in others non-locally like a "psychic aether that acts as a link between consciousness and matter."[110]

Another popular theory is that poltergeist activity or unexplained physical disturbances result from psychokinesis (PK); psychic ability which effects physical systems without physical interaction. An alternative explanation for PK, however, is that electromagnetic brain activity somehow interacts with electromagnetic energy in the environment leading to spontaneous poltergeist events. In other words, the apparitional experience represents a symptom induced by neurological alteration in the brain caused by complex geomagnetic activity. This concept evolved from experiments which demonstrated that the "sensed presence" of a "being" can be reliably evoked by weak magnetic fields applied across the temporal and parietal region of the brain's two hemispheres.[111] This outcome, combined with the finding of existing strong magnetic fields in reported haunted environments, has led researchers to conclude that neurological factors and not the deceased or subjects' beliefs are responsible for facilitating an apparitional experience.[112]

Conclusion: The many thousands of documented cases in the literature indicate that apparitions are an authentic experience which cannot be explained solely on the basis of imagination, psychological disorders, or deceit in each reported incident. And several features of the "postmortem" apparitional experience are especially intriguing since apparitions often appear physically real and behave normally (walking, smiling) as in life; are seen whether the observer knew that the person concerned was dead; and exchange communication in some cases. Despite the numerous compelling accounts of apparitional experiences, however, it is premature to conclude that an apparition proves the survival hypothesis since the evidence is almost always anecdotal in nature involving only one person and not objectively verifiable. Nevertheless, the compelling apparitional evidence should not be completely dismissed and should serve as the foundation for further investigations of this real and perplexing phenomenon.[113]

Discussion

We can see from the anecdotal and experimental results in this chapter that, while intriguing in nature, there lacks irrefutable support in the form of objective, tangible evidence to prove that humans can indeed communicate with the deceased. Those who disagree with this conclusion, however, do so since: (1) unknown information reportedly obtained from the deceased via a medium is difficult to account for by telepathy from the living; (2) cases where the individual receives notification of one's death via an after death communication, a shared death experience, or an apparitional experience, and is unaware that his/her death has taken place; and (3) the high incidence and similarity of after death communication and apparitional experiences.

The primary evidence to support the validity of such phenomena is that they make sense to the individual and the observers when described, and overwhelmingly these visions and/or information contain descriptions of people who are deceased. In the after death communication and deathbed vision cases, however, hallucinations caused by a dying brain should not distinguish between the living and deceased. If hallucinations are responsible for these experiences, as well as apparitions, one would also expect them to contain people, places, and images of the patient's current surroundings and recent life, and not only deceased family members who may have died decades before. This is especially true for Peak in Darien cases where the individual reports seeing and/or communicating with a deceased person despite not knowing the person had died. Peak in Darien cases provide some of the most persuasive evidence for the existence of the deceased, and recent medical advances in end-of-life care provide unique opportunities for further investigation of these convincing cases.

It is indeed reasonable for one to conclude that after death communication and deathbed visions reflect wishful thinking, or a defensive hallucinatory brain response to aid one during the dying process. Attempting to explain such events, which are undeniably inconsistent with medical and scientific principles, presents an insurmountable challenge for researchers since those experiencing them are very close to death. Furthermore, the perceptually real apparition and sensed presence phenomena fail to provide conclusive evidence of an interaction with the deceased since an apparition has never been captured and analyzed, and there is no scientific evidence of an alternate realm for consciousness to exist after death, or that "energy" can remain in a human-looking form after death.[114]

Given this context, phenomenological research of events from the person's point of view may eventually provide sufficient evidence to prove that communicating with the deceased is either a misinterpretation of natural events; a psychological disorder; sleep induced imagery; a fictitious story; telepathically acquired information; and/or a neurophysiological induced experience. Alternatively, one's reported interaction with the deceased may indeed represent a form of energy that survives physical death. If such interactions do represent "beings" from another realm of existence, then verifiable experimental evidence must be obtained before firmly concluding that an aspect of consciousness endures after death. Until then, if ever, the possibility that the deceased are communicating with us via different modes of contact (ADC, DBV, SDE, mediumship (ESP), and apparitions) cannot definitely be ruled out.[115] If any one of these phenomena is someday proven valid, then proof of one's consciousness or "soul" as a non-physical entity existing beyond the natural world, will certainly astonish humankind in unimaginable ways.

CHAPTER 5

UNSEEN FORCES AND THE SPIRITUAL BRAIN

Introduction

Religious teachings inform us of the purpose of life, philosophers explain why life is as it is, and scientists explain the nature of our physical universe. But despite the religious teachings, philosophical perspectives, and scientific endeavors, the nature of spiritual, mystical and extraordinary experiences that comprise the PE remains a mystery. The reason, in part, is that these fundamental perspectives have not been integrated, as they should be. And what is most disturbing is that science often fails to recognize the significance of the PE on one's personal viewpoint and well-being. The frequent incidence and personal significance of the PE alone provide sufficient rationale to learn more about the psychological impact and proper management of this profound and common experience. Survey research, for instance, has indicated that about: 1) one-third of Americans have had intense spiritual experiences;[1] and 2) 10 to 15 percent of the general population experience either an OBE[2] or NDE,[3] with an estimated 200,000 people in the United States and millions worldwide having an NDE annually.[4]

Belief in the supernatural may even be innate. Humans are remarkably prone to supernatural beliefs and especially to beliefs in NHEs. In all human cultures, for instance, "people believe that illness and calamity are caused and alleviated by a variety of invisible person-like entities: spirits, ghosts, saints, evils, demons, Jesus, and devils and gods."[5] But why? It may be the same reason why many people pursue spiritual practices in order to feel more peaceful, more harmonious and content with the world.

The function of yoga, Qi Gong, meditation and other esoteric practices, for instance, is to create a new energy pattern in the body, and to help one's consciousness be more in touch with their body and mind, and ultimately, to achieve peace and oneness with the universe. For many people, this is experienced in meditation for years before they fall into the realization that this is what they are. Others experience this when out in nature and one is swept into a realization that they are everything that is—the mountains, sky, earth, rocks and every being within it. Imagine if everything you believed about yourself was dissolving into space—the realization of who and what you are without the mental concepts and words to hold as truth. This is what people who are evolving into spiritual awakening may experience slowly over time. Others, however, have no intention of "awakening" but instead are unintentionally and suddenly "awakened" by a PE trigger. But again, why?

The Spiritual Brain: The Biology of Spiritual, Mystical and Extraordinary Experiences and Beliefs

Overview: Across cultures and throughout history, humankind has reported spiritual, mystical, and extraordinary experiences of varying kinds. Very little is known, however, about the essence of experiences that facilitate a perceived sense of union that transcends one's ordinary sense of self. But is belief in God, heaven, and an afterlife a natural state of human consciousness? Just what is it that inspirers a voracious need in billions of people to hold an entrenched belief in an invisible, all-powerful being called God? Perhaps the human brain and/or an aspect of our consciousness facilitate a predisposition toward supernatural belief because it gives us a better chance of survival. Maybe this is one reason why hard-core materialists consider you to be nothing more than neural activity arising from the brain alone. Mystics, on the other hand, have historically carried forward the understanding of trans-physical or extreme phenomena that correspond with expanded states of consciousness and the existence of other worlds—the feeling of oneness and interconnectedness with all creation, and a deepened sense of reality where the physical world is seen as limiting.[6, 7]

Who is correct—science or the mystics? While many consider the answer to be of no great importance, most truth seekers certainly do. Your interest in reading this book alone certifies you a truth seeker too. After all, God, spirit, and the paranormal appear as central features of the PE. But is the PE truly "real" or is it just a belief that it is "real"?

Is Spiritual Belief Human Nature? Belief in the existence of supernatural beings is widespread both across and within cultures. In the United States, for example, an estimated 70 percent of individuals believe in the existence of Satan, 78 percent believe in the existence of angels, and 94 percent believe in the existence of God.[8] Apart from cultural and religious indoctrination, such beliefs likely incorporate an innate human tendency similar to your strong desires for certain foods and aversion toward specific things. Evolutionary psychologists tell us, for instance, that our preference for sweet and fatty foods and our fear of heights and snakes represent behaviors caused by the unconscious mind that helped our ancestors to survive.[9, 10]

There is an apparent common foundation in the belief of an order held in common by folk belief traditions and religions around the world that: (1) is objectively real, (i.e., not "all in the mind"); (2) is qualitatively different from the everyday material world (invisible at times); (3) interacts with this world in certain ways (answers to prayer, visits from deceased loved ones); and (4) includes beings that do not require a physical body in order to live (God, souls of the deceased, and angels and evil spirits).[11] In different traditions, this order is considered "the spirit world," "the supernatural," and "land of the ancestors." The question is, why?

Humankind from the beginning of its existence posed the following questions: how was the world created? What is its nature and destiny, the origin of people and where are they going? What is the origin, purpose and meaning of all things? Myths try to answer these questions. Primitive people did not know the philosophical concepts or scientific answers to these questions, so they tried to use the mythical stories, images, and symbols to explain them. The myth is a symbol of the developed language, a language of primitive peoples.

Asking about the reason for the existence of the universe and people, a response was usually found in the world of the gods. The folklore of the supernatural, for example, can be evidenced in all aspects of your life: the things you say (ghost stories, creation myths, tales of skinwalkers, prayers), the things you do (what we wear, what we eat, how we bury our dead, how and when to plant and harvest crops, avoiding bad luck and encouraging good), the things you create (religious symbols, charms, amulets, foods), the things you believe in (gods, devils, spirits, ghosts, interplanetary travelers, healing rituals, life after death), where you go (to church on Sunday, to the cemetery at midnight), and who your friends and associates are (Catholics, shamans, witches, Navajos, the religious, the irreverent). Even if you might not claim any belief in the supernatural, you likely rub shoulders with people who do.

Many people believe that an unseen realm exists beyond your five senses where all knowledge exists. If this is true, then how do you access it, or should you just dismiss this concept as nonsensical in nature? The truth seeker, however, will find it hard to discard thoughts of the possible existence of a Divine Intelligence, the meaning and purpose to life, and am "I" just the brain. This is what makes us human. We as a species intuitively know that you, like your body, are part of an evolutionary process and that your conscious and unconscious intentions and actions enable and affect this process.

104

Humans are predisposed toward spiritual feeling and many purposefully try to achieve a state of self-transcendence—the PE. The quest to expand one's consciousness—to rise above the self and relate to that which is greater than the self—may be driven by our genetic makeup and neurological activity. Some scientists claim humans are born to believe in God. In one study, for example, children as young as age three "naturally attributed supernatural abilities and immortality to God," even if they've never been taught about God.[12] This suggests our basic cognitive abilities bias us toward thinking about an "afterlife, gods, invisible beings that are doing things—themes common to most of the world's religions."[13] Magical and supernatural beliefs may even be hardwired into our brains from birth.

Research has shown, for instance, that children have a natural, "intuitive way of reasoning that leads them to all kinds of supernatural beliefs about how the world works. Children below the age of five, for example, find it easier to believe in some "superhuman" properties than to understand human limitations. As they grow up, "the tendency towards illogical supernatural beliefs remains as religion."[14] The belief in religion and the afterlife, therefore, may be a natural phenomenon that happens for a reason. Your thought processes may be "rooted" to religious concepts. Belief in God may be a part of human nature and religion, and "not just something for a peculiar few to do on Sundays instead of playing golf. It isn't just a quirky interest of a few, it's basic human nature."[15]

If you interpret these viewpoints literally, then spiritual belief may simply result from a programmed innate drive. If true, then modern organized religion may simply reflect an innate biologically-based aspect of behavior that emerges from a spectrum of supernatural beliefs. Most researchers, however, don't believe cognitive tendencies evolved specifically for religious belief. Rather, they likely served other adaptive purposes since we are quick to believe that someone or something is behind even the most benign experiences. Haven't you ever perceived the sound of the wind rustling in the woods as a potential predator? Humans seem to exhibit the tendency to anthropomorphize by attributing human characteristics to animals, inanimate objects or natural phenomena. Spirituality, in other words, may simply be a byproduct of the way our brains work, from cognitive tendencies to seek order from chaos, to attribute human form to our environment, and to believe the world around us was created for our purpose. Consequently, you may have been programmed by our ancestors to believe—just like you are programmed to do just about anything to obtain happiness.

Most people believe that happiness comes from outside themselves, in material objects, acquisitions, fulfillment of desires, money, drugs, alcohol, power, and sex. These things may bring some pleasure, but they are all temporary fixes which can never be permanently fulfilled in this way. This causes suffering. The source of all happiness, and the goal of the spiritual life, may be to awaken your inherent spiritual nature, but the quest for happiness and the spiritual life is interpreted differently by everyone. An ancient text, for instance, states, "In each human being dwells an infinite power, the root of the universe. That infinite power exists in two forms, one actual and the other potential. This infinite power exists in a latent condition in everyone."[16]

Each culture or religion has its own name for this inner energy which serves as the foundation of all happiness. Some call this infinite power the Holy Spirit or Kundalini Shakti. It is conveyed within your being in the forms of love, peace, power, survival, and wisdom. And some people profess that those who secure access to this inner realm will realize this. If true, then is your life's objective to identify with your inner energy to achieve the happiness that lies within? Could this be the essence of one's spiritual quest—the transcendence of the ego, and the primary goal and reason for life?

Maybe we possess an innate tendency for these beliefs just like our common fear of snakes? Well, based on the fact that people of all ages detect images of snakes more quickly than non-threatening frogs, flowers, or caterpillars, this may indeed be the case. Throughout evolutionary history, for example, "humans that learned quickly to fear snakes would have been at an advantage to survive and reproduce."[17] Consequently, those who detected the presence of snakes very quickly would have been more likely to pass this trait in their genes. Similar to your quest for happiness and transcendence, therefore, your fears may also be associated with a specific, innate, emotional or behavioral response.

Consider this experience by those who lived many thousands of years ago. You're in the jungle hiding and waiting for an animal to appear to kill for food. Suddenly, you hear and see bushes close to you rustling. What do you do? Do you stop and think about what might be causing the noise, or do you immediately take action? According to cognitive and evolutionary scientists, those who did not take appropriate action by killing the animal were killed and selected out, while those who survived to procreate were those who had developed a hyperactive agency-detecting device (HADD). The HADD facilitates your innate, rapid decision-making processes of intention and action, and for religious and spiritual patterns of thought. In other words, failure to detect a predator removed the thinkers but not those who acted from the gene pool. Your HADD explains why a rustle in the bushes in the dark prompts the instinctive anxious thought: "There's someone there."

In your ancestral environment, this tendency meant survival and reproduction, but the evolution of a HADD now accounts for your genetically coded predisposition to believe in the presence of NHEs even when none can be observed.[18] Thus, you may be held hostage by your ancestral past. It likely explains why humans today tend to believe in the supernatural, to seek answers in religion and spirituality, and to achieve self-transcendence—a PE. Your HADD, in other words, may be responsible for your tendency to attribute meaning to the actions of things that aren't really there, such as NHEs, God, souls of the deceased, angels, and evil spirits.[19] This is a natural tendency. Whether it's a dead ancestor or God, whatever supernatural agent it is, if you think they're watching you, your behavior will be affected. Is that reason enough to be religious or spiritual? Well, you may not have a choice in the matter, especially since humans seem to have evolved an innate HADD.

Your ancestors explained the natural world, like the threat of lightning or the destruction of a flood, and movements of the sun, moon and stars, through the existence of NHEs with supernatural powers. These NHEs formed the basis for religious and spiritual practices and beliefs. Some scientists even refer to HADD as the "god faculty." Since we all have a HADD, human beings haven't evolved past this way of thinking and making decisions. But not everyone agrees that religious thinking is just a byproduct of evolution. Some scientists, for instance, see spirituality as more of an adaptation—a trait that was inherited across generations because the people who possessed it were better able to survive and pass on their genes. Your predisposition to attribute meaning and purpose to just about everything (volcanic eruptions, lunar eclipses, thunderstorms) isn't necessarily the reason religion came about, but it helps to explain why religions typically involve supernatural elements that describe such events.[20] Consequently, the human belief in NHEs, such as spirits or gods, evolved over time to the present day.

It is well documented that experiences necessary for survival of a species are learned and that this knowledge is passed on to subsequent generations. Are other kinds of experiences saved in our DNA over the many thousands of years when your ancestors were born, lived and died? Is it possible that your DNA contains coded memories of your ancestors? Their life-changing negative experiences may have been passed on to subsequent future generations that are now exerting influence on your present behaviors.

Transgenerational Epigenetic Inheritance: The epigenome is responsible for deciding what genes will be expressed in your body's cells. It tells your cells what to do, how much to do, and when. Your genes change throughout your lifetime. External factors such as physical activity, diet, and stress levels can all make changes to your DNA and can cause errors which can lead to disease and other disorders.[21] This concept has significant implications.

The recent genome project on the search for a biological basis of behavior, called Transgenerational Epigenetic Inheritance (TEI), proposes that the memories of trauma experienced by

108

your ancestors are stored in your genetic makeup. The process called Epigenetics, in other words, can have multiple effects of environmental influences on your genetic makeup. For this reason, your ancestors' painful childhoods or excellent adventures might change your personality, causing anxiety or resilience by altering the epigenetic expressions of genes in your brain. New research findings in epigenetic inheritance are now suggesting that your experiences, and those of your ancestors, may have never gone even if they have been forgotten. They become part of you. Your DNA remains the same, but psychological and behavioral tendencies are inherited. The trauma experienced by previous generations, therefore, may be etched in our genes like molecular scars that activate a dysfunctional response to stress. This outcome, in turn, heightens the possibility of the development of trauma-related symptoms.[22]

Historical trauma may be conceptualized as a combination of symbols, events, actions of real and original historical event(s) that act on the human psyche. They trigger feelings and emotions independent from the individual's knowledge of the specific event(s). A parent's anxiety, for example, could influence later generations through epigenetic modifications to receptors for stress hormones.[23, 24] Epigenetic mechanisms may play an important role in your brain. If diet and chemicals cause epigenetic changes, then certain experiences like child neglect, drug abuse or other severe stresses may also change the brain's DNA.[25]

Consequently, damaged DNA that is replicated may inevitably create alternative states that can affect several generations. Jews whose great-grandparents were chased from their Russian shtetls; Chinese whose grandparents lived through the ravages of the Cultural Revolution; young immigrants from Africa whose parents survived massacres; adults of every ethnicity who grew up with alcoholic or abusive parents—may all carry with them more than just memories.

One of the earlier TEI theories is how traumatic events like surviving the Holocaust might change a person's epigenome and their offspring. One study, for example, suggests that the children of Holocaust survivors inherited a specific response to stress. Like the Jews, others who lived in Europe during World War II experienced unprecedented and extreme levels of stress and anxiety. Five years of fear, hunger, and of losing loved ones was an endeavor when stress hormones were sky-high. They had to be in order to survive. And this cumulative effect of prolonged trauma may have created significant genetic modifications.

Psychologists and sociologists who have studied children of survivors found that they exhibit more anxiety than their controls. While this finding could be the result of living with traumatized parents (environment), studies show that most children of survivors have altered cortisone levels (stress hormones), regardless of how they were parented. Consequently, a child and grandchild of Holocaust survivors may have inherited altered genes that affected their cortisone levels which predisposed them to anxiety.[26, 27] Another example is called the Dutch Hunger Winter Syndrome. Babies who were exposed to famine prenatally during World War II in the Netherlands showed an increased risk of metabolic disease later in life and had different DNA methylation of a particular gene when compared to their same-sex siblings who were not exposed to famine. These changes persisted six decades later.[28]

The concept of TEI is supported by evidence from animal research which demonstrates that memories, such as fear of specific odors, can be passed from parents to their offspring. In one study, a learned aversion to the smell of rose blossoms was passed from the parent onto offspring over multiple generations even though the offspring never experienced that smell. Thus "the experiences of a parent, even before conceiving, markedly influence both structure and function in the nervous system of subsequent generations."[29] This pattern of TEI may have potential implications for how psychological disorders and conceptual memories can be acquired from parents and more distant relatives. But can evidence for HADD and TEI be found in the brain? And, if so, can we then be programmed for religious and spiritual thinking and beliefs, and did what happened to your ancestors directly influence your dreams, your memories or your emotions? It seems quite possible.

Neuroscience and Spirituality

Overview: When you feel a sense of connection with something greater than yourself—whether transcendence involves communion with God, NHEs, nature, or humanity—a certain part of the brain appears to activate. A few neuroscientists consider the brain a "neurobiological home" for spirituality. Neurotheologist Andrew Newberg surveyed about 3,000 people who had spiritual experiences and identified a few common elements—one was a strong sense of what he calls "realness." When you wake up from a dream, he explains, you know it wasn't real, no matter how vivid it felt. Not so with transcendent or PEs, which feel authentic not only at the time but also years later.[30] Another defining attribute is a feeling of connectedness—of not being alone. Spiritual leaders generally consider this as evidence of a supreme power while neuroscientists tend to look for answers in the brain.

The God Spot: Is there a "God spot" in the brain where religious thoughts and feelings arise? Some scientists have speculated that the brain features a "God spot"—one distinct area of the brain responsible for spirituality. Now, researchers have indicated that spirituality is a complex phenomenon, and multiple areas of the brain are responsible for the many aspects of spiritual experiences. In one study, when 40 subjects were presented with auditory phrases such as "God's will guides my acts" and "God protects one's life," areas of the brain involved in deciphering other people's emotions and intentions lit up with enhanced activity.[31, 32] It seems, therefore, that through the use of advanced imaging (fMRI, PET), and noninvasive brain stimulation techniques, we are now beginning to realize that specific brain networks are associated with feelings of self-transcendence and religious thinking.

More specifically, the left inferior region of the parietal lobe (IPL), which processes sensation, spatial orientation, and language, may be the physiological "God spot" responsible for spirituality.[33] One study, which correlated brain-lesion mapping techniques with spiritual and religious beliefs in patients both before and after the removal of tumors from their parietal lobe, may provide an important clue. Those who had tumors removed from the IPL showed a greater tendency toward religious and spiritual beliefs and experiences. In another study, when researchers scanned the brain activity of 27 subjects during transcendent meditative states, all subjects showed similar activity patterns in the parietal cortex—a result that suggests the IPL may "contribute importantly to perceptual processing and other representations during spiritual experiences."[34]

Such evidence may have important implications for explaining the "feeling of oneness" and enhanced sense of unity with the universe and one's surroundings (self-transcendence) often reported by those having a PE triggered by an OBE, NDE, UAP and NHE interaction, psychoactive drugs, and meditation. In other words, when activity of the IPL is reduced, people are no longer able to differentiate between their inner self and external reality. This perceptual distortion, therefore, may be responsible for "self-transcendence" and the PE! Moreover, an increase in the brain's prefrontal lobe activation (associated with attention, concentration, false memory formation, odd perceptions, and unusual beliefs), and associated decreased parietal lobe activity (functions associated with the time concept and spatial activity), may mediate the cognitive process involved in the PE. Remarkably, you may even be able to change your brain.

Meditation practices, for example, have been shown to promote neuroplasticity (brain networks change their connections and activity in response to new information, sensory stimulation, development, or damage) and a mode of consciousness wherein insight can occur.[35] In the meditative and transcendental state, awareness is enhanced, there is a greater restfulness of the body, and brain regions show enhanced activity among specific locations in the brain that are networked together. Individuals who practice meditation and prayer over many years have thicker and more active frontal lobes and thalamus than non-practitioners.

In one experiment, decreased changes in neurological activity of language and orientation centers of the brain were observed in experienced Tibetan meditators.[36] This finding is especially interesting because when the brain's orientation center reduces sensory input, your self-perspective relative to the external world is diminished. This result is similar to that reported in those with reduced activity of the IPL—an inability to differentiate between inner self and external reality.

Experienced meditators, therefore, may be inducing "self-transcendence" and the PE. Moreover, it may be that "religious or mystical phenomena which emanate from meditation or God-like experiences, are not due to dysfunctional or distraught minds," and should not be based on explanations like "epileptic attacks, seizures, or a psychotic hallucinating behavior, as has been emphasized by the reductionist school of thought."[37]

A Stroke of Insight: Neuroanatomist Jill Taylor was 37 when she suffered a stroke that essentially shut down the left hemisphere of her brain—the side that processes language and logical thought. In her book, *My Stroke of Insight,* she described the feeling that resulted as being "at one with the universe."[38] In the hours before she got help, she says, "I experienced an incredible deep inner peace and contentment." She suspects this sense of union came from the brain's right hemisphere, the half that was in control during her stroke. She thinks the right brain, which is associated with intuitive and subjective thinking, is what connects humans to "the bigger picture and the present moment, where there are no boundaries and you're a part of it all."[38] In most people, the brain's left hemisphere dominates, but Taylor suggests that if we can learn to better use the right side, we will increase our natural ability to experience transcendent feelings.[40]

Cognitive neuroscience researcher Michael Persinger explained this concept by stating that: "If the brain is appropriately stimulated, you can have important experiences, with powerful healing effects."[41] Persinger suggests that the brain is hardwired for transcendent experiences and a sense of connectedness—it serves as an evolutionary strategy. As human beings developed language, he points out, we became aware of our mortality. "The anticipation that we would die was devastating, and interfered with creativity and adaptation, as anxiety does. The brain's ability to feel a mystical sense of union with the world may have begun as a coping mechanism for dealing with that existential anxiety, one that frees us to carry on with the business of living."[42]

Despite neuroscientific experimental findings of a correlation between the "God spot" and the PE, it is premature to make any firm cause-effect conclusion between the two, especially since there exists only a paucity of evidence regarding the neural correlates of spiritual practices. Most studies that have explored spirituality have focused research only in abnormal brain models and meditative practices, not true PEs. Consequently, no definitive, so-called "spiritual neuron" or "God spot" has been identified as the neurological trigger responsible for the PE. But the search must continue. For if the brain can be ruled out as a contributing factor, then indirect support for alternative non-physiological theories to explain self-transcendence and the PE can be entertained.

Discussion

The PE has been the focus of more research over the past decade. This emphasis is long overdue, especially since PEs have a profound effect on psychological health not only for the individual but also for society, and possibly generations to come. At this point, however, neuroscience alone cannot tell us whether changes from religious and spiritual practices, rituals, or beliefs are the result of real or illusory perceptions, or are even an aspect of consciousness independent of brain function. The challenge to understand neuroscience's relationship to spirituality and the PE stem from the fact that this experience is difficult to define using agreed upon criteria.

What behavioral criteria specifically describes and delineates the mental state associated in a true PE from meditative, yogic, and religious practice? Based on recent, albeit tentative, physiological study results on the relationship between brain neural networks and consciousness, it appears that meditation, and spiritual and religious experiences, may be a distinct form of consciousness uniquely different from waking, sleeping, and dreaming states. But one important overarching question

114

remains as to whether some, if not all, PEs and associated ASC are facilitated by pure brain-based events.

When the complexities of neuroscience are combined with the difficulties of defining the PE, the result is daunting. Neuroscience cannot tell us where precisely in the brain lies the so-called "God spot" or the symptoms expressed by those who have a PE. At best, neuroscience can provide various models of how the brain mediates aspects of religion and spirituality, and our understanding of how PEs influence well-being and health. While the research to date appears to have identified specific brain regions associated with religious and spiritual beliefs and experiences, the neuroscientific study of religion and spirituality is not likely to offer any absolute answers soon to what governs and regulates the PE.

A paradox also exists with discoveries in physics that tell us matter is profoundly different from what your senses tell you. This perspective, combined with recent neurobiological studies on the effects of ASC on the brain, HADD, and TEI, reinforces the need to further apply scientifically based principles and methods from many related disciplines of study to better understand the relationship between the brain and spiritual effects.[43] More specifically, the nature and impact of PEs must be addressed by the scientific community by incorporating the following research considerations: (1) development of a definition and criteria for characteristics which comprise distinct PEs; (2) relationship between brain activity and true PEs; (3) psychological and genetic factors associated with the content of various PEs; and (4) assessment of the long-term behavioral transformative aspects of the PE on one's personal and family life.

What is believed is not always to the liking of the believer; sometimes, as in the case of night visits by demonic beings and other NHEs, it's absolutely terrifying. The human tendency towards wishful thinking just postpones the mystery. We require an explanation for why humans are so attracted to believing in invisible NHEs and to seek self-transcendence. Whatever the correct explanation for these human tendencies may be, the fact that we are prone to false beliefs should provide caution to anyone who holds a belief in invisible NHEs on that basis. But the innate force within your brain, and possibly even in your DNA, makes this objective difficult to accomplish. You may very well be a hostage of both your brain and ancestral past. These unseen forces are difficult, if not impossible, to defend against, until a genetic surgeon one day comes along.

CHAPTER 6

THE SCIENCE OF UNSEEN FORCES

Introduction

Throughout history people have reported psychic experiences (psi), and in more recent times, thousands of well-controlled scientific experiments have supported the validity of psi effects. Despite this documentation, however, the general scientific community rejects the notion of extrasensory perception (ESP) and psychokinesis (PK). Like the PE, psi is considered an "anomaly"; an unexplained deviation from the norm. They are anomalous since they cannot be convincingly justified by known current scientific theories. Thus, it can't exist. But anomalies should not be considered irrational in any way, shape, or form. The parapsychological literature clearly indicates strong empirical evidence showing that psi does indeed exist, both at the microscopic (subatomic quantum scale) and macroscopic levels (classical physics).

The history of science clearly demonstrates that anomalies can lead to major discoveries and revolutions. History also shows that not all scientists are the model of open-mindedness and rationality. The Wright brothers, who for years claimed to have constructed a heavier-than-air flying machine and to have flown it successfully, were dismissed as a hoax by several American scientists.[1] Most considered it impossible just like electricity—a mysterious incomprehensible entity which is invisible and visible, both at the same time. Even today, no one is absolutely certain what electricity is but we know how to use it. The same can be said for ESP. Despite the lack of scientific principles to justify ESP, its existence has been experimentally proven beyond doubt.

Communication between minds is normal, not paranormal. It is natural, not supernatural, and is common between people, especially those who know each other well. You may, in other words, be able to exchange information that transcends space and time without the use of sensory systems and intentionally effect change in other people and physical systems at a distance (nonlocal communication). After a century of slowly accumulating scientific evidence, we now know that some aspects of psychic phenomena are real. Controlled experiments in ESP and PK, for example, have been validated through replicated, well-controlled experimental studies with "staggering probabilities against chance having produced the results."[2, 3] Even Dean Radin, Chief Scientist at the Institute of Noetic Science, emphatically stated, "There is some way that humans are connected with the rest of reality in nonlocal ways."[4]

Moreover, a statistics professor published a paper in 1999 showing that ESP experiments produced much stronger results than studies showing a daily dose of aspirin helps prevent a heart attack.[5] This chapter, however, is not an attempt to convince the reader to wholeheartedly adopt psi as a provable concept, but rather to present some of the more convincing evidence for one to make a more informed decision of the validity of psi within the context of the PE.

The Biofield

Overview: Are human beings entirely isolated from each other or does a biofield or "subtle connections" exist between you and the world at large? We know, for instance, that our body emits low-level heat, electric, and acoustical energy, but it may also generate a yet to be discovered energy as part of this human energy field. This energy field may provide a scientific foundation of possible connections of living systems through an all-encompassing energy field that incorporates long-range interactions. The implications of its existence for scientific understanding and associated applications in medicine, health, and healing may be profound. For one, this unseen force may eventually help narrow the existing void among science, psi, the PE, and possibly even life itself.

The Torsion Wave: Noted physicist Nicolas Tesla was probably the first to realize that a force exists around the body. He called it a "higher octave of magnetism," and he was spot-on. This extremely ultra-weak photon emission, or "biophotons," has been detected and accurately measured from cell cultures and from the body's surface using sophisticated instrumentation.[6] With the creation of each biophoton there is also a torsion wave—a form of radiation that connects subatomic particles and spreads through space as a rotating energy current. Biophotons form an electromagnetic field, whereby frequencies of waves determine the strength and timing of a biological event and provide the main signals and physical basis for cellular biological regulation.[7]

The torsion wave concept was developed by astrophysicist Nikolai Kozyrev using pendulums and gyroscopes. Like time, he described this "torsion field" energy flow as a sacred geometric spiral that controls time, space, matter, gravity and electromagnetism.[8] According to physicist Claude Swanson, this "torsion" force is everywhere, and when its "spin pattern changes, it causes a twist in space that carries effects."[9] This "spin"—the quantum version of angular momentum—is used to describe the properties of nuclei, atoms and molecules. Spins of molecules within the human body have even been observed to

119

couple with other molecules several inches away.[10] This form of communication or information exchange may even represent a cellular version of ESP or nonlocality. And if this is indeed the case, then a physiological basis and explanation for ESP may exist in the form of a torsion force that interacts with consciousness.

The Torsion Field and Consciousness: The torsion field, concomitant with the four conventional fields of the Unified Field Theory (electromagnetic, gravitational, and the two nuclear forces), may allow for the manipulation and even possible manifestation of consciousness. This higher dimensional field may be linked with your consciousness. Your biological biophoton torsion field, an energy which is over one million times greater than the body's magnetic force, exists in a holistic form of coherence in electromagnetic waves, [11,12] biophotons,[13] and human intention. The torsion field, therefore, may be the "missing ingredient which makes it possible to develop a true science of consciousness."[14]

Torsion may interact with and possibly even represent consciousness itself. Kozyrev's most controversial theory, for instance, was that human thoughts and feelings generate torsion waves of biophotons, and that even sudden changes in one's thoughts, feelings and actions influence torsion fields. Consciousness may be a "detectable force which can act on the environment both locally and remotely."[15] These effects have been studied for decades and the most important conclusion is that torsion force is a subtle energy; a higher dimensional field that may interrelate with consciousness itself.

Kozyrev claimed to have developed a complicated meter to measure the physical effect of his own psychological changes. When he realized that his emotional thoughts had a greater effect on this device than did his intellectual thoughts, he considered this interaction between torsion and consciousness as rationale for "spiritual phenomena," and the "physical" understanding of consciousness within a model of reality.[16] As Kozyrev points out, consciousness is related to vibrations within a fluid-like "aetheric" medium, and acts like an unknown form of energy—time itself. Physicist Swanson took this concept to the next level in his contention that torsion energy gives rise to the "subtle structure

120

of the aura and chakras, and also the long-range signals used in distance energy healing."[17] The body's DNA, therefore, may play an active role in ESP and may even be the receiver as well as the transmitter of your permanently evolving consciousness.[18]

Torsion waves are a fundamental feature of the physical universe. Like torsion waves, consciousness may possess quantum-like properties—nonlocality, superposition, and complementarity of a real and detectable force that acts on the environment both locally and remotely—biophotons. For this reason alone, the torsion field, combined with these forces, may provide for a "unified field theory that will extend the realm of science to include the effects of consciousness."[19] In other words, your mental intention alone releases energy in the form of a torsion field which causes a "ripple in the wave of time."[20] Consciousness, therefore, may be explained as quantum particles that carry information through a vacuum faster than the speed of light. This may explain the mechanism that governs and regulates ESP.

Even leading physicist David Bohm considered the existence of subtle energies in his statement that, "The implicate order has many levels of subtlety. If our attention can go to those levels of subtlety, then we should be able to see more than we ordinarily see."[21] Like Tesla, Bohm may also be correct. Experimental evidence demonstrates that the "torsion field operates holographically, without regard to time and distance."[22] Consciousness, therefore, may be a nonlocal electromagnetic system that does not exist in the physical world. And if this is indeed true, then your consciousness operates as a torsion/scalar biofield. But don't go bragging about this just yet until more evidence emerges, especially since supportive evidence for this concept is still evolving.

Experimental evidence has shown that photons released from chemical processes within the brain produce biophysical pictures during visual imagery. In one study, when subjects were dark adapted and asked to think about white light, reliable, physiologically dense photons were emitted and measured from the right side of the brain's cerebrum. More specifically, increases in photon emission from the head occurs while imagining light in the dark and is correlated with changes in EEG power.[23]

Scientist Tom Bearden got my attention to the point of almost "bragging" when I read his statement that, "all mind operations are time-like—they are comprised of scalar electromagnetic photon and wave functions." We see this in plants and insects. The fact that plants grow more quickly when spoken to may be related to torsion waves created by human intention. The "cavity structural effect" created by bee nests is another example. Entomologist Viktor Grebennikov, for instance, discovered that the unique shape of the nest allows bees to "harness and throw off large amounts of torsion waves" and this energy was even detected by human hands when the nest was shielded with thick metal.[24] Torsion waves may also act as a guide to trees. As trees detect them, their roots grow around the bees' structures rather than growing into them.[25]

If you are still unsure about the biofield, then ask physicist Buryl Payne, who alleges to have measured this unseen force using ordinary materials of just a piece of string, a few sticks of wood, metal, or plastic, and a few magnets. With these items, Payne constructed and suspended a frame with magnets over a subject's head, and when the frames and magnets were placed in airtight bottles while the subjects placed their hands around the bottle, the frame consistently rotated a few degrees. Over a series of experiments using this technique, Payne noticed that healers and young children usually produced greater rotation of the frames, and the direction of this rotation reversed when the moon was new or full, and when solar flares and geomagnetic activity increased.[26] This bioenergy, therefore, may be the interconnecting force between you and the entire solar system.[27] It seems there may be more science behind astrology than initially thought. Now, go ahead and read your horoscope for today.

Discussion: If torsion waves serve as connections in the realm of time-space, then instantaneous telepathic communication between people may seem plausible. Phenomena such as ESP and the PE may, therefore, be facilitated and explained by torsion waves through nonlocal correlations—the ability of objects to instantaneously know about each other's state, even when separated by billions of light years. But we do not yet fully understand the implication of the biofield on the human

THE SCIENCE OF UNSEEN FORCES

condition. Theoretically, however, since the biofield may exist as quantum information flow that regulates the body's cellular and neurological activity, effective alternative approaches in the treatment of psychological and physical illnesses may eventually be at hand.[28]

This is not a far-fetched idea, especially since biofield healing has existed for thousands of years in a wide range of cultures. Even today, physiological evidence is accumulating which suggests its therapeutic value in complimentary alternative medicine (CAM) techniques of healing. Energy medicine or bioenergetic therapies of healing, for example, are used by so-called energy healers who claim to sense and modulate "subtle energies" of the body to promote healing in the form of Reiki (Japanese spiritual healing) and Qi Gong therapy (an ancient form of Chinese energetic medicine). Since we do not fully understand how biofield energy can be effectively applied to the human condition, medical research must continue to explore its potential benefits on the mind and body. Any alternative to adverse side effects of ineffective drugs is something we all need, especially since time, at least for us old folks, is quickly evaporating.

Human Entanglement: Are Minds Linked?

Overview: Theories in quantum mechanics (QM) tell us that your focused intention or consciousness can influence external events. Consciousness, in other words, is vital to the existence of physical events being observed. In other words, this so-called "nonlocality" enables you to make reality real. This paradoxical notion must be taken into consideration to understand the nature of reality. This is so, since a nonlocal connection may allow for communication by thought transfer with other people's consciousness, regardless of distance.[29] Proof may be found in well-controlled experiments in parapsychology.

The discipline of parapsychology, the scientific study of interactions between humans and their environment, serves as part of the broader study of consciousness and the mind,[30] and typically includes three major areas:

(1) Extrasensory perception (ESP or the sixth sense: sensory information that an individual receives beyond the ordinary five senses). Extrasensory perception includes: (a) telepathy (mind-to-mind communication—being affected by someone's thoughts or emotions, unmediated by the senses or logical inference; (b) clairvoyance (obtaining information about a distant state of affairs, unmediated by the senses or logical inference, such as in remote viewing—someone accurately describes details of a place chosen at random by someone else); (c) precognition/presentiment (acquiring knowledge without the mediation of human senses or logical inference about a future event—being affected by an event taking place in the future that could not have been foreseen, as in dreaming about an event before it occurs); and (d) retrocognition (acquiring knowledge without the mediation of human senses or logical inference about a past event).

(2) Psychokinesis (PK—the ability to influence a physical system or move an object without any known physical methods).

(3) Survival of physical death; the concept of consciousness being able to operate separately or independently of the physical body and brain. This includes the notion of discarnate human spirits who have survived the death of their physical bodies (ghosts, hauntings, and apparitions), mediumship and channeling (communication between physically embodied and other intelligent beings), near-death experiences (NDEs), out-of-body experiences (OBEs), and reincarnation.[31]

These concepts are more than just theory. As a matter of fact, both physiological (electroencephalography—EEG) and psychological (consciousness and intuition) based experiments tell us that one can even respond to external stimulation before consciousness processes the event; that is, intuitive perception may occur from nonlocal characteristics of particles at the subatomic scale—the "observer effect," and quantum entanglement.

Entangled Minds: The experience of having our well-being impacted by the actions of others occurs all too frequently with both positive and negative consequences. The negative comes from those who are argumentative, stressed, or pessimistic, while the positive can be felt from those who are compassionate, empathetic, and optimistic. This is true for the friend you meet on the street, the physician explaining your blood test results, and the driver who unexpectedly cuts you off with only inches to spare.

These experiences are common, and you've dealt with them accordingly, but there are those few indescribable awe-inspiring moments that must have shocked you to your core. How do you explain, for instance, your absolute connection with the love of your life, the profound emotion you felt the moment your child was born, the horror and sense of connectedness with others following a major world event like 9/11, or the spiritual sensation of ineffability and unity with a divine force? This unseen force hits you hard and resides in the pit of your stomach. This gut-wrenching feeling is far beyond the "fight or flight" reaction induced by your body's elevated cortisol levels from extreme stress. It is a powerful connection with others and almost feels non-physical in nature with resulting impressions and memories that can last a lifetime. It feels as if an unseen force is in control. This unseen force may be you.

Your intentions create your experiences and your reactions express your intentions. It is like a box of chocolate with different flavors. When you pick one, you experience the sweetness and the bitterness of your choice. Life is similar to that. Whatever decisions you choose and pick in your life, you experience the sweetness or the bitterness of the choices you make in your life.

This often occurs unconsciously. Your intentions facilitate an action or a type of energy whether you are conscious of it or not. This is seen by our unconscious intention to marry to enable the survival of our species, to love and to be loved, and for spiritual growth. You create your own personal heaven or hell through unconscious intention. You are always being given chances to love and be loved, but how many times have you regrettably squandered this chance?

Telesomatic Events: Actual feelings and physical sensations triggered in one person by the intention of another, despite the distance between the individuals involved, are called "telesomatic events." This may be what is called "karma" in action. Negative karma means that the person who produces harmful intentions toward another will experience that same behavior from that person. The same is true for positive karma. Studies now suggest that its effects may be associated with linked minds.

Interpersonal connection or linked minds is frequent among identical twins in which one twin feels the pain suffered by the other and is aware of traumas and crises even if he or she is far away. The unique connection of mothers is also seen in incidents where they knew when their son or daughter was in grave danger or was involved in an accident. Amazingly, objective physiological evidence for an unseen connecting force that links the minds of people through conscious intention alone has been observed. Information produced by stimulating an individual's brain, for example, has been shown to somehow be transmitted and instantaneously measured via EEG in a distant individual's brain.[32] This information transference was more likely to occur if the individuals were closely related or emotionally linked, while meditating, or when attempting to communicate with the subject intentionally.[33]

In one study, EEG results from individuals who were placed in separate rooms and asked to feel the presence of each other showed that their electrical activity in each brain hemisphere synchronized.[34] When one individual in one room was visually stimulated by a flickering light, a significant increase in brain activity was observed in another person in a distant room.[35] These results have also been observed in separated identical twins. In two pairs of twins tested, eye closure in one twin produced not only an immediate alpha rhythm in his own brain but also in the brain of the other twin. What is especially significant is that this startling finding was reinforced by ten replicated studies by independent research groups around the world, and of these studies, eight reported positive findings which were published in respected peer-reviewed journals.[36-40]

Moreover, this confirming evidence was reinforced after a successful experiment by EEG expert Jiri Wackerman, who emphatically announced that, "no biophysical mechanism is presently known that could be responsible for the observed correlations between EEGs of two separated subjects."[41] This

126

evidence indicates that you are indeed connected through space and time at the level of consciousness with others.

In another experiment to test the validity of nonlocal intuition, physiologist L. Hendricks observed an interpersonal EEG coupling between healer and subject pairs by which the healer produced a "connection between the healer and the subject."[42] Similarly, psychologist Dean Radin asked subjects to imagine that they could perceive and alter a low-intensity laser beam in a distant interferometer. Astonishingly, the subjects were able to do so—their intuition alone modified the photons' quantum wave functions and the pattern of light produced by this device. This result led Radin to conclude that "intuitive knowledge arises from perceptions that are not mediated through the ordinary senses,"[43, 44] and that "conventional explanations" for these results were "implausible."[45, 46] The notion of communicating on "invisible pathways" has also been documented in experienced meditators who were able to willingly effect change in the pH of water in an electrical device using their intent alone.[47] One study also showed that individuals successfully increased the energy field output of very weak emissions of light by up to 70 percent through conscious intention alone.[48]

The process of nonlocal communication appears to function outside normal physical evolutionary processes and may be related to higher unknown aspects of consciousness. Highly respected scientists are now emphasizing the importance of what is still commonly overlooked in the mainstream scientific community—physical matter is not the only reality. Thus, it is not too far a stretch to suggest that psi study results enhance our understanding of the physical world—it extends to the non-physical or "spiritual" realm, especially since ESP experiences are often accompanied by feelings of profound ineffable meaning. Consequently, an unknown aspect of consciousness and associated cultural influences may represent the key unifying characteristic that explains why different triggers facilitate similar subjective PEs.

Are Autistic Savants Telepathic? An autistic savant is an individual with autism spectrum disorder. These individuals seem to possess certain extraordinary cognitive abilities, naturally exceeding the abilities of those who may have practiced similar skills for a lifetime.[49] Despite their severe disabilities, they demonstrate remarkable memory and calculation, as well as musical and artistic talents. Evidence also suggests that some autistic savants may also have an enhanced capacity for telepathic abilities. Autistic savants have not undergone rigorous scientific investigation for psychic ability, although many of their skills are very psi-like. Some are capable of correctly calculating cube roots of over five-digit numbers without knowing how to perform simple mathematical functions like addition or multiplication, and with no conscious derivation of the answers. These remarkable skills are even accepted by mainstream science because they have been reliably replicated.[50]

Neuropsychiatrist Diane Powell conducted an experiment with a severely autistic child named Haley. In this experiment, Haley and her therapist were seated at the same table separated by a partition. The therapist was given various pictures and equations and would glance at them one by one. As she looked at the images or equations, the therapist would hold another card with numbers, letters or images in front of Haley who would point to the number or image that she was thinking of. Incredibly, the numbers or images that Haley pointed toward were the same numbers or images on the therapist's hidden cards. In one test, her answers were 100 percent accurate, and through all the tests, she never scored below 90 percent.[51]   ·

To verify this result, Powell conducted two controlled sessions with two therapists who presented randomized numbers, sentences, fake words, and visual images out of view of the girl. She was then asked to "read the therapist's mind." The therapists were asked to write their own verbal descriptions of the images for comparison to the girl's answers. Haley was asked to give all the numbers in the equations and to duplicate the answers generated by the author with a calculator. Results from the first session with one therapist were amazing. She scored 100 percent accuracy on three out of 20 image descriptions containing up to nine letters each, 60 to 100 percent accuracy on all three of the five-letter nonsense words, and 100 percent accuracy on two random numbers: one eight digits and the other nine. Results from the second session also showed 100 percent accuracy on six out of 12 equations with 15 to 19 digits each, and between 81 to 100 percent accuracy on sentences of between 18 and 35 letters.

In light of these extraordinary results, Powell concluded that: "The data is highly suggestive of an alternative, latent and/ or default communication mechanism that can be accessed by people born with severely impaired language abilities."[52] These results, in combination with other successful ESP experiments, led psychologist H. Eysenck to conclude: "Unless there is a gigantic conspiracy involving over 30 colleges and several hundred highly respected scientists in various fields, the only conclusion the unbiased observer can come to must be that there does exist a small number of people who obtain knowledge existing either in other people's minds, or in the outer world, by means as yet unknown to science."[53]

Synchronicity

Overview: Are things indeed "meant to be" at some deeper level? Or is the universe revealing random events as we seek to find the thread that links them together? It may be "synchronicity"—a term often used as a synonym for coincidence, as in, events that trigger the exclamation… "What a coincidence!" or "What are the chances?" At times, however, coincidences are perfectly designed as an unbelievable experience of timing and meaning that is impossible to ignore. We've all had them. They happen when you see a meaningful connection between an external event and your own internal state. Such events can be relatively minor occurrences or, in some cases, significant events that alter our lives. The impactful significance and profound life changing meaning of a synchronicity has long fascinated humankind. It may even help us to understand the nature of the PE.

There is a fine line between intuition—a feeling that makes it possible to know something without any proof (internal), and synchronicity—something totally unexpected and timed to wake us up to our connection with reality (external). The difference between intuition and synchronicity is this: Intuition is having a sudden desire to phone a friend whom you haven't talked with in a while when they suddenly call you. In contrast, synchronicity is feeling a sudden desire to talk with this friend and as you begin to phone, they suddenly call you. Your intention initiates the act (first event), and synchronicity answers your intent (second event).

Synchronicity is the meaningful relationship of related internal (first) and external (second) events that go a step or two beyond an unusual chance occurrence. They are totally unexpected and timed to startle and wake us up to our connections with other realities around us in a way that cannot be explained by cause and effect. One is left bewildered trying to make sense of it. Or not? When the seeming absurdity of such random, improbable events occur, rare and fleeting though it may be, our sense of reality is momentarily questioned. Something happens within us that may shock us at our core—as if there is some kind of meaning behind it all. For some, there is a feeling of profound awe.

Synchronicity and One Mind: We have all experienced the sense of understanding the way things really are, especially when synchronicity is accompanied by a feeling of compassion and love. Anyone who has been deeply in love experiences the inexplicable fusion of two people, like the love of a mother for her child, or the love between true "soul mates." People who are emotionally close often exchange thoughts, feelings, and emotions despite being apart. In this nonlocal effect, a parallelism cannot be explained causally. Is it an invisible field effect linking multidimensional spaces, as the PEr believes it to be?

Synchronicity is in control when the experience contains significant meaning to the individual, and which occurs at a specific time, that makes the experience all the more meaningful. The classic example is a mother who "just knows" that her child is in danger, even though far away, as if the mother and child have a linked mind. Not to her surprise, the mother arrived just in time to prevent the child from serious injury. Synchronicity, in other words, represents the boundary between meaning and time.

Now, here's an old gambler's joke: A man wakes up and looks at his alarm clock, which reads 5:00 AM. He turns on the TV to see that the five o'clock news is on channel 5. He takes 55 minutes to get ready for work, goes down to the street level and takes the number 5 bus to Fifth Street to where he works at 555 Fifth Street. He takes the fifth elevator to the fifth floor and notices his office is on the fifth door to the left. And it is his 55th birthday so he figures this is a message from God and that there's got to be some way to take advantage of all these remarkable coincidences. So, he sits down at his desk and he finds the cleaning staff has left a racing form on his desk. He looks at the number five horse named Lucky Fives in the fifth race, and figures this is a sure bet to make a lot of money. So, he bets $5,000 with his bookie for that horse to win. He waits 'til five o'clock to call back and says, "How did my horse do?" The bookie says, "He came in fifth."[54]

This poor attempt at humor aside, these sequences happen to people all the time. What materializes is that one's conscious or unconscious intent influences the person's future experiences. If we are "seeing" our "own projections," then we may be creating our own reality. But while intriguing to contemplate, it may not be all good. It's an unexpected puzzle that can make people think they're going crazy, especially when caught in a series of synchronistic events of their own making.[55]

Synchronicity is a part of life that has no definite explanation. To explain such remarkable events, psychologist Carl Jung coined the term "synchronicity": "The coming together of inner and outer events in a way that cannot be explained by cause and effect and that is meaningful to the observer."[56] One such example is as follows:

"In 2012 I was doing research for a novel. The story would hinge upon an unlikely combination of geopolitical events that might lead to the collapse of civilization. To get to grips with the subject I bought an excellent academic book titled *Collapse*, by Jared Diamond. Diamond is a Pulitzer Prize-winning author who has made a lifetime study of these things. After I read the book, I composed an email to Jared Diamond. I wanted to explain the central concept of my novel to see if he thought it was realistic enough to be defensible. But he's a professor in Los Angeles and I'm a writer in England. Could I ever get through to him? I tried to guess his email address, but all my attempts failed. So, I gave up and took a vacation. We were off to Indonesia to look for the world's rarest rhinos. In a remote forest in Sumatra we found ourselves staying at a tiny eco-lodge. But there were two other tourists at the lodge—so we shared a table at dinner and got to talking about birds and rhinos. One of tourists was an American—it was Jared Diamond. And I promise—I had never come across him before."[57]

Such an experience seems to defy all logic and mere coincidence. It can certainly be debated if meeting Jared Diamond at this time, and in this way, was a coincidence and nothing more. But the nature and the timing of the event, which provides profound significance and meaning to the individual, makes it something uniquely different that a mere coincidence. This is synchronicity at work.

Discussion: Synchronicity is an aspect of consciousness which may not have its origin in the material world, but instead, in the nonlocal energy field referred to as the biofield, semantic field theory (SFT), and the collective unconscious. Like consciousness, this field may operate as a nonlocal interconnective force that unifies us in real-time, without regard to space and time. Whatever it is called, an unseen force may represent the missing link that facilitates synchronicity, ESP, and even aspects of the PE. According to the SFT, one "injects meanings into the semantic field, modifying its organization, while the modified organization is 'retrojected back' to the subject; this loop continues as long as the person continues to generate new meanings about the event, and may start all over again the next time one thinks about it."[58] In other words, our intentions may influence our future life events in an "interactive way" that may allow for synchronicity.

Those who believe that they've had a meaningful coincidence in their lives often experience feelings of wonder and amazement attributed to a form of destiny, mysticism, or existential importance. But meaning, a central component of synchronicity, cannot be obviously recognized or adequately defined since "meaning" is not scientifically testable. Thus, one major obstacle is in trying to scientifically explain what a meaningful coincidence is, and the possible mechanism that facilitates it. This mechanism may have its roots in the illusion of time.

The Illusion of Time

Overview: Time is an illusion. It doesn't really exist, but we are taught that it does. We have all learned to consider the past as something that happened, and that the future is about to occur. But that's an illusion because the past and future really don't exist at this very moment. The past and future are just simple language-based words to describe a present moment; instead, they are all transpiring simultaneously through our individual consciousness. Time, therefore, is interrelated with our consciousness—the brain archives and can recover past experiences. Our past memories and reflections, along with our thoughts and intentions toward the future, are one of the same. We're just experiencing them from different sides of time's illusion.[59, 60] With this in mind, physicists are now telling us that the past and future are not absolute and depend on the reference point of the observer. But how can this be explained for it to be understood on a personal level?

Physicists contend that everything that ever has existed, does exist and will exist. Confused? Well, if we assume that the past, present, and future all exist simultaneously, then it may be theoretically possible for you to access the future "you" that is experiencing your highest and best reality and outcomes. You may feel like you're postulating intentions of future actions, but instead, you may simply be receiving the memory of that version of you. This is practical in the sense that if the memories of our future self exist right now, then it may be theoretically possible to make strategic, purposeful decisions based on thoughts coming to you from the future "you" that has already experienced it. If reality is indeed flexible in this way, then foreseeable possibilities can be transformed into certainties.

Try to access the illusion of time by feeling for those thoughts that are the most aligned for you right now. Maybe this is the "gut feeling" we have all experienced and regard as being true. And how many times do we remind ourselves that "we should have acted on that feeling"? Maybe life becomes more manageable when we begin to practice it.[61, 62] This may be what neuroscientist Christof Koch implied about intuition and that "meaning" exists in the universe. Koch said: "I can't really describe it. I just feel the universe is filled with meaning. I see it everywhere and I realize it's a psychological mindset. I fully realize other people don't have this. I have it. It's very difficult to explain where it comes from. I just have this firm belief and the experience of numinosity. It's difficult to put into words."[63]

What may be difficult for Koch to "put into words" may be more easily explained by what psychologist Imants Barušs described as "meaning fields."[64] According to Barušs, "meaning fields affect reality through whatever mechanism it is that human beings use when they are remote viewing and remote influencing (ESP). They structure the form that events take at any level of existence. They are not only spatially nonlocal, but temporally nonlocal, in that the content of meaning fields can be modified by events from the past or future. Events are "tuned" to one meaning field rather than another. Meaning fields can "interact directly with human meanings so that human beings can 'tune' to different meaning fields as well as modify meaning fields according to some weighting algorithm."[65]

The concept of "meaning fields" may represent a major step toward the elimination of time from the description of the universe. This idea may have been established by physicists John Wheeler and Bryce Dewitt who developed an equation in which time had no role. This theory was advanced by physicist Julian Barbour, who believed that "time" is nothing more than changes that lead to the illusion of time.[66] It is important to note, however, that such concepts are inconsistent with the Newtonian concept of linear time and that of the fourth dimension proposed by Einstein.

While theoretical evidence in the world of math can provide the needed foundation to support the illusion of time, empirical evidence is also required to verify the concept of synchronicity and its interrelationship with this illusion of time.

Science has not yet determined the nature of time itself or why it seems different (both perceptually and in the equations of quantum mechanics) than the three dimensions of space but the answer may help to explain synchronicity. The proof likely requires yet-to-be-realized scientific principles to test under controlled experimental conditions in humans.[67]

Is the Future Now?

Overview: Studies in ESP indicate that it possible to detect information about an event before it occurs. Precognition experiments, for instance, indicate that information can indeed be transmitted via intention across space (nonlocality). In fact, a meta-analysis of over 300 precognition studies published before 1990 have produced odds against chance of 10 million billion to one. Chance can't be in control with these odds.

Knowing future events may even change the past.[68] More specifically, precognitive events or the ability to respond to a future event that could not be anticipated by any normal inferential process, usually appear to individuals as a flash or spontaneous vision. For example, a mother who has a vision of her child injured at the park quickly arrives to find her child about to fall from a swing. Another example is of a person who is about to board an airplane and has a vision of a crash that is so meaningful he decides not to board the plane. He finds out later that the plane crashed.

These occurrences illustrate how information can flow from the future to the present. But this notion doesn't "feel right" because our common sense impression of time is purely linear: at a given moment we are at one point on a dimension linking the past, the present, and the future. It may be possible, however, to move about this linear channel to another time where the past and the future may be observed. There are, of course, no agreed upon scientific principles of the physical world that can explain this, but experimental evidence suggests this may be true.

Experimental Evidence: In the quantum world, time runs both backward and forward whereas in your reality, it only runs forward. A recent discovery, however, has added a major new spin on this concept. A subatomic particle, for instance, not only moves backward in time, but its state in the past can also be altered by knowing its future outcome.[69] While seemingly confusing, this finding is significant. For one reason, it supports the first testable framework for the investigation of anomalous psychological properties in the groundbreaking studies by research psychologist Daryl Bem. His experiments demonstrated that future practice might influence present performance—retroactive influence.[70]

One of the most impressive findings from Bem's precognitive experiments was that practice on a list of words after a word-memory task was correlated with significant improvements in recall for the words that would subsequently be practiced. That is, instead of presenting the stimuli and then measuring the response, Bem reversed them in time and measured the response before the stimuli were presented—"retroactive causation."[71] Incredibly, the subjects were significantly better at recalling words that they would later type. Thus, the cause became the effect. But does this prove that people unconsciously know what will happen in the future? Possibly.

Several experiments, which have shown that brain activity and unconscious emotional arousal occur appropriately before a stimulus is presented, provide some support for Bem's findings. This is called presentiment—the sense that something is about to occur, but without conscious awareness of a specific event.[72, 73] As a matter of fact, compelling evidence from an analysis of experiments from many independent laboratories has consistently showed that humans do indeed unconsciously react to future stimuli. Researchers have shown that physiological measures such as heart rate, blood volume, and skin-conductance activity can be used to determine precognitive effects while participants viewed a randomized series of emotionally stimulating images.[74]

Psychologist Dean Radin pioneered a novel way to study precognition experimentally by exploring whether further emotional states (future feelings) are detectable in nervous system activity. With subjects seated and affixed with electrodes to measure their emotional reactivity, he observed that skin-conductance activity reacted appropriately consistent a few seconds *prior* to randomly shown emotionally calming or upsetting computer pictures.[75] Most of the pictures were emotionally neutral, but on randomly selected trials, a highly arousing erotic or negative image was displayed.

As expected, participants showed strong physiological arousal when these images appeared. But the important "precognition" result was illustrated by the significantly different physiological changes *preceding* future emotional events, as compared with calm events. This arousal occurred between two to four seconds *before* the picture appeared on the screen— even before the computer randomly selected the picture to be displayed. Bodily functions, in other words, began to change several seconds before the image was randomly selected by the computer and shown on the screen.[76] This is a convincing result. But even more persuasive was that subsequent studies by various researchers successfully replicated this outcome over 20 times.[77-79]

Radin's many presentiment experiments revealed the same striking outcomes with combined odds against chance of 125,000 to one. These results were also replicated by independent researchers using an fMRI scanner while subjects looked at computer images.[80] After each picture presentation, they were told to remain as calm as possible and to avoid thinking about the previous pictures. On each trial, the pictures were presented randomly—no one knew in advance which picture was about to be presented. Incredibly, specific areas of the brain involved in emotion were activated in 10 subjects *before* erotic pictures appeared.[81] This suggests that the brains of the subjects were somehow responding to future events. And this remarkable outcome has been validated by over 40 replications of the presentiment experiments with physiological measures.

In another presentiment experiment, researchers measured the time it took for a touch stimulus on a patient's skin to reach the brain as an electrical signal.[82] The patient was also asked to push a button when he or she became aware of being touched. Surprisingly, the brain transmitted the stimulus in 0.0001 of a second *after* it occurred, and the patient pressed the button 0.1 of a second *after* the stimulus was applied. However, the patient didn't report being consciously aware of either the stimulus or pressing the button for almost 0.5 seconds. Thus, the decision to respond may have been made by the patient's unconscious mind—an outcome which forces one to speculate if "free will" does not even exist.[83] Similar findings by neuroscientist R. Hunt, for instance, led her to conclude that, "I think we have way overrated the brain as the active ingredient in the relationship of a human to the world. It's just a real good computer but the aspects of the mind that have to do with creativity, imagination, spirituality, and all those things, I don't see them in the brain at all. The mind's not in the brain. It's in that damn field."[84] This so-called "damn field" may even be responsible for the finding by researchers of EEG correlations between the brains of spatially separated people mentioned prior (entangled minds). In other words, objective measures of a subjective sense of connection via nonlocal intuitive perception may be reflected in brain activity.

Collectively, this evidence suggests that the brain's regulatory mechanism may be activated just before conscious will to allow a brief period for consciousness to override a decision—the unconscious mind allows one to bring information into conscious awareness. For this reason, nonlocal intuitive perception appears to be predictive of randomly selected future events; that is, the mind somehow anticipates these events more often than chance and is based on physiological activity in the autonomic and central nervous systems. In other words, you can perceive your future. The question remains as to whether the perception of your future is a pure unconscious related outcome or if the brain somehow interacts with a field of information (SFT) for the answer.

Discussion: Experimental evidence shows that people can somehow access information that does not exist in the present time. Time, therefore, not only runs both backward and forward in the quantum world but also in your physical world. Although the awareness of future events that are eventually realized (precognition) appears to exist on an "unconscious" level in experimental settings, this awareness is also reported as an unusual "conscious" occurrence during a PE. The PEr typically reports alterations in time, and the ability to retrieve information from the past as well as the future. For this reason, another piece to the PE puzzle fits. That is, additional experimental evidence provides supporting corroborative evidence to the anecdotal descriptions of the PE.

The many controlled replicated studies demonstrating a compelling unconscious reaction in the form of changes in physiological activity just *before* conscious awareness indicate that you may very well have an unconscious ability to know the future. So, do you unconsciously know the future before our conscious awareness does? Well, based on these positive study outcomes, several well-respected researchers provided a definitive answer to this question by stating: "Barring widespread collusion among independent investigators, it appears that nonconscious access of future, unpredictable information is possible."[85] I accept this conclusion, especially since it has been verified by numerous independent investigators. But I am still left wondering how this is accomplished. After all, only theories exist to explain it. One popular, albeit controversial, theory, is that you are able to construct "concrete" reality by interpreting information from another dimension which transcends time and space. While this may sound more "woo woo" in nature than agreed upon scientific principles, prepare yourself, because this may be true.

Global Consciousness

Overview: Evidence to support nonlocal intuition is an important step toward understanding how consciousness is not limited to the brain and how it may relate to the PE. If the mind interrelates with the physical universe, then your awareness—the thinking, feeling part of yourself—may not even be confined to the physical body. We have seen that many physicists believe you are connected with the universe through nonlocal intuitive perception via a biofield, and that physical systems such as the brain or mind can be moved, changed, or influenced without being physically touched by anything else. Some of history's most notable discoveries may have evolved in this way.

A prime example is when people acquire knowledge of things in ways that are inexplicable. The inventor Thomas Edison, for example, said, "I have never created anything. I get impressions from the universe at large and work them out... Thoughts come from the outside."[86] The amazing life of Srinivasa Ramanujan provides another example. Born in 1887, he had no formal training or prior knowledge of mathematics before he began to see the Hindu Goddess of Namagiri in his dreams. Remarkably, nearly all the mathematical formulae he acquired in these dreams proved correct. They even paved the way for later success in many other fields.[87] Like Ramanujan, chemist Dmitri Mendeleev said he discovered the Periodic Table from dreams. The instant he awoke, he made notes of this table and the elements fell into place. Similarly, the grandfather of quantum physics Albert Einstein said the Theory of Relativity came to him in a dream, and the founder of Apple Inc., Steve Jobs, alleged his daydreams inspired the development of the iPad and iPhone.[88]

When the mind is at rest and free of everyday distractions, the sudden awareness of the solution to a problem—the so-called "Aha!" moment—has a greater tendency to emerge from the subconscious into conscious awareness because it occurs with little or no conscious effort leading up to that solution. Some people think the information for the "Aha!" moment was "downloaded" from the universe. That is what Edison thought when he said, "I get impressions from the universe at large and work them out." The mind slightly relaxed or when in a sleep state allows it to explore different combinations of ideas to test out different solutions. Once it arrives at one that looks promising, that is what pops into your head as an "Aha moment." You may, therefore, think about solutions at an unconscious level prior to solving problems.[89] Distinct neural processes in the brain may underlie the sudden flash of insight that allows people to "see connections that previously eluded them."[90] But don't start taking more frequent naps just yet—other non-brain-like possibilities for your "Aha!" moments may exist. And some neuroscientists think the answer lies in that "damn field." As a matter of fact, its possible existence comes from the startling results of the Global Consciousness Project.

The Global Consciousness Project: Is an unseen force or "global consciousness" created when people worldwide feel a sense of coherence or resonance among each other? If so, is this force strong enough to affect physical systems? The possibility that human intention alone can affect physical systems was demonstrated after a decade of rigorous experimentation as part of the Global Consciousness Project (GCP) at the Princeton Engineering Anomalies Research Laboratory (PEAR). The results were dramatic and hard to ignore.

In this unique study, the output of a worldwide network of 100 computer random event generators (REG), which continuously emitted ones and zeros in a random pattern, was analyzed by a supercomputer at PEAR to identify any statistically significant deviation from randomness influenced by major world events. Remarkably, such deviations were reported when major events elicited the attention of millions of people to a single point in time. This result occurred simultaneously with the terrorist attacks on September 11, the tsunami that devastated Southeast Asia, and the election of President Obama, among others. The odds against chance of this consistent result were less than one to one billion!

Researchers at PEAR also conducted a meta-analysis of about 600 REG studies by 68 different researchers. The overall results generated odds against chance beyond one trillion to one. In a separate series of experiments, over 100 subjects were asked to try to intentionally influence the REG outputs to drift above the chance-expected average (the high aim condition) then the below-chance average (the low aim condition). The results showed that when the subjects wished for high scores, the REG outputs drifted up, whereas when they wished for low scores, the REG outputs drifted down. Estimates made of the results produced odds against chance of 35 trillion to one! Remarkably, in some of the PEAR experiments, the subjects were thousands of miles away from the REG, and no decline in effects was found as a function of distance.[91] This conclusive result, combined with thousands of experiments with hundreds of subjects over the past two decades at PEAR, convincingly demonstrate, at least to some, that one's intention alone can influence REGs to produce a significant change in the direction of their will. Furthermore, the extraordinary results from the GCP led physicist Robert Jahn to conclude that changes in REGs were caused by a "field of consciousness strong enough to affect artificial intelligence," which proves "we are all one."[92]

While it is certainly encouraging to know we may be "all one," what does this imply? Well, how about this—humans can indeed exchange information without the use of their sensory systems and intentionally effect change in other people and physical systems at a distance. There exists overwhelming evidence to support the concept of a deeply interconnected "conscious universe."[93] It is impossible to ignore, as too many closed-minded scientists do, the numerous studies which convincingly demonstrate that perception of reality without the use of physical senses is indeed possible.[94-100]

It is important to sit back and take serious note of the conclusion by GCP researcher Roger Nelson who concluded that "we don't yet know how to explain the correlations between events of importance to humans and the GCP data, but they are quite clear."[113] The extraordinary statistical odds against chance of the GCP results, replicated numerous times by independent researchers in various ways, provide strong support for the existence of an interconnected, unified field of awareness (nonlocal communication). This field of awareness, generated by the strong emotionally charged reaction from billions of people focused on a specific global event (mental state), has a measurable effect on physical systems (output of random number generators). Consequently, the mind can affect physical matter – nonlocal communication seems very real indeed! Curiously, hard core scientific materialists still disagree with this possibility, despite the fact that many of their strong experimentally derived beliefs do not even come close to the conclusive power of the overwhelming GCP statistical research outcomes. It seems that for many scientists, realism and Newtonian physics must prevail in order to maintain their perspective that is threatened, both psychologically and intellectually, by evidence which contradicts their view of reality based upon established scientific principles. Despite the growing trend by many scientists who are beginning to see that realism and Newtonian physics are limited in their ability to explain nonlocal communication in all of its manifestations (anecdotally, experientially, experimentally), many still ignore that their long held traditional scientific model is outdated and in need of a new paradigm shift.

The GCP outcomes, combined with many other similar experimental results, are generally considered "implausible" and "anomalous," especially since scientific principles cannot explain how intuition can both affect physical systems and obtain knowledge from the minds of other people from perceptions that are not mediated through the ordinary senses. Not surprisingly, these outcomes have caught the attention of the CIA. For example, one declassified CIA document on psychic ability titled, "Research into Paranormal Ability to Break through Spatial Barriers" stated, "A total of 50 experiments in the ability to break through spatial obstacles were conducted," and of these, "25 were successful."[101] These results are precisely why the American Institutes for Research concluded: "The statistical results of the studies examined are far beyond what is expected by chance," and that "the data reviewed constitute genuine scientific anomalies for which no one has an adequate explanation."[102]

Discussion: Parapsychological studies indicate that conscious intent is a real and unseen force. An invisible connection between individuals does indeed exist and one's intuition is capable of "gaining knowledge about the world."[103] Although evidence of how one's intention can influence other people and physical systems has been justified, the mechanics of this transmission cannot be explained by traditional scientific models. This does not mean, however, that intention can't exert influence on the physical world or the notion of "linked minds" isn't valid. It is valid. The overarching question is simply this: If minds are linked—then, so what? Well, one potential implication is that your "cooperative intent" may have "subtle but real consequences," especially since you may be capable of communicating with others on "invisible pathways."[104]

Science and the Peak Experience

Overview: An obvious paradox associated with the nature of PE triggers, like a NDE and OBE, pertains to the reported sense of one's existence from outside one's body during a PE. For example, during a PE individuals allege to: (1) possess knowledge of existence in another dimension without a body; (2) perceive time as if the past, present and future exist simultaneously and instantaneously (nonlocality); (3) be linked with the memories and consciousness of oneself and others, including deceased relatives (universal interconnectedness); and (4) experience a loss of "universal wisdom and love" they had experienced during their PE upon return to their body and wakeful consciousness.

Attempting to explain such incomprehensible experiences that are undeniably inconsistent with medical and scientific principles presents a unique and insurmountable challenge to say the least. But given the high incidence and pronounced behavioral impact of the PE on those who experience it, it is important to at least try.

Theories and Anecdotal PE Evidence: Scientific theories have been advanced to provide insight into the PE and the means by which consciousness and memories interact with other minds, the deceased, and NHEs. Evidence on the PE and NDE, for instance, suggests that the experiencer often returns from an apparent unseen realm with a firm understanding of the holographic interconnectedness of all things.

The PE is typically described as a dimension beyond where one has access to an infinitely interconnected informational realm. If we assume this to be true, as experiencers firmly claim it to be, then an aspect of consciousness likely behaves independently of the brain during a PE. Consequently, a critical question emerges as to whether the brain inhibits cognitive function rather than facilitating it by normal embodiment. If consciousness is a byproduct of the brain, then if the brain is injured, consciousness should also be adversely affected in some way. But this is not the case in those who report to have had a NDE or those with terminal lucidity. Their reported experience contradicts what would be expected if consciousness is dependent on normal brain function, especially since the brain is severely compromised during these near-death states.

Indirect evidence to support the notion that consciousness is not the brain comes from anecdotal reports by those who claim to have an OBE. In an OBE study of "objective perceptions," about half of the subjects (N = 48) reported "precise perceptions corresponding to verified details in the environment and/or to scenes which took place just as described, thus giving a precise idea of when the actual experience occurred."[105] The following anecdotal accounts of four individuals, who reported to have explored their surroundings during their NDE, exemplify how one's consciousness is not adversely affected by their compromised near death brain state:[106]

(1) "My displacements were subject to my will with instantaneous effect. Instant zooming of my vision, without any displacement on my part. When I was on the outside in the park at tree level, I remember experiencing this zoom effect very clearly since I could see inside a tree without having moved."

(2) "I see everywhere at once, except when I target an object toward which I am "hurled" at great speed, as if I was zooming onto it. It is like a rapid zoom to be there where I am looking. It is very pleasant and fun."

(3) "My consciousness, like a beam of light, can move around very fast, nearly instantly. This gaze, just like thought, can move about very rapidly."

(4) "Moving around is done as if time does not exist anymore. We "think" about where we wish to be and we make a volitional effort and we get there instantaneously since there is a sensation of movement, but very fast."

If you believe these accounts to be valid perceptions of events without the use of one's sensory system, then intuitively you may believe your personal identity, intention, and free will are not facilitated by the brain. In contrast, the traditional scientific viewpoint is that only matter exists, and that everything about one's uniqueness and "self" is facilitated entirely by poorly understood neuro-electrochemical activity in the brain. These opposing viewpoints raise a critical question: Is an aspect of one's consciousness or "I" (spirit or soul) absolute, unbounded by space and time, and not entirely defined and controlled by the brain? If you believe that a PE provides the means to access another reality and interact with NHEs, then this must be the case!

These similar PE accounts may be explained, at least, in part, by integrating theories in physics and consciousness studies. My interpretation, if I may cut to the chase and spare you the details, is that consciousness: (1) is not limited by spatial and temporal parameters; (2) may function independently of the brain; and (3) may be capable of experiencing other realms of existence. Theories in QM essentially support these and other types of characteristics unique to the PE. Similarities may be found between components of the PE and quantum field concepts of nonlocality, universal interconnectedness, and an alternate dimension beyond our time-space; that is, all events are related and influence each other instantaneously.[107]

The Quantum Hologram Theory (QHT) may provide the essential underlying principle to explain the PE. The QHT addresses how at the quantum level, everything, such as atoms, cells, plants, animals, and people, are connected within a network of information. According to many physicists, the PE may be explained by the QHT—a "shift" in consciousness from one dimension of the hologram to another. This abstract concept may be represented in the PErs descriptions of "no time," "eternal present," and "being out of time"—a form of time alteration not consistent with your physical reality.[108]

In a holographic universe, the past, present, and future all exist simultaneously; a phenomenon documented in the PE trigger—the NDE. This concept may be supported by the following testimonies by individual NDErs:[109]

(1) "Feeling that time no longer existed."

146

(2) "In fact, there was no time, it was like a moment of eternity."

(3) "Time did not exist. Now it's a real knowledge for me, time does not exist."

(4) "On the other side, time does not exist. One truly realizes it. Time is a completely mental concept. A thousand years may be instantaneous."

(5) "I had a horrible feeling of eternity. I had an experience where time no longer unfolded. Furthermore, no past, no future, just an eternal present. I had the feeling that all that was real, the feeling of 'living' in eternity."

(6) "Past, present and future are merged in a single concept, that's what I experienced."

(7) "The notion of time has nothing to do with ordinary life, that's for sure. Physical, material time does not exist. Time does not flow. To say that there is another 'time system' I do not know."

(8) "Time is no longer linear. Your own life is in 3D and the fourth dimension is fully integrated. At that time, if I had watched a man, I could have known everything about him. His age, height, blood type, his siblings, the amount of all his taxes, his diseases. All in a single concept."[110]

The unique similarity of such anecdotal reports suggests that consciousness could be the result of interactions between 4D and 5D phenomena and/or universes, a theory supported by neuroscientists, cosmologists, and philosophers. This paradox may best be explained by assuming that if we try to take apart something constructed holographically, we only get smaller wholes instead of the pieces of which it is made. This "whole in every part" nature of a holographic universe may represent the mystical features reported in the PE.

Now, if we take this to the next level, as many more physicists seem to do each day, it is not outside the realm of possibility that the universe is holographic in nature. That is, light energy, interacting with holographic information in a two-dimensional realm, produces a holographic projection of our three-dimensional world—the universe. This holographic information, therefore, may be the result of information existing outside the universe itself. My old friend, Harvard professor and astrophysicist Rudy Schild, even proposed that "black holes"—super-dense, massive, collapsed, evolved stars and galaxy-center quasars—store "quantum holograms" and may even function as "nature's hard drives" by holding copies of the "quantum holograms generated by each new moment of human experience."[111] This notion has been repeatedly proposed by eminent scientists—especially since the universe is comprised of interfering electromagnetic waves—just like the holographic image that you marveled at years back in a science museum.

Theories and anecdotal evidence are all we have to support the "holographic universe" concept. But that's an important initial step in a long-needed and evolving process to explain the PE. For example, you saw how time may be altered by a PE, but what about space? Well, PErs often report a change in normal visual perception and claim to: (1) be "everywhere at once," (2) have an "enlarged vision," and (3) experience perception by transparency. Seven individual accounts consistent with the holographic concept are as follows: [112]

(1) "I visited various places I managed to identify afterward. I remember a window in a village, a building with very white plaster, sand-carved windows. My curiosity was attracted to details. This is quite important, since we cannot do this normally, like seeing inside and outside at the same time, an impression of a quasi-holographic vision. Not a panoramic view, but seeing in front, behind, all details simultaneously which is completely different from ordinary sight. It is very rich."

(2) "I had a 360-degree spherical-like vision. I saw everything and had different points of observation: above, sideways, from the front, underneath, it was really extraordinary to see and be all of it at the same time. When I saw the sofa, the furniture and the room in which I was, I was simultaneously above, sideways, from profile, facing forwards...it was very clear."

(3) "Here you see this, then elsewhere you see something else, you know everything, from one place to another from the spot where you are. For example, if I want to go to the window,

I have to move. But there you don't move, you're everywhere. Unbelievable, but it's great."

(4) "I could see everything at once and if I focused on one thing, I could see this thing through any obstacle and in every detail, from its surface to how its atoms were organized, truly a global and detailed vision."

(5) "I could see in front and behind oneself simultaneously, through objects, a holographic view."

(6) "I felt like a soap bubble with eyes strolling about above at ceiling level, in a space which seemed a little "closer" than real space. Behind a wall was a woman dying in the resuscitation room. I saw the instruments, the doctors' gestures and their conversation, I could see through the curtains which hung in front of the glass partition."

(7) "I could see up close and also transparently. I remember seeing a stick of lipstick in one of the nurse's pockets. If I wanted to see inside the lamp which illuminated the room, I'd manage, and all of this instantly, as soon as I wanted to."

These individuals are convinced that what they experienced during their PE is a reality and not an illusion. Quantum theory supports their personal accounts. That is, consciousness behaves in a nonlocal manner that is free of both time and space.

Discussion

A fundamental, yet seemingly elusive question is whether QM may provide the conceptual framework for understanding the PE. Quite interestingly, the reported subjective PE characteristics do seem analogous to QM principles of time and space. The overarching issue remains as to how consciousness may be experienced independently of the body during the PE. That is, is our consciousness itself a nonlocal phenomenon? Unfortunately, the answer will likely remain tenuous at best since explaining the PE using QM principles has not been seriously considered, let alone attempted, using an objective, testable framework. This major limitation is further compounded by the fact that mainstream science equates consciousness with the brain. This is regrettable, especially since the initial first step toward explaining the PE should, at the very least, require the consideration that separation of consciousness from the body may be possible. This obstacle, however, may be circumvented by studying the inner workings of the brain itself. The PE may possibly be explained by studying the brain's holographic-like behavior.

Despite objective evidence of correlations between nonlocal intuition and associated physiological measures, however, further justification is required to validate this cause-effect relationship. This is a necessary step to help explain the possible force which may govern and regulate the means for such information transmission; that is, consciousness is not constrained by time or distance. As far as I'm concerned, ESP is indeed real, and will one day provide the foundation to explain the connection between one's own consciousness and that of other living persons and the PE.

The supportive evidence of communication on "invisible pathways" justifies the existence of ESP. This is critical for understanding the PE, especially since PErs report communication with deceased relatives and NHEs via telepathy. Linked minds, therefore, may not only exist in your present reality as research studies indicate. They may also be a normal behavioral mode of communication during a PE. Thus, the pieces to explain the PE puzzle continue to evolve into a more coherent whole. The unique properties of torsion fields, and the results that conclusively prove minds are linked on invisible pathways, demonstrate the emerging view of life as information and energetic flows. This theoretical and experimental foundation may provide a model for understanding the PE and associated psychic phenomena.

CHAPTER 7

THE PEAK EXPERIENCE

ANOTHER REALITY, PSYCHOPATHOLOGY, OR A PHYSIOLOGICAL DISORDER?

Introduction

The strong impression by those who have had a PE is one of encountering a different reality, a higher state of mind than that of everyday waking experience, and/or the sense of cosmic or universal consciousness to which we are all connected. Although subjective descriptions are critical for understanding the nature of the PE, this evidence is scarce, subjective, and not amenable for study under well-controlled laboratory conditions. Consequently, there lacks sufficient objectivity and reliability for mainstream science to determine the specific psychological and biological factors that give rise to one.

To the scientific community, the PE is explained by reference to the abnormal neurological workings of the brain and associated hallucinatory phenomena. It has been well documented that on occasion, and for different reasons, our brain fails to distinguish between a visual or auditory stimulus that is occurring in the outside world, and one that is just a product of our mind. This occurs in the form of visual and/or auditory hallucinations in those with schizophrenia which involve a hyper-stimulated auditory/visual cortex that results in random sounds and visions being generated; in those with Parkinson's disease who have an overactive visual cortex that produces images of things that aren't there; and in those who take psychoactive drugs which upset the relationship between the sensory processing parts of the brain. The overarching question, therefore, is whether faulty neurological processes are also responsible for the altered perceptions reported in most, if not all, PEs.

Quite surprisingly, abnormal psychological experiences in the form of either normal dissociative or imaginative states to more severe psychotic and schizophrenic mental states are not rare in occurrence. According to a 2015 World Health Organization mental health survey, about 1 in 20 people in the general population has experienced at least one psychotic experience in their lifetime not associated with drugs, alcohol or dreaming.[1] Hallucinations are also fairly common with almost two out of three healthy people reporting benign hallucinations—hearing their name being called, the phone ringing or seeing someone sitting at the end of their bed while falling asleep.[2] Hallucinations also frequently occur in people during bereavement, life-threatening situations, and stressful traumatic situations, such as sensory deprivation, sleep deprivation, and solitary confinement, and in physiological disorders like Parkinson's disease and dementia (hallucinations of people alive or deceased, or guardian angels). Given this context, the consistency of reported PEs, whose features challenge the materialistic view of human consciousness, the concept of mind as a byproduct of the brain may be critical for understanding the nature of the PE.

The Peak Experience: Is it in the Brain?

Overview: The general scientific community contends that spiritual and mystical experiences are facilitated by brain regions that regulate emotion, self-representation, and cognitive conflict.[3-7] They consider an aspect of brain physiology to be responsible for all "non-pathological visions" illustrated in varying spiritual and mystical ways among cultures throughout history.[8] As mentioned prior, PE triggers have been correlated with the activation of a large network of the parietal system (integrates sensory information) in the brain which may play a crucial role in self-transcendence.[9] Furthermore, this line of reasoning has been used to explain the altered state of consciousness (ASC) elicited by "life-threatening situations (both organically and psychologically), in psychiatric and neurological disorders, and also in hypnosis and meditation, role transitions and, more generally, all deep existential crises."[10] The ASC induced by hallucinogens (DMT, LSD), hypnosis, and meditation may also stimulate specific brain regions resulting in a broad range of experiences perceived as being "spiritual" in nature.

One neurological theory is that hallucinations are caused when something goes wrong in the communication between the brain's frontal lobe and sensory cortex. The brain may be more susceptible to generating realistic illusory perceptions when this delicate and complex process is compromised by lack of sleep, and stress from extraordinary or life-threatening experiences.[11, 12] Surprisingly, hallucinations are a common part of the grief reaction, with as many as 70 percent of bereaved people experiencing illusions of their deceased loved one.[13, 14] Direct stimulation of the brain's visual association areas has also been shown to produce complex and vivid images of "Lilliputian-type" individuals, animals, various objects, and geometric figures.[15, 16]

Abnormal neurological activity such as tumors, traumatic brain injuries, epilepsy, and cardiovascular events may also cause hallucinations induced by compromised brainstem regions and areas involving the occipital and temporal-parietal pathways.[17] One popular neurological explanation, for instance, incorporates a "reverberating circuit" initiated by electrical activity in the right prefrontal cortex that represents the "intent to eliminate thoughts from the mind."[17, 18] This activity may inhibit input to the parietal lobes resulting in a sensation of pure space that is subjectively experienced as "absolute unity or wholeness, and the obliteration of the self"[19] — core subjective features of a PE. Although the brain may indeed facilitate the general essence of an ASC, however, the specific content and meaning of the experience is likely dependent on one's personal and philosophical values, emotional state, and cultural background.[20, 21] But while many theories attempt to explain self-transcendence, considerable debate persists as to whether the PE is real or imagined.

Peak Experiences — Real or Imagined: Our poor understanding of how the brain facilitates your sense of self and reality make it virtually impossible to firmly conclude the PE is either real or imagined. Although materialists generally consider PEs a hallucination, there exists some evidence that this may not be the case. For example, if consciousness is a byproduct of the brain, then if the brain is injured, consciousness should also be adversely affected in some way. This may not be true since NDE evidence suggests that when one is close to death, consciousness may be unaffected. Consequently, consciousness and the brain, while clearly interrelated, may also function independently of each other. No one can say for sure, although many contend that one or more theories of compromised brain function elicit the NDE.

A common brain-based explanation is that even when NDErs accurately report events that occur while their brain and heart are not functioning, their consciousness is not truly separated from their body. Instead, the perceptual content of their NDE may arise from prior knowledge, false memories, and hallucinations generated by an abnormal functioning brain concomitant with the mind's attempt to "fill in the gap" after a period of brain inactivity. More specifically, reports of visiting heaven and/or seeing angels and God, may include one of several possible contributing factors that create a surreal, yet realistic experience caused by a stressed or dying brain. These include oxygen deprivation (i.e., hypoxia or hypercapnia), abnormal sensory input, endorphin-induced euphoria, and the body's neurochemical responses to trauma.[22] When the person recalls the NDE, therefore, perceptual experiences may be interpreted as spirit beings, alternate realms of existence, and conversations with God and deceased relatives.

In contrast to brain-based explanations, many consider the NDE as evidence of the separation of consciousness from the brain, especially since most NDErs frequently report their experience as more real and vivid than waking consciousness.[23] The vast majority of NDErs report that when their brain was significantly impaired (flat-line EEG), their thought process and control of cognition were clearer and faster than ever before— as if their mind had been suddenly released from the brain's impeding influence.

Supportive evidence for this concept was provided by the founder of the Near Death Experience Research Foundation, Dr. J. Long, who reported that 74 percent of over 1,200 NDErs claimed to have "more consciousness and alertness" during their NDE; 47 percent reported enhanced vision; 41 percent had unchanged vision; and about 35 percent claimed to have had increased awareness and mental activity. Long considered these results to be "quite remarkable, given that these patients were in a severe medical crisis and often unconscious."[24] In a study to test this theory, researchers who employed the Memory Characteristics Questionnaire to compare memories of real and imagined past events in groups of individuals that survived a coma (one group was characterized as having had a NDE, while the other was a non-NDE control group), concluded that NDE memories had more features than any kind of memory of real and imagined events and cannot be considered as imagined events.[25-27]

While these findings have often been interpreted as strong evidence that the mind is independent of the brain to many who wish it to be true, it is, nevertheless, premature to formulate any firm conclusions based on these results alone. If these findings are valid, the question then arises as to what physiological activity governs one's reported enhanced cognitive perceptions under severely comprised brain conditions? If no activity can be found, these outcomes would then serve as indirect evidence, albeit controversial, that consciousness may be independent of the brain and exist in a non-corporeal form that may be capable of interacting with other realms of existence. Or is it simply all in the brain?

Am I Really Dead? Reports of those who claim the ability to see and hear events that their body shouldn't be able to perceive are difficult to explain. It is a mystery how a clear consciousness can be experienced at the moment the brain no longer functions, during a period of clinical death with a flat EEG. One explanation is that they may not be dead. Even when pronounced "clinically dead," it may be possible for one to still experience sensory input and recall prior knowledge, which are incorporated into their NDE. For this reason, existing medical criteria for "death" may not accurately represent one being truly dead.[28]

This possibility presents a confounding variable in NDE research and medical practice and serves as the primary argument against the validity of an NDE. It implies that there may be no justification for declaring one clinically dead if the person subsequently can be resuscitated. If one is resuscitated and has an NDE, some degree of neurologic activity must have been present. Accordingly, the NDEr may still be alive and able to process environmental information despite their flat EEG: an important clinical criterion to define "brain death." Many scientists, for instance, contend that despite the medically accepted clinical sign of death following a cardiac arrest (i.e., a flat-line EEG within 10–20 seconds of the arrest), active brain function may still exist but is undetectable by current EEG technology.[29] Consequently, one may still be conscious during an NDE despite being pronounced "clinically dead." Another possibility is that the NDE arises during the rapid transition from consciousness to unconsciousness and/or in the reverse process from unconsciousness to consciousness and not specifically during the period of clinical death.[30]

Supportive evidence for this finding comes from EEG studies in NDErs who have flat EEGs. Under normal circumstances, whenever a person is engaged in speaking, thinking, imagining, or even hallucinating, their EEG illustrates heightened brain activity. But there are many cases in which people with flat EEGs have had NDEs, and even if their NDEs were a hallucination, that event would also have been indicated on their EEG. In other words, "even if neurological evidence is found to account for experiencing or recalling a NDE, that evidence alone still does not exclude the possibility that consciousness survives bodily death."[31] This conclusion, however, is contradicted by findings which allow for a neural component for NDE memory storage in a brain that is partially functional (in coma or cardiac arrest patients), regardless of a flat-line EEG which measures only surface cortical activity, the moment when the NDE occurred.[32-39]

The controversy over the clinical criteria to define "death" is one reason why the medical and scientific communities reject NDEs as compelling evidence to support the existence of consciousness outside the body, especially since those reporting NDEs are "alive and their bodies were still functioning sufficiently to be revived."[40] Even when "a person is deemed "brain dead" by strict clinical criteria, brain activity can often still be demonstrated days later, raising the question of when, if at all, death had occurred."[41] These perspectives raise important questions about both the definition of death and the associated NDE. In other words, what does "near death" really mean if the definition of "death" itself is a topic of debate within the medical and scientific communities? Maybe dying isn't a new road as some may think?

Psychological Factors: The role of psychological factors in influencing one's susceptibility to PEs has been a focus of much research. Some consider that PEs are not a pathological psychological disorder but rather a non-pathological experience that involves the psychological mechanism of dissociation as a normal response to extreme stress.[42] Thus, a depersonalization reaction by the brain may elicit a feeling of being separate from one's self and reality—a "processing impairment" caused by stress-response hyper-stimulation or a state of "semi-emergency readiness."[43] When we perceive danger, for example, stress hormones that are released for immediate action (fight or flight) induce many physiological, psychological, and emotional reactions for survival purposes, which, in turn, can create depersonalization symptoms.

A strong relationship between "fantasy proneness" and NDE phenomena has been reported in individuals while in "meditative states or under intense psychological distress" where no actual threat to their lives existed.[44] This outcome suggests that one's traits and beliefs might strongly influence the appearance of such phenomena in a range of different contexts. Consequently, one may experience anomalous sensations, emotions, and perceptions, which can also include the belief they are outside or separate from oneself, as if they are having an OBE and/or NDE.

The psychedelic and near death states reported by experiencers appear to be sensitive to contextual factors such as prior psychological traits and state, the environment in which the experience occurs,[45] and the cultural context in which they are embedded.[46] Certain personality traits (absorption and neuroticism) can also predict the intensity and quality of a psychedelic experience.[47, 48] Similarly, the prevalence and nature of NDEs appear to be sensitive to environmental, demographic and personality variables, such as etiology and prognosis of the NDE, age, absorption and a propensity to report paranormal experiences.[49] Cultural factors can also influence the psychedelic experience and the content of NDEs.[50-52]

Related to this concept are the findings from a questionnaire survey, which found that while PErs were not more fantasy-prone than control subjects, they experienced greater sensitivity to non-ordinary realities as children, a higher incidence of child abuse and trauma, and scored higher on a measure of psychological dissociation.[53] Some researchers have also considered that the reported observation of deceased relatives and a beautiful landscape during an NDE represent an illusion produced by expectations of what will happen at death.[54] This concept is represented in a cross-cultural study of NDErs from two different cultures, whereby researchers reported the deathbed experiences of 442 persons living in the USA with those of 435 individuals living in India to be significantly different.[55] This finding may explain why individuals seen during the reported NDE differ considerably among those with different socio-cultural backgrounds. The reason for this may be twofold: the brain facilitates the altered perceptions reported in an NDE and OBE, and the individual's memory, expectations, and personality provide the content and meaning of the experience itself.

Temporal Lobe Pathology and the OBE: Neurological disorders, from brain lesions to extreme emotional states, can alter your body schema—your body's relationship to the world and position in space. A disruption of your brain's network patterns of activity, for instance, may create sensations of being separated from your own body, perceiving the body from "outside," and shifts in perception of place and time. The association between brain stimulation/pathology and altered perceptions (the sensation of floating, interactions with NHEs, induced memories, disorientation of body image and time and space, and loss of one's sense of reality, etc.) support a physiological basis to explain PEs triggered by NDE, OBE, and psychoactive drugs. More specifically, the function of the brain's temporal parietal junction (TPJ) suggest that abnormalities in this region are the primary cause of an OBE, and may even account for most, if not all, PEs. This perspective is largely based on the TPJ's function to mediate the conception of our own body in space and its role in thinking about thoughts— the part that lets us explicitly conceive of "thinking" or "wanting" something to be true, which then interacts with many other brain regions to place these ideas in context and sense other presences.[56]

The association between temporal lobe pathology and the PE has been tentatively established in both healthy and pathological subjects.[57] This is evidenced by those who had a stroke that damages the right TPJ. This damage often causes an impairment in reorienting attention resulting in left-hemisphere neglect, characterized by reduced or an absence of awareness of spatial events (objects or people) on one side of their body. What is especially interesting is that symptoms induced by external stimulation of the temporal lobe correspond with the symptoms experienced in many with temporal lobe epilepsy, represented by subjective "feelings and things" that become suddenly "crystal clear," of "having the truth revealed to them," or of having achieved a "sense of greater awareness and of a new awareness such that sounds, smells and visual objects have greater meaning and sensibility."[58]

Moreover, psychological evidence suggests that OBEs result from a disruption in the processing of one's body image.[59, 60] Individuals with brain injuries, who show enhanced brain activity within the parietal and temporal regions, have frequent OBEs, paranormal episodes, as well as mystical accounts, including the feeling of a presence.[61] This was demonstrated by neurosurgeon and Nobel Prize winner Wilder Penfield, who induced memories of the past, experiences of light, sound or music, and even an OBE in patients via localized electrical stimulation of the brain's temporal and parietal lobes.[62,] Stimulation of the temporal lobe may also induce experiences in the form of conversing with spirits, angels, or gods,[63, 64] and some with temporal lobe epilepsy visualize ghosts, demons, angels, and even God, or claim to have left their body.[65-71] More specifically, electrical stimulation of the right TPJ has been shown to elicit an OBE and individuals suffering from temporal lobe epilepsy have reported "religious or spiritual experiences in between, during, or after seizures."[72] Additionally, enhanced EEG activity originating from the right TPJ region has even been reported in an OBE during an epileptic seizure.

Similarly, another study demonstrated that a whole-of-body illusion or a type of OBE could be elicited using virtual reality goggles on subjects standing in an empty room. More specifically, when an image of themselves standing six feet ahead was projected into the goggles while their backs were stroked with a pointed stick at the same time, they perceived their virtual self being touched. When the real and virtual touching was synchronized, the subjects reported the sensation of being in the projected body. Subsequent experiments involved projecting an image of the participating subjects into video goggles from two cameras placed six feet behind them caused the subjects to sense they were looking at their own bodies from six feet away, as if disconnected from their physical body, like an OBE.

Collectively, therefore, the association between brain activity and unusual psychological experiences implicates possible neurological disturbances as the mechanism responsible for facilitating the NDE and OBE and their content, in the form of complex imagery, entity encounters, and vivid autobiographical recollections.[73,74] Some individuals may even have a predisposition for an OBE. Individuals who hold strong beliefs in the paranormal, for instance, are more likely to report a "sensed presence," sensation of "being uplifted," and distortion of time and their own body.[75] Since these sensations occur in those without temporal lobe pathology, processing distortions may also be responsible for OBEs in healthy individuals. The TPJ region of the brain, in other words, may be the mechanism for anomalous perception (OBE and NDE) in both individuals with (pathological) and without (non-pathological) TPJ abnormalities.[76,77]

Sleep Disorders: Am I Asleep or in Another Reality? Physiological explanations have been implicated for the content of sleep related illusions that occur when falling asleep (hypnagogic) or when waking up from sleep (hypnopompic); during lucid dreaming (the dreamer is aware that they are dreaming); sleep paralysis (inability to move one's body upon waking); and narcolepsy (a neurological disorder that affects the brain's ability to control sleep-wake cycles).

Sleep transition phases (hypnagogia and hypnopompic) enable one to observe their unconscious mind and interpret its contents as vivid and real events. The strange nature of hallucinations occurring during the initial and final sleep stages, unlike the unreality of normal dreams, is a common occurrence and may explain some PEs. Studies have shown, for instance, that about 40-80 percent of the population report sensory perceptions that seem quite real during transitional sleep states that persist once they are fully awake.[78] About one-third of the population have experienced a hypnagogic hallucination at some point in their life, and two-thirds may hallucinate when they are falling asleep.[79]

In these states, people report feelings of peace, being separated from reality, and sensing or visualizing the presence of NHEs, deceased relatives, and/or a "Supreme Being."[80,81] A range of auditory (music, voices, repetitive words), visual (images are fleeting but sometimes they form entire dream-like scenes), and proprioceptive (feelings of floating and OBEs) hallucinations have been attributed to hypnagogia. It is also common to experience multiple forms of hypnagogia, whereby visual memories from the day appear as a display of physical sensations and sounds.[82]

Hypnagogic hallucinations are different from other sleep-related conditions such as lucid dreams and sleep paralysis. Lucid dreams are realistic dreams that can make one feel as though they are having an OBE. In contrast, sleep paralysis is a waking dream accompanied by an inability to move since the body remains in the sleep mode;[83] a state when the "brain is caught in the borderlands between waking and rapid eye movement (REM) consciousness."[84] Features of REM, like sleep paralysis, can intrude into our fully awake consciousness which can cause one to see, hear or feel things that are not there, or to think that another person is in the room with them, and to even have an OBE.[85]

Sleep-based perceptions, such as observing a divine entity at the bedside, one's own body from a distance, or a bright light encompassing the room, are likely to be inspirational and considered a supernatural experience. They raise an important and fundamental question regarding the validity of some PEs. That is, are transitional sleep states responsible for eliciting hallucinations interpreted wrongly by the individual as a PE (OBEs, NDEs, and deathbed visions), or can such states be responsible for triggering a profound personal event that allows the mind to access spiritual realms? The OBE may simply be an illusion created by the brain that corresponds with the experiencer's psychology, culture and life experiences. A religious person, therefore, may report seeing a religious figure consistent with the person's beliefs; a Christian will likely see Christ, and one who practices Hinduism will see Buddha.[86] The hypnagogic state of being "awake while dreaming" has been known to mystics for ages. This sensation may generate a sense of belonging to a greater "union," similar to the reported "mystical states" described as "Absolute Being," or union with spiritualized encounters and the divine.[87]

An OBE has also been implicated as a symptom of sleep paralysis since it occurs during the dissociated REM sleep state. During REM sleep stage, the TPJ, which allows you to know where you are in space, is turned off. This may explain why most OBEs occur during REM.[88] Irritation of the primary and association visual cortical areas may also cause visual hallucinations. One study reported 17 such OBE cases associated with sleep paralysis in which the individuals viewed themselves lying in bed, generally from a location above the bed.[89] Our assumptions regarding the clear REM sleep dividing line between dreaming and non-dreaming visions, however, may be flawed, especially since intense visual images occur during theta states during meditation or when transitioning into sleep. Accordingly, some PEs may represent an expression in both the NDE and sleep paralysis states, and persons with NDEs may have an "arousal system predisposed to both REM intrusion and OBEs."[90] So, if you think you're having an OBE, or seeing, smelling, hearing, tasting, or feeling things when you're asleep, you may not be dreaming. It's possible you're experiencing a brain-based, sleep-induced hallucination. Or not?

The Peak Experience: Psychopathology or Spiritual Awakening?

Overview: The largely positive behavioral transformations incurred from a PE present a unique paradox. That is, does the PE reflect a pathological condition rather than a true spiritual awakening or expansion of one's consciousness? If one should describe their PE to a psychologist, for instance, he/she may automatically be diagnosed as having an abnormal symptom in the form of a bizarre delusion or hallucination. Such a diagnosis should not be surprising, especially since the psychiatric bible published by the American Psychiatric Association—the Diagnostic and Statistical Manual of Mental Disorders (DSM-5)—defines a mental disorder as a "syndrome characterized by clinically significant disturbances in an individual's cognition, emotional regulation, or behavior that reflects the dysfunction in the psychological, biological, or developmental processes underlying mental function. Mental disturbances are usually associated with significant distress or disability in social, occupational, or other important activities."[91] Research has shown, however, that most individuals presenting with anomalous and paranormal experiences and beliefs do not fit this definition. This is certainly true for the PEr.

Psychopathology or Spiritual Awakening: As part of a "spiritual awakening," a person may have involuntary movements and visual disturbances; be unable to relax due to increased energy; have an OBE or NDE; become more sensitive and attuned to the thoughts, feelings, and energies of one's self and others; and experience overwhelming emotions and realize a greater sense of purpose. While these commonly reported PE symptoms are considered a psychopathology to some, they may instead represent a psychological crisis triggered by a "spiritual awakening" called a "spiritual emergency"; a "critical and experientially difficult stage of a profound psychological transformation that involves one's entire being."[92]

The diagnosis of a psychopathology must be made within the context of cultural norms and practices. Those who claim to have conversations with a supreme being are less likely to have functional impairment if they interact with those who accept or even admire their experience than if they are immersed within a culture that does not accept this as normal behavior. It is not considered normal in mainstream U.S. culture to have directly heard the voice of God or to have witnessed spiritual beings. But certain hallucinations are considered normal, and indeed encouraged in some cultures, and in some cultures, it is even acceptable to hear the voices of one's dead relatives. The DSM-5 specifically states: "Mental disorders are defined in relation to cultural, social, and familial norms and values. Culture provides interpretive frameworks that shape the experience and expression of the symptoms, signs, and behaviors that are criteria for diagnosis."[93]

Thus, diagnostic assessment must "consider whether an individual's experiences, symptoms, and behaviors differ from sociocultural norms and lead to difficulties in adaption in the culture of origin."[94] Clinicians assessing for schizophrenia in socioeconomic or cultural situations different from their own must take cultural differences into account, especially since, "in some cultures, visual or auditory hallucinations with a religious content may be a normal part of religious experience (e.g., seeing a non-human entity, the Virgin Mary or hearing God's voice)."[95]

While many people with psychosis do hallucinate at certain times in their lives, most people who do (as much as 10 percent of the population) are not mentally ill. For them, hearing voices or seeing NHEs and/or the deceased is a normal mode of experience. This is perfectly demonstrated in those with Charles Bonnet Syndrome in which mentally sound, lucid individuals with severe or slight vision loss actually see vivid figures and faces. Brain imaging techniques performed on those while hallucinating, demonstrate heightened activity in specific sensory processing brain regions consistent with their hallucination (seeing faces, hearing voices, smells, etc.). Thus, hallucinating should not always be synonymous with insanity. In fact, there is a "very high prevalence" of "post-bereavement hallucinatory experiences" in those with no history of mental disorders. Among widowed people, for instance, 30 to 60 per cent have reported seeing their dead spouse sitting in bed or hearing them call out their name. These hallucinations may be either a spontaneous, externally generated contact of the mourner by the deceased loved one, or an internally generated contact by the mourner. But are the contacts real, or are they hallucinations? Well, for the approximately 70 million mourners who have had them, these contacts, are indeed real and comforting. However, one cannot dismiss the possibility that such unique hallucinations in the bereaved are similar to the flashbacks experienced by people suffering from post-traumatic stress disorder.

In light of these psychological criteria, would you question your sanity if you had a PE? Would you write it off as absolutely crazy because it doesn't fit with sociocultural norms and your daily routine, or would you accept it as an inspirational and constructive life-altering event? Consider the following transformative PE accounts by James Goll and Sarah and then decide for yourself.

James Goll and God: James Goll, while serving as a pastor of a congregation in Missouri, described this unique experience in his book, *Hearing God's Voice Today*:

"A strong current overwhelmed me. The next thing I knew, I was lying on the platform. I began to see a vision of a man's hand with a globe rotating in it. A sort of ticker tape with words on it came before my sight, listing the names of nations. I could read the list clearly as they rushed before my mind: Guatemala, Haiti, and Israel, etc. Then a word came to me, 'You cannot perceive and receive this in your natural mind, because in your natural mind there is self-doubt. You can only perceive and receive this in your spirit through faith.' The Holy Spirit continued to hover over me, and a second time I saw the same vision. A globe was turning in a man's hand with names of nations circulating before my eyes. I began to analyze what was happening, skeptical that it could be from God. The voice came to me a second time, clearly whispering the exact same words, convincing my heart as the words settled deep inside of me. The vision occurred a third time and the names of nations were burning in my heart. Faith was awakened inside of me. God spoke other things to me as I lay there—promises from His throne and conditions that had to be met. I sat up. I was dazed. I arose. I was changed, and I believed what God had promised. I had very little understanding of what this meant, the cost it would entail or any other details. But I knew that I knew I knew—that I was born for a ministry of the nations."[96]

Goll's PE motivated him to the extreme. He has since ministered in every one of the nations revealed to him that day, about 30 in all. He considered the many sacrifices made to accomplish the objective of the messages received that day through his "increased intimacy with Him."[97] Historically, people like Goll, who have undergone similar PEs that were passed on to the rest of humanity as symbols of faith, have been esteemed, and enjoyed privileged status as shamans, prophets, or saints. In contemporary Western society, however, experiences such as seeing visions, hearing voices, and communicating with a religious figure, are too often viewed as symptoms of a psychotic disorder. But this is not necessarily true for all PErs. But did Goll really communicate with God, and if so, how can it be objectively confirmed by the scientific community? Maybe the subjective validation by the recipient, who believes it to be real, is proof enough and all that really matters. Or, should they be prescribed medication to help prevent similar experiences in the future? And what about Sarah?

Sarah and God: Sarah was awakened by a bright light shining in her eyes. When she opened her eyes, she saw a sphere of light about four feet in diameter floating in her room. "It was about six to eight feet from my bed," she said. "It looked like a luminous, wispy fog, and it was swirling within itself, very gently rotating from my right to left. I was immediately filled with a sense of great peace and tranquility. All of my troubled feelings immediately vanished. And then this sphere of light spoke to me." A clear, soft, male voice asked Sarah if she were afraid, and she told the light being that she felt no fear. "I was nearly overcome because he was radiating something of unspeakable beauty. I felt his light envelop me and flow through me. It was a light which was not limited by boundaries of physical matter. It was a light of great gentleness and compassion beyond words," she said.⁹⁷

"The light within, around, or generated by the benevolent being became even brighter as he spoke. "You are loved unconditionally," the voice said. "The Creator Spirit is not filled with wrath and vengeance as so many Earth religions have taught, but that which you call 'God' is pure love beyond comprehension. What you humans have mistaken as punishment from your fierce concept of God is nothing more than the effects of your own actions."

Sarah said, "The light coming from the celestial being went through me—and I experienced unconditional love for the first time in my life. It was searing—and exquisite. It was though I was being bathed in a light which entered every cell in my body and filled everything it passed through with love. As the light washed through me, it removed all traces of fear, anxiety, guilt, and loneliness, and I felt clean and profoundly at peace. I began vibrating, as though to the sound of light, and I suddenly became aware of each cell in my body and I felt love and compassion for them. I knew the light was coming from a source that was endless and was equally available for all people. I knew that I was not being singled out. This same love was available for all of creation. And this realization only added to my elation, because there was great comfort in discovering that I was not a single entity, that I was a part of all creation. I was feeling joy, relief, peace, love beyond any level I ever thought the human body was capable of achieving. Again, there was no way for me to express this sensation of wild joy. I wanted to sing with the light, although I had no breath."[98]

Conclusion: Goll's and Sarah's life altering experiences violate our current understanding of the nature of physical reality. They transcend the scientific paradigm of space and time, matter and energy, dimensionality, and the nature of causality—nonlocality. Most would consider Goll's and Sarah's experiences not part of the physical reality external to us as part of normal waking consciousness, but rather as an inner, subjective one. Not surprisingly, such accounts are seriously questioned and often considered a psychological disorder—a delusion. For this reason, it is critical to distinguish PEs from psychotic disorders. The issue at hand is knowing whether an individual who experiences a non-physical realm and/or interacts with a religious figure, deceased relative, or a NHE is experiencing another reality. In other words, is the PE an actual self-transcendent-spiritual awakening or a pathological illusory brain-based or psychological event?

Discussion

Neurobehavioral factors which characterize atypical perceptions of the PE have been attributed to: (1) depersonalization symptoms; (2) stimulation or pathology of the temporal parietal junction (TPJ) and left inferior region of the parietal lobe (IPL); and (3) the process of unconscious inference. Briefly, unconscious inference is a process based on expectations of one's surroundings which incorporate the "perceiver's knowledge of the world and prior experience with similar input evidence." For example, consider two trees of the same height but different distances from the perceiver. The images of the trees that appear on the retina are of different sizes, but the knowledge that one tree is farther away than the other leads the perceiver to infer, without conscious effort, that the two trees are the same size. This same effect occurs when the faint illumination of a bulb and a near-threshold tone presentation are consistently paired—subjects report hearing tones, even when none were presented. Those with psychosis may even be more susceptible to this effect.

Auditory stimuli can also cue expectations: a salient 1-kHz tone can, through repeated association with a faint visual stimulus, induce visual hallucinations. These examples incorporate what psychologist Ivan Pavlov described as classical conditioning. Such conditioning may be the mechanism for anomalous perception that gives rise to the PE, especially in those who may be more susceptible—delusion, dissociative, or psychotic disorders.

It seems that sometimes the brain has the capacity to overpredict. It can expect something that isn't there, and this expectation can be so strong that we perceive the nonexistent thing. The precision of sensory evidence appears to depend critically upon neurotransmitter (cholinergic) signaling which can bias one's perception of sensory stimulation. If the cholinergic receptor is blocked, then sensory sensitivity is reduced leading to a decreased reliance on incoming sensory evidence during perceptual inference. In turn, this event can cause spontaneous hallucinations and enhance conditioned hallucinations.

Those who have glimpsed an alternate reality where they encountered other beings believe to have developed new insights, inspiration, and a more positive outlook on life. Although clues to explain the PE exist, firm conclusions based on supportive evidence from a biological and psychological standpoint remain elusive. The associated evidence addressed in this chapter, combined with the consistent description of the PE, however, lead many to interpret it as a pure, brain-based, believable hallucination. Subsequently, the general scientific and medical communities, who regard the PE as a physiological or psychological disorder, largely ignore the significant and positive transcendent after-effects it provides to the experiencer. Their position is understandable, especially since many PE symptoms resemble specific neurological (temporal lobe pathology, sleep disorders) and psychological (delusions, dissociative, and schizophrenia) disorders.

The PE is an enigma to all concerned. The psychological community has not even developed criteria for what constitutes a transcendent experience, let alone recognizing the PE as part of a "normal" psychological state in a well-balanced individual. The overarching question, therefore, is whether PEs fall into the area of psychopathology or into the area of enhanced mental health? This is a valid point, as there are both unique similarities and differences between psychotic or schizophrenic episodes and certain aspects of transcendent experiences. An established clinical criterion to distinguish a true PE from a psychotic disturbance, for instance, is the impact of the experience on one's overall wellbeing. But despite some similarities, the two are distinguishable. Most PEs, for example, provoke feelings of joy, serenity, wholeness, and love, which can lead to improvements in psychological health and awareness of the life's spiritual dimension. Any adverse symptoms which may appear in the initial stages of a PE often resolve spontaneously with appropriate support.

Psychotic episodes, on the other hand, typically generate feelings of confusion, fear, and judgment by an angry God which increasingly isolates the person from society. For this reason, the PE should not be diagnosed as a psychopathology, although some PErs are indeed suffering from a disorder that requires immediate professional help. Since the majority of PErs do not have a psychological disorder, the PE must be considered a distinct non-pathological state and not the pathological state that it resembles. This is especially true since PErs show signs of more, not less, adequate adjustment.[99] The PE should be viewed as healthy growth toward higher states of spiritual awareness—a spiritual awakening.

Despite the apparent PE enigmas and controversies, the PEr believes it to be true. But is that all that really matters? Yes and no. It is indeed real to the person who appears to benefit from their PE. But you, like me, are truth seekers. I, like you, feel a sense of urgency to know if the PE represents an objectively real alternate realm inhabited by various non-humans. If true, the implications are inconceivable. Maybe this potential revelation alone drives me with fierce determination to find the answer.

So, what pieces to the PE puzzle exist? Well, even if the PE is caused by a brain-based event, the PEr believes their experience to be real, derives significant benefits from it, and is not suffering from a mental disorder. Whatever the catalyst may be, the fact that the PE is credible in the mind of the individual makes it a spiritual awakening. At least, it does to me!

170

CHAPTER 8

CONNECTING THE DOTS

Introduction

Most scientists today consider the world a collection of subatomic particles governed by the nuclear, gravitational, and electromagnetic forces of Einstein's Unified Field Theory. But if that is all there is to physical reality, then no easy or rational way remains to explain the phenomenon of the PE, and the associated issue of how consciousness emerges from a physical brain. The center of this debate is whether you are your brain, and the PE may provide significant evidence to help resolve this burning question which humankind yearns to know.

Materialistic scientists who contend that consciousness is nothing more than a byproduct of complex neurochemical processes can never explain how feelings of awe and universal connectedness arise from the spiritual and mystical experiences reported by millions worldwide. If the explanation lies solely within the brain, a jellylike mass of fat and protein comprising some 100 billion nerve cells, the answer surely won't be discovered any time soon. Conversely, if consciousness is nonlocal, and somehow extends beyond the body to perceive things not accessible to our sense organs, as experimental research suggests, then consciousness must be something qualitatively different than the brain.

Within the Western materialist framework, unexplained personal PE triggers in the form of NDE, OBE, communication with the deceased and Supreme Beings, meditation, entangled minds and ESP, and interactions with UAP and NHEs, are dismissed as an underlying psycho-cultural phenomenon, and/or a psycho-biological pathology that manifests as memory disturbance, sleep disorders, wishful thinking, or misinterpretations of natural events. These experiences, therefore, are not considered true perceptions of the conscious mind, soul, spirit, or "self." Yet many of these same debunking scientists, who denounce and dismiss the PE as a neurological or psychological disorder, routinely attend church to pray to a disembodied Supreme Being for guidance, healing, and forgiveness. This is the ultimate paradox. That is, how can someone believe in and interact with an unseen and scientifically unproven Deity on Sunday, and then denounce and dismiss one's PE on Monday?

This contradiction, generated by biased viewpoints fostered by psycho-religious and cultural factors, greatly impedes our objective understanding of the true nature of reality and the diverse range of PE triggers revered throughout history to the present day. This contradiction is a matter of perspective which reminds me of a quick story: A man checked into a hotel for the first time in his life and goes up to his room. Five minutes later he called the reception desk and said: "You've given me a room with no exit. How do I leave." The desk clerk said, "Sir, that's ridiculous. Have you looked for the door?" The man said, "Well, there's one door that leads to the bathroom. There's a second door that goes into the closet. And there's a door I haven't tried, but it has a 'do not disturb' sign on it." I think you get my point.

Science has consistently misunderstood, misrepresented, and largely ignored the spiritual dimension, the supernatural or paranormal, and the PE. They consider it suspect and in opposition with scientific principles, especially since spirituality has been so closely tied to unproven religious teachings. This seems unwise, but at some level, it is understandable. A scientist is committed to physical laws, not faith, bias, and speculation that cannot be proven with scientific logic and empirical evidence. Consequently, it is virtually impossible for either the scientific or spiritual perspective to prevail over the other through logic or force of argument since these beliefs are based on faith and not compelling evidence.

The apparent endless gap between science and consciousness begs for some kind of overarching bridge to connect and integrate modern scientific principles with those that emerge in studies on consciousness, the brain, parapsychology, the social and natural sciences, and the PE. A fundamental goal of physical science has been to explore and explain deeper levels of reality associated with atoms and molecules, often using the controversial explanation of Quantum Theory. By the same token, mathematicians have attempted to develop equations to describe ever more abstract levels of consciousness. Since mathematics has described so well the physical laws of nature, from the macroscopic (cosmology) to the microscopic (quantum field theories), scientists are now following suit by seeking to explain consciousness as a by-product of brain processes using principles drawn from Quantum Theory. This is seen in the form of nonlocal information, as well as the String Theory and the Unified Field Theory. But despite these recent efforts, a wide and seemingly impenetrable gap between science and spirituality remains. This is unfortunate for many reasons.

Despite the extraordinary advances in science and tech-nology over the last three centuries, the subjective experience, especially the essence of consciousness and nonlocal communication (ESP), has been largely neglected by mainstream science. However, there now exist hundreds of peer reviewed scientific publications showing that parapsychological experiments support the concept of ESP. Despite the skeptics, who continue to either disregard or refute the validity of ESP, there is clear documentation that some aspects of psychic phenomena are real.

Research in parapsychology, for instance, has provided us with keen insight about human potential. We now understand that focused intention can promote information transfer and reception (telepathy and clairvoyance) and alter physical systems and matter (psychokinesis), but we haven't yet mastered the rules sufficiently to significantly influence such nonlocal effects. The small effects measured, however, clearly demonstrate that intention can indeed influence reality. Still, larger effect sizes must await a clearer description of the rules by which conscious intention interacts with matter, energy, and information to unfold and actualize the structure of physical reality. Highly respected and well-recognized scientists are now emphasizing the importance of what is still commonly overlooked in the mainstream scientific community—the fact that physical matter is not the only reality.

Connecting the Dots

In light of the information presented in this book, there are a few interrelated critical points or "connecting dots" presented in this chapter that should be strongly considered if we are to better understand the nature of the diverse range of profound personal and extraordinary experiences of the PE and its associated triggers, and reality itself. This objective is essential since the PE alters one's viewpoint on the meaning of life and the nature of reality in those who experience it from that moment forward. Consequently, the major "takeaway" or "connecting dot" is this: There will come a time when an existing energy, which dwells beyond our known laws of nature, will be discovered to confirm that "consciousness" is a distinct unseen force independent of brain function. This discovery will serve as the missing link that will co-exist with the other known physical forces that comprise Einstein's Unified Field Theory. That is, what may be considered by current scientific mainstream standards today as "anomalous" or "paranormal," may be related to and explainable by concepts inherent within the hologram, biofield, torsion energy, and/or other yet-to-be-realized unseen forces.

Of key significance, however, is whether we can extrapolate from the enigmatic properties of microscopic subatomic particles—the stuff we are made of—to phenomena experienced in our macroscopic world. This possibility deserves far greater attention by mainstream science, especially since experimental results mentioned prior indicate that a subtle unseen force (the biofield) may link the mind and brain of individuals with each other and with the world at large.

But if the eminent theoretical physicist who originated quantum theory, Max Planck, is correct in his statement that: "Science cannot solve the ultimate mystery of nature...because, in the last analysis, we ourselves are part of nature and therefore part of the mystery that we are trying to solve," I could be seriously mistaken. Planck's perspective raises an interesting paradox. That is, how do humans who have consciousness explain consciousness when human consciousness itself represents "the mystery that we are trying to solve." I know, I had to synthesize Planck's irony again too. But the point is this: how can we solve unexplained aspects of altered perceptions associated with the PE and its triggers when we ourselves are part of that mystery? Our brain and consciousness, each a poorly understood entity, are the only resources available to solve an enigma analogous to the mysterious nature of life itself. After all, what is life? Well, maybe my dear friend, Frank DePasquale, nailed it in his comment that: "Life is not knowing what the hell it's all about"[55]—a humane and insightful truth seeker indeed.

Given this ironic context, my most plausible "connecting dot" attributes the PE and associated phenomena to a yet-to-be-discovered physical energy. Although an atom is to electrons and protons like the sun is to planets, this energy, which may be so small that it does not interact with matter, may be mediated as a field effect from each of us. But similar to the elementary particle theory (protons, neutrinos, etc.), there is no widely accepted and uniform agreement that such an energy with the required characteristics exists.

This mystery is further compounded by our lack of understanding how PE triggers enable one to interact with and

175

utilize this energy, if at all. For this reason alone, we are dealing with several possible interacting phenomena; the PE itself; the different triggers that gives rise to it; and the manner in which one's consciousness may interact with a yet-to-be-discovered physical energy (biofield). Each phenomenon, and the manner of their possible inter-relationship, serve as one of humankind's most sensational and significant enigmas to resolve.

Collectively, the anecdotal and experimental evidence addressed prior should serve as the initial foundation for researchers to build upon to empirically demonstrate and measure a currently unknown aspect of energy called "consciousness." This foundation leads to another "connecting dot"—that is, there is an unknown aspect of reality that has a pronounced effect on the lives of millions of individuals who interact with it. To comprehend reality requires us to explore the role of consciousness and its interaction with physical systems. If mainstream science analyzes this evidence using a systematic and multidisciplinary approach, some "outside the box" thinkers may also recognize with fierce determination, as I do, that this area of study deserves far greater attention from the scientific community than the "drop in the bucket" currently allocated. The theories and associated supporting evidence in this book should serve as the basis for a call to action: the need for a new paradigm shift.

Science today knows the shape of the Earth and elliptical orbits but still has no clue how your brain facilitates the first-person conscious experience. Who and what am "I"? This is the essential issue of our time. All else is secondary and evolves from the answer to this question. Consequently, a new paradigm is needed to explain the many important unresolved issues that beg to be answered from a scientific, societal, and personal level. We still know very little about the nature of the PE, nonlocality, and existence of other possible alternate realities.

Long ago, our best science told us the Earth is flat and everything in the night sky circles the Earth, including the sun. Fast forward a few centuries and today's best science now says the world presented to us by our perceptions is not true reality. If true, then what is a first-person conscious reality? This is the so-called "hard problem" of consciousness and the questions about the nature of reality. The answer likely exists as a yet-to-be-discovered force that interrelates with brain activity and explainable by a scientific theory that may eventually evolve from quantum physics. At this point in our embryonic development, we are only scratching the surface of what will eventually become an integral component of the Unified Field Theory. But the first step towards this discovery requires a new paradigm shift.

The Peak Experience and the Mind-Brain Connection

Overview: Essential to the development of a new scientific paradigm is the quest to better understand the mind-brain connection and the essence of you. More is unknown than is known about matter and the relationship between the mind and brain. Your mind is the new frontier of science and future generations will advance our understanding of the mind. Quantum theory may prove essential to this evolution because classical physics inappropriately downgrades consciousness to the role of physical events explained only by mechanical laws of physics.

Believe it or not, they got the whole enchilada wrong, and it is time to right the ship. The mind-brain connection is becoming recognized as the most important objective of science. Co-discoverer of the structure of the DNA molecule, Francis Crick, and neuroscientist Christoph Koch, for example, considered that "the overwhelming question in neurobiology today is the relationship between the mind and the brain."[1] But how does the set of processes we call "mind" emerge from the brain? These processes are not well understood because the traditional laws of science significantly impede our understanding of the mind-brain relationship and the PE, especially since they are based mainly on scientific principles that consider you just a mechanical biological system.

Well, I don't know about you, but this perspective conflicts with my deep intuitive sense of who and what I am. It diminishes my inner voice of reason that I am not just a three-pound mass of 100 billion neurons between my ears. In contrast to classical physics, however, quantum theory incorporates humans in a critical way. This shift, though slow in nature and appeal, is sufficient to allow quantum theory to provide a causal explanation of how consciousness acts on the brain and physical systems. You saw the results of this from several neuro-psychological and scientific-based experiments addressed prior. It is ultimately up to you to determine their potential implications since answers from the scientific community will likely evolve long after your last breath.

This process of discovery proceeds at a snail's pace, especially since neuroscientists ignore the progress in quantum physics, and physicists focus exclusively on non-biological phenomena. Someday, the person who successfully integrates principles from each discipline will contend for the Nobel Prize. Neuroscientists, for instance, maintain that quantum physics is not critical to the aspects of brain function and consciousness. Instead, the answer must exist in the discipline they are most familiar with and studied most of their life—neurobiological activity. Neuroscientists can't admit that the mind-body problem might reside in a discipline they know little about. That acknowledgement is self-defeating and ego shattering. By doing so, they continue to follow one well-known path taken many times before which, if followed, will not get them lost. Confidence can certainly be misleading and biasing. They are certain the answer to the mind-body problem can be found in the properties of neural activity in the form of frequency of neuron firing and connection strengths at synapses.

This analysis is outdated Newtonian physics, where time is absolute, and objects exist absolutely. For this reason, neuroscientists ignore anomalous experiences and fail to acknowledge or adopt the theories of quantum physics and experiments in ESP to the level of the brain to help complement and refine their insights and research focus. They are stuck like glue to the apple landing on Newton's head and remain centuries behind the curve. In doing so, neuroscience will never solve the "hard problem" of consciousness. Are they sly as a fox or stubborn as a mule? The existing contradictions, theories, and experimental evidence suggest the latter.

Over the past four centuries, Western scientific inquiry has operated firmly within the boundaries of Realism—everything our basic senses experience is all there is to existence, and anything else is imagination, hallucination, or delusion. To scientific realists, what you experience is what you get in the form of reality.[3] Nothing else exists. But there appears to be a slow evolving shift to disprove scientific realism by demonstrating it to be an optical delusion of consciousness. Many scientists are beginning to embrace Instrumentalism. In other words, the reality you think you see when having a morning coffee is an imaginary construct of your mind.[2] Since less than 10 percent of learning comes from training and the rest from experience, science should place more trust in one's reported experience that seem beyond their capabilities as critical evidence towards solving a problem. Quantifying data using calibrated recoding techniques is important but should not serve as the only measure to define reality, especially since aspects of reality cannot be measured objectively in this way with existing technology.

Instrumentalism was advanced by philosopher John Dewey, who considered concepts and theories as just useful instruments in explaining and predicting phenomena. This theory lies in stark contrast to Scientific Realism. To Instrumentalists, the value of concepts and theories is not measured by whether they are true or false, or if they correctly depict reality. Instead, the truth and value of an idea is determined by its success in the active solution of a problem, as determined by human experience. In other words, practical consequences constitute the essential criterion in determining meaning, truth or value.[4]

The Mind-Brain Filter: William James, considered the father of psychology, may have been right when he made a bold proposal about the brain over 100 years ago. The process James described is the filter theory, and he said that what the brain filters out is a supremely expanded consciousness. James proposed that the brain acts as a partial barrier and gives us only the surface of what is possible for us to perceive—the brain filters our access to a vast consciousness which extends beyond the limits of neural activity. We are just now realizing what James had considered long ago, that

179

these experiences occur when the brain is inactive or minimally active. The brain's amazing capacity to filter sensory information is critical to forming coherent perceptions of the world.[16] How can this be accomplished? Possibly the new paradigm shift will help achieve this fundamental goal and resolve the "hard problem of consciousness."

Critical to this "hard problem" is the research by neuro-scientist Candace Pert with the brain's electro-chemicals—neurotransmitters and hormones. Her findings have forced scientific realists to confront the fact that a human being's ability to be an objective observer of reality seems to work much better in theory than in fact.[5] Pert discovered that when we think different thoughts, our brain generates neural activity that stimulates the expression of visual images which correspond to those thoughts. This electrochemical process enables subsequent mental, emotional and physical actions and reactions to take place to better understand how you interpret and react to life's experiences.

The two sides of your brain filter information differently through attentional pathways. The left controls information important for language abilities and goal-directed actions. The right controls a broader visual-spatial attention that enables you to interpret new experiences of awareness.[6] An example of this filtering process is described by neuroanatomist Jill Bolte Taylor in her book, *My Stroke of Insight*, where she described changes in her attention following a stroke to the left side of her brain.[7] She found it very difficult to interpret what someone was saying. But once she allowed herself to rest in the experience of her right brain, she was aware only of the present moment.

She described her experience in the following statements: "In this altered state of being, my mind was no longer preoccupied with the billions of details that my brain routinely used to define and conduct my life...As my consciousness slipped into a state of peaceful grace, I felt ethereal...I have gained access to the experience of deep peace in the consciousness of my right mind when the language and orientation association areas of the left hemisphere of my brain became nonfunctional."[8] The greatest benefit she received from the experience was an understanding that a "deep internal peace is accessible to anyone at any time."

Is it possible that the experience of expanded consciousness, like the PE and deep meditation, occurs when the normal filtering mechanisms of the brain are reduced? This question must be asked since the PE seems analogous to Taylor's experience resulting from the left hemisphere damage due to her stroke. According to Taylor, "If I had to choose one word to describe the feeling I feel at the core of my right mind, I would have to say joy. My right mind is thrilled to be alive! I experience a feeling of awe when I consider that I am simultaneously capable of being at one with the universe, while having an individual identity whereby I move into the world and manifest positive change. This joy is simply being inhibited by more anxious and/or fearful circuitry of the left mind."[9]

Based on the research by Pert, and the personal accounts by Taylor, it seems that the left hemisphere impedes your natural capability of expanding consciousness by getting in the way. After all, the brain evolved on this planet. As a result, it is only capable of functioning in a 3D world, not a spiritual one. In other words, if you are not your brain, you may be able to perceive a wider aspect of reality beyond the physical 3D world of your morning coffee. Current research supports Taylor's experience—the left side of the brain may selectively filter and, thus limit, access to this broader awareness—3D+. Since this experience is similar to that reported by many meditators, it is reasonable to assume that by reducing activity of attentional areas in the brain's left hemisphere, the brain's filtering influences may then allow one to experience an expanded consciousness.

Interestingly, Taylor's anecdotal account seems to correspond with studies that attempt to find the so-called "God spot" area of the brain responsible for spirituality. Recall from prior discussion that the left inferior region of the parietal lobe, which processes sensation, spatial orientation, and language, has been tentatively identified as the brain's "God spot." Taylor's altered state of consciousness may reflect this experimental finding; it may even account for other phenomena like the PE and its triggers, terminal lucidity, and after death communication, among others noted prior. The core issue is to determine if the brain's reduced activity allows you to become less dependent on the brain, whereby an altered and expanded consciousness becomes accessible. Alternatively, this reduced activity may create a neurological state that somehow enables this expanded state of consciousness.

Case evidence of patients with long-term dementia and other severe neurological disorders who exhibit a brief return to mental clarity and full memory shortly before death may also be significant for understanding the mind-brain connection. The phenomenon of "terminal lucidity" is attracting renewed interest on the part of scientific researchers, particularly in the context of NDEs.[10] Patients with severely destroyed brains (such as in terminal stages of Alzheimer's disease, tumors or strokes) who become fully lucid shortly before death may serve as an appropriate experimental model to assess the possibility that consciousness is not entirely generated by the brain, but that the brain functions as a kind of filter or transmitter organ.[11, 12]

But this makes no sense to neuroscientists who are at a complete loss to explain how a severely dysfunctional brain in an individual who was non-verbal and not receptive to others for many months and even years can suddenly appear alert, converse with others, and then die moments later. This is more than a surprise to family members who experience terminal lucidity in a loved one—it is a blessing. It is also not uncommon for terminal lucidity to be accompanied by deep spiritual experiences, especially since near-death states regularly contain anomalous characteristics (after death communication, deathbed visions, nonlocality, and NDEs). By studying terminal lucidity, concomitant with related subliminal layers of the human psyche, evidence for post-mortem survival or the continuation of consciousness following bodily death may be obtained.[13]

Research also shows that meditation practice can expand the way we perceive the world. Long-term meditation training increases right hemisphere activity and expands one's awareness to greater and more joyful aspects of reality. Meditators possess a highly activated anterior cingulate cortex (ACC) that grows larger over time with continued practice. The ACC is also active during hypnosis and energy healing which appears to facilitate a more expanded consciousness to modulate the activity of the brain and body.[14]

It seems, therefore, that by reducing the dominance of the left hemisphere and modulating the activity in the ACC, the brain's impeding filter is eliminated to allow one to experience true consciousness. This might even explain the mystical experiences and "paranormal" phenomena reported during the PE and its associated triggers—they facilitate an expanded level of consciousness accessible to our awareness. The issue at hand for subsequent research, therefore, is to figure out a way to remove the brain's apparent limiting influence in order to experience awareness of this expanded level of consciousness.

Taylor's description is also consistent with computerized tomography imaging of the brains in meditators. More specifically, when meditators report the instant they attain their meditative climax or felt united with the universe, there is a corresponding decrease in the left hemisphere's language and orientation centers. This region helps you identify your personal physical boundaries and when this area is inhibited or receives decreased input from your sensory system, you lose sight of where you begin and end relative to space around you. According to Taylor, when the left hemisphere language and orientation areas are silenced, consciousness shifts from feeling "like a solid," to a perception of "feeling fluid—at one with the universe."[15]

The key takeaway from this evidence is that the PE and its corresponding sense of unity with reality may be allowed for by a change in brain hemisphere activity. This makes sense, especially since these symptoms are reported in the following cases: (1) when the brain is severely depressed and compromised—NDE, terminal lucidity, and stroke, among other types of adverse physiological events; (2) in those who have altered states of consciousness from psychoactive agents like DMT; (3) during sleep transition states; and (4) in those who silence their brain through meditation. The PE, therefore, may represent a mind-brain event that is indeed real. The critical question remains, however, as to whether the brain is capable of providing us with a greater sense of awareness of reality. Your brain's right hemisphere may provide the answer toward achieving eternal peace.

One way you can initiate the process to accomplish this goal is by quieting the mind through meditation training. A meditating quiet mind inhibits your internal analytical, left-brain, ego-centered dialogue. This increases your awareness. While achieving pure awareness or a state of nonlocal consciousness is possible, it is not an easy task. It is something that should be taught early on in life and cultivated throughout one's life to help improve one's mental and physical well-being. But what is occurring in terms of accessing this aspect of nonlocal consciousness where thoughts subside and an energetic awareness of love and joy, and a sense of unity with others and the world emerge? By simply quieting your mind, beneficial changes occur over time in the form of thicker regions in key areas of the brain, and enhanced neural circuitry.

Experienced meditators can achieve a so-called "non-dual state of awareness"—a state of consciousness where you can truly experience the actuality of what is here and now. It allows you to diminish or eliminate, at least for a period of time, your mind's clutter of to-do lists—the stresses and worries, fears and desires, and memories and random thoughts. When your internal thoughts and the external world subside, the brain's electrical activity reduces and facilitates a sense of oneness and unity—a type of PE. Deep meditation states, a flat line EEG during a NDE, terminal lucidity, sleep states, and psychoactive agents create this neurophysiological event and its associated altered state of nonlocal consciousness. People in this state perceive things they otherwise would not perceive—an unseen force.

Unseen Forces

Overview: When Newton felt that apple land on his head, he assumed that human beings were separate from that apple, the universe was four-dimensional, and only emptiness existed between particles, people, planets, and solar systems. Newton and his followers believed that everything was intelligently designed, and that our sensory systems interpreted all that existed. His theories became physical laws and these laws served as the primary materialist viewpoint that humans could be only observers and not active agents for universal change.

With this footing, scientists have created mathematical processes from Newton's gravitational theories to Einstein's $E = mc^2$. These equations are still used for validating or dis-proving scientific hypotheses.[18] The problem here is that these equations, while purposeful for numerous reasons, are limiting in their application to prove all theories. This pertains to anecdotal evidence in the form of the PE among other associated extraordinary personal experiences measured or validated using traditional materialistic equations and Newtonian principles. Times have changed and new principles are needed to prove hypotheses that relate to aspects of consciousness and extraordinary subjective experiences.

Einstein believed that if a model to explain why all the energy and matter in the universe should behave in a predictable and orderly way could be proven, it would mean that an objective reality exists beyond human perception and consciousness. This must be the case since no two human beings perceive or process reality the exact same way. This means that you are not wired in an objective fashion. You are wired, in part, by your experiences, like the PE. But hardcore materialistic scientists believe that the closest anyone comes to existing in a reality beyond the brain corresponds directly to hormones created upon interaction with neurotransmitters in the brain. To them, what you see is what you get. Only when this interaction occurs can the brain tell the sensory organs like eyes and ears what to see and hear. And only when that sight or sound takes place, can anyone experience anything at all.

To the materialist, any notion of an alternate realm is a fictitious representation of a chaotic brain with a loose screw or two. Physicist David Bohm, however, attempted to bridge science and consciousness in his proposed theory of the "implicate order"— the glue that holds everything in the universe together that your eyes see as four-dimensional, physical space-time.[19] Implicate order patterns are programmed to generate orderly forms and sequences of events that filter down from the energy-frequency level (or the 95 percent) to the mass matter (or the 5 percent) level. Bohm's experimentation allows for a concrete foundation for the interwoven fabric of consciousness and reality as two distinct, yet interdependent, entities within our universe: The physical and the non-physical person.[20]

Time is fluid and things are constantly changing. Sometimes we wish for time to stop just to catch one's breath to keep up with these changes and make sense of it all. This applies to just what we are able to see, let alone that which we can't see. Before 2000, for instance, astrophysicists were adamant that they understood the contents of the universe very well. But then in 2009, scientists at the National Accelerator Laboratory and Stanford University shattered this understanding when evidence for dark energy was discovered. These measurements of the cosmic microwave background—an unseen force of a faintly glowing relic of the hot, dense, young universe—provided support for the standard cosmological model. This result confirmed that dark matter and dark energy make up 95 percent of everything in existence, while ordinary matter makes up just 5 percent. The remaining 95 percent of light energy in the universe is not visible to the eye—it is literally obscure. People are able to see only approximately 5 percent of the entire light-based color spectrum. Nevertheless, it is incredibly real and consequential. Apparently, there is a heck of a lot more in existence that you don't see than you do.[21] But what about the internal little, wet mini-receiver of your reality—the brain? This question leads to another "connecting dot"—one day a wiring diagram will describe the brain in "mathematical, physical, neurochemical, and electrical terms" with all the precision of a "differential equation."[22]

Biophotons and Torsion Energy: Our daily existence in this world may be momentarily interrupted by the transcendent experience of an unseen world which parallels that which we normally feel on a daily basis. While this may seem bizarre in nature, keep in mind that many widely accepted scientific discoveries initially sounded incomprehensible in theory. These original "far-out" notions were often dismissed since they defied logic when proposed. For example, the Earth is not the center of the universe, Albert Einstein told us that time slows down at high speeds, and quantum mechanics tells us that pairs of particles can be linked, even if they're on different sides of the room or opposite sides of the universe, and that alternate dimensions co-exist with our own. Thanks to ESP experiments, there now exists dramatic evidence that we are connected through space and time at the level of consciousness—nonlocality. There are, in other words, compelling reasons for science to take many aspects of what is now considered "paranormal," such as the PE, much more seriously than is currently the case. Thus another "connecting dot" is: today's "paranormal" is tomorrow's "normal."

Like many historic examples in science and medicine, theories once considered implausible become accepted through research and practice. One of Albert Einstein's most significant discoveries, for instance, was not just the equivalence of matter and energy and the relationship between light and time, but that space itself is an energy field and everything in it arose from the energy of this field. Taking this concept to the next level, an unseen force like the "biofield" could very well be the next significant discovery. Torsion energy may be the most important aspect of the biofield that facilitates anomalous events associated with consciousness; a real force that needs to be "integrated in modern physics." This energy may even be responsible for the human aura, Qi Gong (which kills cancer cells), and ESP, among many other paranormal phenomena of today.[23]

Unknown aspects of our external physical and internal physical world abound. Phenomena not explainable by known laws in the physical universe requires "something" beyond the four fundamental energies of the Unified Field Theory. This "something" may very well be the potential source of the reported non-physical perceptual characteristics of anomalous events that may trigger the PE—a biofield that is governed and regulated by torsion energy.[24] The next step is to understand the implications of an unseen force—ultra-weak photon emissions such as biophotons; a constituent of the metabolic process of any living system. Researchers are now attempting to develop models of biological regulation of biophotons from the cellular level up to the formation of consciousness using detectors based on photomultiplier techniques.

Preliminary results using this technique have shown that: (1) states of DNA influence biophoton emissions; (2) reactions to stress increase emissions; and (3) meditation decreases emissions. Consequently, another "connecting dot" is that: as biophotons gain acceptance and become the focus of continued study, numerous medical and scientific applications may eventually be developed to provide a reliable basis for examining and further advancing our understanding of the interrelationship of biology and consciousness.[25, 26]

By developing our understanding of the biofield, ESP, and the PE, a paradigm mediated by unseen forces and processes of a yet-to-be-discovered energy field may evolve. Once applied in a practical way, this discovery may have profound implications on both a personal and societal level.

The physiological role for photons of light produced by living matter of biophotons and its potential impact on human beings is what makes the biofield an imperative concern for understanding the "subtle connections" between us. It is evident, for example, that biophoton regulation acts as a carrier field of electromagnetic interactions that interferes nonlocally in a spatial and temporal pattern. This activity provides for a variety of informational processes in living systems that is in stark contrast to traditional materialistic principles. This regulation is allowed for by physical laws of quantum coherence. That is, all objects have wave-like properties.[27] We saw many examples of nonlocality in the form of ESP experiments and the PE and its triggers in our prior discussion. Another example is found in a new discovery of the behavior of hydrogen atoms.

Hydrogen atoms can recognize one another's histories, and if the histories are similar, then they can copy each other's properties. According to physicist Lee Smolin, "There's no need for the two atoms to be close to each other for one to copy the other's properties; they just both have to exist somewhere in the universe."[28] This finding is significant because it raises important questions fundamental to the concept of nonlocality. In other words, how is a "similar" history recognized and how do they "copy" properties? Are atoms psychic? This mechanism of action, like all nonlocal events such as ESP and the PE, remains to be discovered. The mechanism of its action may lie beyond you—in nature itself. In other words, an unknown aspect of nature may have inherent intelligence that is compatible with your own. We may not be interacting with just physical systems but, rather, "with an intelligence that is responsive to the meanings that we attach to it."[29]

This concept raises another "connecting dot"—that is, if torsion energy is indeed a carrier wave for consciousness and serves as a nonlocal interrelated force linking minds in real-time, this force may be the key component or the so-called "missing link" that facilitates phenomena to access information from anywhere in the universe. In other words, if torsion waves act as the mechanism for "connected minds," then telepathic communication between people separated by vast distances may be explained.[30] Torsion energy may be responsible for facilitating quantum processes occurring in individual atoms between people, objects, and even in unseen parallel dimensions that are recognized and allowed for by the String Theory.

Quantum Mechanics and the String Theory: The revolutionary science of quantum mechanics (QM) has challenged scientific materialist principles and perspectives of the physical laws of the universe. This discipline, sometimes referred to as the "theory of everything," is a relatively new science of unusual concepts such as superstrings, extra-dimensions, and parallel universes. The scientific community acknowledges the existence of "strings" (the smallest constituents of pure energy—matter and force—interacting in our universe) and are hopeful that it will someday explain one of the biggest mysteries of the universe, namely the relationship between gravity and QM.

But I mention the String Theory not to possibly confuse you even more than you may already be, but rather to emphasize an important point within the context of the PE. That is, there

189

is credible physics behind QM and the String Theory which allows for the possible existence of alternate realms beyond the subjective reality we perceive in our everyday waking consciousness. Physicists have demonstrated the validity of the String Theory and are now applying it to study black holes—places in space where gravity pulls so much that even light cannot escape. Science even acknowledges that the universe we live in could be just one of an infinite number of universes making up a "multiverse." In other words, there could be more to the universe than the three dimensions we are familiar with but are hidden from us in some way, perhaps because they're warped—they exist in our time and space but at a slightly different frequency or phase. Thus, other dimensions could be right in front of our face, but we can't see them.

Even if they're invisible, they still affect what we observe in the universe. There are lots of things we cannot see with the naked eye, such as dark energy, and acoustic and electromagnetic energy, that exist and are based in reality. Many complex and exquisite mathematically derived theories have independently revealed that the existence of hidden universes is more likely than not—they could exist parallel to our universe. Consequently, there may very well be a much deeper and complex reality out there than can ever be imagined.

Now sit back and contemplate how this concept may relate to the PE and its triggers. Recall, for instance, that people describe their PE as an interaction with another dimension or universe. The physical body remains here but they somehow perceive an unseen realm vastly different than our 3D reality where no time and space is sensed and where all information can be retrieved. Since science adopts the validity of the String Theory, and that people who report their PE to be as real as this book in your hand, it is conceivable that the String Theory may allow for one to access another parallel time and space via a PE. This causal relationship between the String Theory and the PE cannot be completely dismissed. Accepted scientific theory may allow for access of one's consciousness into an alternate realm. A greater understanding of quantum processes in our brains and nervous systems is essential if we are to find answers never before considered. The PE may even provide the means by which subjective experience can be applied to QM to either prove or disprove theories that address the possible existence of parallel universes.

Such implications have enormous potential to better understand the essence of the spirit, soul, or "I." Similar QM principles may also be applied to explain how one's conscious intention is capable of affecting physical systems, as previously addressed; i.e., altering random event generators, collapsing the quantum wave function, and modifying other people's brain activity at a distance (telesomatic EEG events). This experimental evidence, combined with associated scientific based theories, seem to justify nonlocal intuitive perception (ESP and psychokinesis) and serve as a necessary prerequisite condition to explain the relationship between QM and the PE triggers. Consequently, QM may help bridge the existing psycho-spiritual gap between the social and hard sciences. The PE, which incorporates the sensation of "instantaneous knowledge," and a "timeless moment" with its accompanying flash of illumination, suggest there may be two realities in human experience; one visible and experienced by our senses, and one that is not—an unseen force. This unseen force may be allowed for by QM and measured in the form of a torsion wave—the biofield.

Modern Day Mystics and the Quantum Hologram: The mystics of the past proclaimed that we are all part of the universe and each one of us contains the whole universe. Now, physicists, or shall we say, modern day mystic scientists such as Einstein, Schroedinger, Eddington, Bohr and Heisenberg, have discovered that the physical world cannot be broken down into building blocks of solid matter existing in a particular time and space. The atom itself, which exists as both a vibration and a particle; a fine line between existence and nonexistence, suggests that matter, energy, time and space are all one reality—a reality referred to as the quantum field or the Quantum Hologram Theory (QHT). Consequently, the QHT must be considered a critical "connecting dot," especially since it tells us that our physical world is an illusion created by our sensory systems. Experimental evidence

191

suggests this may be true. The observable physical realm exists on a vast ocean of energy called the zero-point energy field or the quantum vacuum field from which virtual particles emerge and disappear, mediating all electromagnetic forces.

Related to this matter is that quantum physicists consider that everything and everyone in all universes may be a hologram. If this is indeed true, then each minute part of the universe is both connected to the whole and contains the whole; changing a fragment of it changes the whole. Our body, therefore, may be composed not only of cells and atoms but also of interrelating energy fields similar to a hologram. Thus, what we regard as "reality" may not consist of distinct things and boundaries but may, instead, be a quantum hologram. If this is indeed "true reality," as many contend it to be, then this holographic universe may be the reality of an alternate dimension described by PErs.

Reality is like a rainbow or like the electromagnetic spectrum. Each organism has evolved so as to be able to detect the electromagnetic energy that will be most useful for its survival—each has its own window on reality. Humans, for instance, can perceive the part of the color spectrum between infrared and ultraviolet. But bees can't see red at all. Scientific theorist Ervin Laszlo described this phenomenon as a "holistic, interconnected matrix" (the zero-point-field or the quantum vacuum),[31, 32] which eminent physicist David Bohm referred to as the "implicate order of being."[33] One of Bohm's most significant ideas is that the physical reality of our everyday lives is an illusion—a holographic image. Underlying it is a holographically organized primary level of reality that creates your physical world,[34] which may explain why reality becomes nonlocal at the subatomic level.

Shamanic accounts, OBEs/NDEs, and interactions with the UAP and NHEs, with their descriptions of strange beings and ventures into alternate realties and other worlds, seem to closely correspond with QM theories of similar dimensions of reality embedded within or parallel with our own. The scientific community, however, does not uniformly agree that such experiences are valid in a "real" sense since they obviously can't be "proven" using traditional scientific methodologies.

Given the similar reported physical features and psychological after-effects associated with the PE triggers, however, indirect evidence to support an interdimensional basis for the PE cannot be conclusively ruled out. QM proves that matter is energy and not tangible matter and does not even exist with certainty; it tends to exist.

Thus, according to QM, our so-called reality is an illusion because an illusion that is seen cannot really exist. Then, what is true reality? Well, I don't have a definitive answer other than that you ("I," spirit, or soul) may be particles of energy capable of free will and intention which makes you a conscious being. True reality, therefore, may simply be a type of non-three-dimensional conscious energy that exists apart from your physical brain. You interact with the brain but the brain and associated sensory systems are not capable of perceiving a non-three-dimensional reality. Since the brain evolved in a three-dimensional physical reality, it is designed to process and interpret only energy that exists in this physical reality (3D). The brain is only compatible with your physical reality, not the assumed alternate non-physical reality of the PE triggers.

The critical "takeaway" from these concepts is that the QHT may explain the unusual perceptual characteristics described by those who have had a PE and its triggers. Certain features of the PE, for example, appear to have quantum-like, holographic properties that correspond with some of the basic principles from quantum theory. This includes: (1) nonlocality, coherence, and instantaneous information exchange in a timeless and placeless dimension, and (2) experiments which demonstrate that "telepathy" is not affected by distance (outside space), and "precognition," which provides information of future events (outside time).

By extrapolation of this evidence, a case can be made for the existence of an aspect of consciousness, or you, which may remain unaffected by death and continue to function in some undefined realm of existence beyond our 3D, space-time continuum. Although this suggestion is a bold leap, especially since this concept is impossible to validate at the present time using traditional scientific methods, supportive evidence may be found in my book, *Life after Death: An Analysis of the Evidence.*[35] Within this context, it is important to consider that research on the OBE and NDE cannot give us the irrefutable scientific proof of the continuity of our consciousness upon death. This conclusion is premature since people who had a NDE did not die. What they all had was a severely compromised, barely functional brain that left them knocking on death's door.

Although the OBE and NDE evidence suggests the possibility that death may represent a transitional phase from one state of consciousness to another—from this three-dimensional reality to an alternate holographic reality—the notion that consciousness can be experienced independently of brain function should remain tenuous until stronger supporting evidence emerges, if ever. If proven valid, as suggested by the QHT, the implications will no doubt have a profound effect, not only on a deeply personal philosophical and spiritual level, but will also greatly modify the scientific paradigm in western medicine, and have practical implications in ethical problems such as the care for comatose or dying patients, euthanasia, and abortion, among others, including the PE.

Further, the perplexing aspect of the NDE and OBE, concomitant with the experimental results in QM and para-psychology (ESP and consciousness), suggests that consciousness may be separate from our physical body and/or capable of affecting events remote from our body. More specifically, if sensory information processing is nonlocal, it may explain the reported altered perception, life review, and images often described as a dimension without time and space associated with the PE trigger; the NDE. These reported similarities suggest a common underlying cause to all NDEs. This cause could be either physiological—a common brain event in a particular brain region, or non-physiological—the separation of consciousness as a distinct energy of awareness from the physical body.

CHAPTER 9

THE NEW PARADIGM SHIFT

Introduction

The long-established materialist paradigm dismisses the anecdotal reports of millions who contend with fierce determination to have pierced the veil of another extraordinarily real world that dramatically changes their perspective on life and who and what they are. Moreover, although sufficient evidence exists to support ESP and nonlocality, the force which governs and regulates its behavior cannot be explained by current scientific principles since they are based purely on objective and measurable aspects of physical reality; they cannot be appropriately applied to study aspects of non-physical phenomena like the PE. But here's the crux of this paradox. The PE appears to be non-physical in nature. Because it is likely non-physical, or at least non-quantifiable, established scientific laws based on the physical are inconsistent with the PE. This inconsistency begs for a new paradigm which incorporates newly developed principles that can be appropriately applied to study such phenomena.

195

For this reason, a new paradigm with agreed upon laws and principles that incorporate the non-physical aspects of reality must be developed. It is not only essential for traditional materialist science to evolve into a new paradigm—it is mandatory! And once developed, the paranormal may very well be considered normal. Just wait and see. But that wait may not accommodate your body's lifespan. So, in the meantime, just take my word for it, or at the very least, think about it while gazing upon an awe-inspiring scene of nature.

The New Paradigm Shift

A paradigm is a theory of reality. Some well-known examples of major paradigm shifts are the Darwinian theory of evolution, the Copernican revolution in astronomy, and the relativity and quantum theories in physics. A new paradigm shift is needed. It is needed because there are acknowledged anomalies that do not fit into the current scientific paradigm. These anomalies, addressed throughout this book under the overarching nature of the PE, are rejected entirely, debunked, or ignored. Those who either reject entirely or debunk the PE and its triggers, do so without a clear understanding of the comprehensive and persuasive anecdotal and experimental evidence. The few who take the time and effort to carefully interpret this evidence generally fail to accept its validity, especially since our traditional scientific framework doesn't include unexplained anomalies—ESP, the PE, and its triggers. It is unfortunate that Einstein's insight that: "All religions, arts and sciences are branches of the same tree," has long been forgotten. It doesn't apply to today's existing paradigm, but it certainly should. It is a crime it does not.

This concern, combined with those mentioned prior, require newly developed theoretical and conceptual frameworks for this new paradigm shift as follows:

(1) The scientific and medical communities should allocate greater attention towards understanding a uniquely complex personal experience that changes the lives of many people who yearn for explanations, guidance, and support following their PE. The similarity of anecdotal PEr accounts from healthy, well-

balanced individuals, of interactions with alternate realities and associated NHEs, suggest that people are somehow experiencing a non-physical reality considered to be "realer than real," often associated with pronounced psycho-spiritual outcomes. Despite the different modalities which trigger them, the similarities of their reported interaction(s) suggest a common underlying mechanism, process, and/or an internal or external force that governs and regulates this altered state of consciousness. This state may help to improve our understanding of the mind-brain relationship and even the possibility of an alternate reality—as strange as that may sound.

(2) Consciousness is likely intrinsic with the universe, not bound by space and time. We are connected through space and time at the level of consciousness. Quantum physics, for example, shows that the fundamental units of nature, including photons and electrons, are temporal as well as spatial, and consciousness, which is interrelated with the brain in space and time, cannot be explained only by mechanical laws of science. Over time, quantum interactions evolve into the free will and self-awareness of higher biological beings; the emergence of higher-level consciousness enhances the entropy-production ability of biological entities.

(3) The essence of materialism that matter is the only reality is wrong. In consciousness studies, materialism is being challenged by panpsychism—all self-organizing material systems have a mental and physical aspect. Consciousness may arise from non-spatiotemporal ingredients; experience is the underlying nature of the properties that physics identifies.

(4) A biofield that is governed and regulated by torsion energy (biophotons), concomitant with the four conventional fields of the Unified Field Theory (electromagnetic, gravitational, and the two nuclear forces), may allow for the manipulation and even possible manifestation of consciousness. This higher dimensional field may be linked with your consciousness. Biophoton regulation acts as a carrier field of electromagnetic interactions that interferes nonlocally in a spatial and temporal pattern. If torsion energy is indeed a carrier wave for consciousness and serves as a nonlocal interrelated force linking minds in real-time, this force may be the key component or the so-called "missing link" that facilitates

phenomena to access information from anywhere in the universe. Torsion energy may be the most important aspect of the biofield that facilitates anomalous events associated with consciousness; a real force that needs to be "integrated in modern physics."

(5) We have only just begun the process of explaining the mind-brain relationship, and there are still large explanatory gaps to fill. The brain is the most intricate of complex adaptive systems in which the whole is greater than the sum of its parts. Its emergent property consciousness, the "mind," or one's subjective sense of self, is different qualitatively from the billions of interconnecting neurons and synapses which form its parts.

(6) New methods are required to objectively verify aspects of consciousness that do not conform to traditional principles. Mainstream science must shift away from Realism to Instrumentalism—the belief that what a human being sees is based wholly on their beliefs about what does or does not exist to be seen in the first place; everything our senses experience is not all there is to existence. Practical consequences should constitute the essential criterion in determining meaning, truth, or value.

(7) Many aspects of paranormal activity should be considered normal, not abnormal. Extrasensory perception (telepathy, clairvoyance, precognition) and psychokinesis are valid, and nonlocality is a normal feature of human performance that should be cultivated and reinforced throughout one's life. Numerous experimental studies have been replicated by independent researchers showing that focused intention can facilitate the transference and reception of information and affect physical systems despite time and space—nonlocality.

(8) Evidence to support the UAP is overwhelmingly convincing and sufficient to accept its validity. Millions of people worldwide and throughout time have and will continue to interact with this phenomenon. The fundamental issue of concern is the essence of what governs and regulates its behavior. The UAP may be intelligently controlled by NHEs, a psychic projection from one's mind (PK), or both. If the former, then what is their objective, and if the latter, what are the implications for human potential?

(9) The multiverse theory asserts there are trillions of universes besides our own and reality may be the physics of

the virtual. Contemporary theoretical physics is dominated by superstring and M theories, with 10 and 11 dimensions respectively. (10) The concept of "reality" must be concisely defined and uniformly agreed upon. Through the synthesis of existing theories from noted scholars such as B. Kastrup, D. Chalmers, C. Koch, and G. Tononi, it would appear that three to four distinct levels of reality exist as follows: (1) Reality exists only upon the act of observation by an individual, and each individual world is coupled with, and follows the same rules which govern the world of all others. The act of one's subjective observation (internal world) represents an aspect of reality which is connected or entangled with all other individuals; (2) Reality exists in your mind—it represents the structure of conceptual thoughts facilitated by observation of your external world; (3) Reality is based on probabilities of occurrence governed by the laws of physics and mathematics that describe the probabilities of observation; and possibly (4) Each individual provides input to "pure consciousness"— the collection of all subjective observations into one objective "mind."

Consciousness and the Peak Experience

Overview: Consciousness may represent the key unifying characteristic that explains the PE and each distinct altered state of consciousness that facilitates it (NDE, OBE, psychoactive drugs, meditation, the UAP, and interactions with NHEs, etc.). This conclusion may even be analogous to the fundamental question, "What is the meaning of life? My answer is that the meaning of life is the meaning you give to life. It is solely dictated by aspects of free will and intentions governed by your conscious energies. As far as the answer to the question, what is consciousness? Well, my gut feeling tells me that you need the brain and the brain needs you. But once the hard drive crashes and the screen fades to black, you won't need this three-pound interpreter of 3D physical reality anymore. It'll then be time for you to move on to who knows where. Life may indeed be a long and winding infinite road.

Realization of the Unrealized Peak Experience: How does conscious experience and the subjective sense of "I" arise from lifeless matter? The same unanswerable question also applies to

199

the diverse range of phenomena referred to as "anomalous" or "paranormal" events. Can these phenomena, considered more real than real by those who experience them all be reduced to brain events, as material reductionist scientists maintain? Those who contend they do also ascribe to the belief that consciousness and the PE are delusions created by the brain. If this is true, then humans cannot have a transcendent experience that puts them in contact with a reality beyond themselves because there is no such reality. Or should I believe there is? If consciousness is indeed a fundamental physical law like our known principles of space, time, and gravity, it may represent a universal construct that facilitates free will, abstract thought, intuition, and one's sense of "self." The subjective perspective of "self" suggests that we are truly conscious only when our "self" is realized.

There is indeed a relationship among the subjective characteristics of PE triggers with symptoms of certain neurological (temporal lobe epilepsy, dementia, and sleep disorders) and psychiatric (schizophrenia, dissociative) disorders. By studying the neurological and cognitive aspects that contribute to such experiences, psychological models of how stable behavioral attributes emerge from sensory processing may contribute toward a better understanding of human consciousness. While most scientists acknowledge that consciousness exists, they consider it a philosophical issue best left to philosophers to explain or that we should focus research on other aspects of brain function because the neurological substrate mediating consciousness is unlikely to be identified.

Historically, an awakening out of one's self and into the transcendent has been the end of the path in many ancient traditions. It is virtually impossible to know how to interpret the reported experiences throughout the historic literature by visionaries and mystics who claim to have interacted with NHEs. Is it possible that in certain circumstances our consciousness can be purposely hijacked by NHEs to experience an alternate realm in the form of a PE? Does the brain impede an expanded awareness of this reality? It may just be that PErs are the modern-day version of shamans and visionaries of the past. If this is indeed the case, then it appears we may be seeing evidence of the same phenomenon that manifests itself throughout recorded history through our mind.

This evidence is depicted in the literature from religious texts, to folklore, to modern day accounts of the supernatural. Those who interrelate with this phenomenon via different contact modalities, whether it is in the form of a UAP, apparition, grey aliens, angels, or demons, experience an alternate reality from which it may arise. The intelligence behind this phenomenon, if one should exist, may be us or a possible external agent who can interact within our reality and psyche, but the potential objective and associated implication(s) makes little sense to us now.

Experiencing the transcendent realm is like an escape from reality. It is as if there is a sudden transition from the everyday experience one identifies with into the realization that they are everything that is—the mountains, sky, earth, rocks and every being within it. But is it the natural evolution of consciousness? This is the paradox of the PE. Is the PE an illusory event created by a misinterpretation of reality caused by a sleep disorder, a neurological abnormality, or a psychotic-based hallucination? Or is the PE a manifestation of a true reality that somehow incorporates vivid encounters of the deceased at one's bedside; a Supreme Being and/or NHEs in a heavenly realm; the perception of the environment and one's self from a location outside their body; and the altered perceptions and indescribable feelings of the intensity of love felt while in another reality?

The PE has the potential to trigger a transcendent experience that dramatically alters one's viewpoints and values. The PE is a life-changing event; a spiritual awakening—a path to true freedom and reality and a realization that life and "I" are the same thing. The PEr senses a dramatic shift in who and what they are for the first time. They feel overwhelming bliss, spaciousness and expansion, and realize they are not their mind, ego, emotions, and body. They speak of a beautiful "oneness" with all of life and a truth of what they are—not a self-centered ego who desires to control but rather to act with the highest wisdom for the highest good. But why do PE triggers wake them up and shift their perspectives out of their ego into something new and unlimited? To them, their PE created a new beginning. The question is whether this "new beginning" is true reality, something we must all strive to attain as part of spiritual evolution; to become more humane in all respects toward others and yourself.

Such changes are not surprising. How would you react if you experienced what PErs describe as an interconnectedness with the consciousness of other persons and of deceased relatives; instantaneous and simultaneous (nonlocality) review of your life in a dimension without our conventional bodies; to perceive altered aspects of time and space, where all past, present and future events exist; and to have clear consciousness with memories from early childhood, with self-identity, with cognition, and with emotion, and the perception of being out and above your body, etc.?

This transcendent-like awakening has not been sufficiently analyzed by science but must be of paramount importance to science to better understand the nature of the PE and its potentially profound implications to the experiencer and world at large. This commitment, in turn, must motivate others to study the PE in great empirical detail. If that scrutiny displays aspects that are inconsistent with established scientific principles, then science must be challenged to refine observational techniques and theories to better understand non-physical phenomena.

We need to make sense of what seems to be nonsense in the form of the PE and its triggers. As we are still debating the nature of reality, we must incorporate both objective experimental evidence and subjective anecdotal evidence of what mainstream science considers "absurd." This outdated perspective, which is consistent with Newtonian laws that do not apply to every aspect of human experience and ability, provides significant impedance to adequately test the hypothesis "what is the ultimate nature of reality?" Initially, however, the recognition of this possibility is a required prerequisite that will hopefully motivate scholars from many disciplines to integrate their efforts for research purposes. Further, hints of an alternate reality exist in many ways, as described in the literature on parapsychology, QM, paranormal activity and the PE and its triggers. If the validity of experimental and anecdotal evidence can somehow be established using newly discovered techniques, humanity will then be able to better understand the true or ultimate nature of reality. But trying to integrate what has already been established objectively in order to appropriately inform the development of appropriate theoretical questions to address, requires that a multidisciplinary effort be established by "outside-the-box" objective researchers who are brave enough to explore what is now considered "nonsense."

One major problem, however, is that major granting agencies are reluctant to fund research in this arena. It doesn't "fit" into prevailing traditional scientific principles and associated areas of research topic endeavors. Consequently, even motivated academics are reluctant to study this topic, especially since they know the chances of receiving funding would be more remote than winning at the slot machines. Thus, they bury their head in the sand, remain in the closet, and just read books on topics such as this, instead of pursuing research on one of the most critical issues of our time.

Part of the reason for this lack of actionable interest is that the PE and associated phenomena have not been verified—there is no proof. In addition, the information reportedly obtained from NHEs has "never been relevant information or information unknown to humankind."[47] However, it has been documented that these experiences have an important spiritual part, as if these entities were half physical and half psychic. In fact, "even one's own experiences seem to develop on a confused border between two opposing universes—the physical or the material and the psychic or spiritual."[48] The question, therefore, is not only whether NHEs are real beings but also why all the reported interactions with NHEs in the form of "descriptions of the entities, in the messages, or the actions undertaken by the entities," have "illogical or absurd components?"[49] One can't help but wonder if these illogical or absurd components contain an important clue as to their nature and purpose. If you bought this book to find the answers to these questions, let me be the first to apologize, because your guess is as good as mine.

Research Directions

Ideally, an initial major goal for researchers should be to establish agreed upon theories to be tested by scholars among different scientific disciplines and supported by independent studies to verify behavioral outcomes in PErs. Unfortunately, however, this imperative objective is impeded by the following study limitations: (1) intangible personal accounts serve as the primary source of the PE evidence; (2) established scientific principles cannot explain the phenomena—it lacks a widely accepted theory to test; and (3) research cannot be performed and replicated upon demand or be controlled in a laboratory setting; a pre- versus post-behavioral analysis cannot be accomplished since the PE is not predictable in occurrence—it occurs spontaneously and cannot be induced in an individual under well-controlled experimental conditions.

Despite this lack of validation, the similarity of reported psycho-spiritual outcomes engendered by contact experiencers warrant the need to further study aspects of these results within the physical, behavioral, and social sciences. The difficulty for researchers in this arena is that one can't control when such transformational experiences specifically occur. This makes studying them directly nearly impossible. In spite of this, it is clear that such behavioral transformative outcomes may result from the reported PE, a psychological aberration, or possibly something else which cannot be conceptualized at the present time. Consequently, the PE catalyst, which appears to alter aspects of consciousness and personal attitudes and viewpoints, is very difficult, if not impossible, to research (e.g., psychological and physiological) since the PE and associated symptoms spontaneously emerge; it generally occurs when one is having an OBE, NDE, and/or UAP and NHE interaction.

We must rely, therefore, on newly developed and creatively applied technology and methods to assess individuals who report to have a PE facilitated by different triggers. Once accomplished, if ever, the potential findings and associated implications will be of profound importance in unraveling the etiology of the PE and, by default, the possible nature of consciousness itself.

The research limitations associated with the PE beg for a behavioral analysis both within and across PErs of different cultural, ethnic, and demographic backgrounds to determine possible psycho-cultural influences of the PE itself. Although it is convincingly clear that the PE manifests in profound ways with lasting behavioral transformations in those who experience it, the PE is not amenable. It simply doesn't fit with the principles and methods of traditional Western science, and for that reason alone, the PE has been largely ignored by the scientific community. Even if it wasn't ignored, Newtonian physics, which has served us well, is becoming outdated and is limited in application to studying non-3D phenomena in the form of consciousness and the PE. For these reasons, among others noted prior, the lack of sufficient and well-controlled physiological, psychological, and cultural research evidence impedes our ability to develop agreed upon conclusions that can be made with confidence, despite those who contend to have done so.

A fundamental concern underlying further research is the issue of what type of evidence represents "proof" of an actual PE. The development of criteria and associated methodology to evaluate such "proof" may facilitate a greater understanding of the elusive mind-brain relationship; that is, whether consciousness is a direct outcome of brain function or is instead an interrelated but distinct aspect of energy that exists apart from the brain. Moreover, the nature of consciousness itself may be better understood through the comparative analysis of both physiological real-time brain activity and psychological assessments when an individual is experiencing an altered state of consciousness induced by each different PE trigger. By doing so, the altered state of consciousness produced by a PE in those diagnosed as psychologically "normal" may be differentiated from those states of consciousness consistent with various psychological conditions.

This assessment is critical if we are to accurately diagnose those individuals whose symptoms result from various psychopathological (schizotypy, psychosis, and delusional disorders) and neurological-based disorders that can cause an altered state of consciousness (non-PE) from those whose have a true PE. If both physiological and psychological assessments rule out an underlying abnormality that may give rise to it, the validity of the PE in the "normal" population may then be justified as non-pathological or a "true PE."

The concept of an "altered state of consciousness" emphasizes the need for continued research to determine if the PE and its triggers cause one to "see a different world" or instead, to "see the world differently" in a non-spatial/non-temporal context. Further investigations of the perceived characteristics of the PE, which include spiritual insights and encounters with an unseen, non-physical realm, may contribute toward a better understanding of both the many phenomena that facilitate the PE; the feeling of separation of consciousness from the physical self; and the associated similarity of psycho-spiritual transformations incurred by the PE in the form of changes in personal and philosophical viewpoints.

To better understand the nature of the PE, it is also necessary to determine the similarities and differences of changes in perceptual and psycho-spiritual attributes incurred by each distinct PE trigger among those who experience them. By doing so, the contributing factor(s) which facilitate different types of PEs may broaden our understanding of the nature and validity of the PE and of consciousness itself.

If science would focus more research attention toward the mysteries of the PE and consciousness, we would be in a better position to address critical questions, such as, can the PE and unconscious impulses, desires, and feelings be willfully raised to the level of the conscious self, and, if so, would the realizations of the mechanisms involved lead to authentic self-knowledge and self-actualization? If the unconscious is a source of intuitive and creative inspiration, how might a more expansive understanding of consciousness help one to improve their psychological and spiritual well-being?

Furthermore, there exists a critical need to extrapolate from laws of theoretical physics that relate microscopic quantum processes of the subatomic world to the macroscopic scale of the human brain and behavior. The persuasive evidence that a form

THE NEW PARADIGM SHIFT

of energy associated with consciousness and mental intention may be capable of both affecting events and receiving information remote from our body, combined with the compelling parallels drawn between aspects of human behavior/consciousness and the mathematical terms describing quantum processes, are significant interrelated issues that most researchers often neglect. These features directly pertain to the perceptions that everything in the universe is interconnected and that normal time and space is dramatically altered. If sensory information processing is nonlocal, it may explain the reported altered perception and images often described as a dimension without time and space associated with each PE trigger contact experience.

Conclusion: A critical initial step is for science to acknowledge that nonlocal perception or ESP is real, and to then develop a new paradigm to guide research to attempt to interpret and rationalize it. The elusive underlying processes of how ESP and synchronicity are represented and explained require research on the means by which information is shared between the unconscious and conscious mind, and its relationship to time. That is: (1) how does a conscious decision to receive information about a future event influence one's ability to accurately perceive that information (synchronicity)? and (2) how does information travel from one place or mind to another place or mind, and how does the element of time interact with such information transference (ESP)?

The mechanism which governs and regulates how the mind and time are interrelated should be of particular importance to researchers among many disciplines (physicists, psychologists, and neuroscientists, etc.), especially since the PEr often reports altered perceptions of time and space, where all past, present, and future events exist in a timeless and spaceless reality. It is one thing to demonstrate that many forms of ESP and synchronicity are valid, but it is quite another thing to determine the ways in which it manifests in the individual's consciousness and behavior.

Unfortunately, research to explain how interactions between people and their environment that seem to transcend the known physical laws of nature, endure as a small fringe field with only a handful of scientists actively pursuing research in this arena. This major research limitation begs for the development and application of comprehensive multidisciplinary research efforts in future studies.

The reported consistency of encounters with an unseen realm cannot be either irrefutably dismissed or accepted as a pure brain-based pathological aberration or a psychological manifestation. For this reason, there is a need to integrate consciousness more thoroughly into the framework of science than is presently the case. More specifically, the apparent transformative power of PEs on one's attitudes and values should be a major focus of future study to help resolve fundamental questions such as: (1) does the altered state of consciousness facilitated by the PE present evidence about additional states of consciousness beyond the central three; waking, dreaming and deep sleep? and (2) does the "self" exist at all, and if so, what is the role of the "self" in transcendent experiences such as the PE and its triggers? The primary question to this all is simply this: Are you the brain?

Closing Remarks

It is a daunting challenge to develop a coherent, all-encompassing explanation of the PE. In our still infant evolutionary cycle, we are merely scratching the surface wearing bearskins, using stone knives, and repeatedly grumping to make sense of it all. But in time, a few yet-to-be-born futuristic thinkers with non-existent egos and brilliant minds will apply newly developed principles and creatively applied methods to realize the answer. But since we will likely not witness this moment of discovery any time soon, it is essential to maintain an open and unbiased perspective of the conclusions made by those who proclaim to know what this phenomenon is all about. For this reason, to those who believe they have the irrefutable answer to what governs and regulates the triggers that facilitate the PE, let me emphasize in no uncertain terms that your steadfast conclusion is highly premature, tenuous at best, and that your egotism is showing.

Anomalous experiences facilitate curiosity. This same level of curiosity served as the required prerequisite condition and state of mind necessary for solving the nature of mysterious streaking bright objects, small flickering dots, and the changing shadows of that large, bright circle we see in the clear night sky. The PE is analogous to these ancestral mysteries and parallels many of today's mysteries, such as how the pyramids and other great ancient structures were built. Since we cannot determine how they were built, many believe "space aliens," often referred to as "ancient astronauts," must have been responsible for their construction. The argument, in other words, is that if you cannot disprove a claim it must be true also applies to defining the nature of the PE.

For instance, since you can't prove that Santa Claus does not exist or that UAPs are not governed by alien beings, does it mean Santa exists and aliens have visited earth? Achieving a confident, unbiased perspective when trying to decide if the PE is real in nature is not an easy task. That is, if you believe that you: (1) are not the brain and persist after death to be reunited with deceased loved ones; (2) have experienced an alternate realm of existence apart from your body; (3) interacted with NHEs in this or another reality; (4) know firsthand what heaven is like; and/or (5) communicated with deceased friends and relatives—it will be difficult to accurately interpret evidence that either supports or refutes your position, and you may perceive opposing viewpoints to be weak in principle and resist revising your belief. These experiences are not uncommon. They should be considered normal and not abnormal. Largely ignoring them, as mainstream science continues to do, greatly impedes our understanding of a unique human experience of which the PE and its triggers are a significant part to many millions yearning for an answer.

Without the bias for superiority, proponents of science must realistically appreciate and enhance the contributions and complementary aspects of spirituality and the PE. But science is missing the boat since Newtonian laws don't apply—they are inconsistent with the nature of the PE. This is unfortunate since focused research on the PE has the potential to yield important insights into the nature of reality, the mind-brain relationship, and how our brain facilitates conscious events and the sense that "I am aware of being aware."

My scientific-based education and research endeavors have caused this trained analytical and overly curious truth seeker to attempt, with fierce curiosity, to find answers to these puzzling aspects of reality and the human experience that only future generations will realize. Despite our modern-day scientific principles and discoveries, we are still barely out of the primordial soup from which we evolved. Our knowledge of reality is still in its infancy, and we have a long journey ahead to fully understand the true nature and potential of us and the world around us. At this stage in our evolutionary cycle, the collective PE evidence clearly indicates that "something" significant is occurring in varying ways that cannot be adequately explained using today's scientific principles. This "something" should be considered a much more important endeavor by mainstream science than is now the case.

The lack of acceptable research protocol applied in the study of the PE has contributed to our inability to adequately define, with sufficient confidence, the nature and origin of many unexplained personal events. Part of this difficulty is trying to apply the scientific method to spontaneous intangible PEs which cannot be controlled in a laboratory setting or in any other setting, for that matter. For this reason, in part, this limitation leaves mainstream science skeptical about the validity of the PE. But skeptical analysis serves as a necessary component to the scientific process. Skepticism is incorporated in the scientific method, which integrates the observation of a phenomenon, the development of a hypothesis about the phenomenon, experimentation designed to demonstrate the truth (or not) of the hypothesis, and a conclusion that supports or amends the hypothesis. This traditional approach, however, cannot be adequately applied in the study of the PE, at least not yet.

Consequently, when the general scientific community hears extraordinary claims of one observing their body from above, experiencing a heavenly realm and communicating with NHEs, and feelings of unity with the world without time or space, they know it cannot be adequately studied, let alone, proven. So, it is ignored.

But it is presumptuous to firmly conclude that all "realer than real" personal descriptions of PE triggers are nothing more than symptoms resulting from either a dysfunctional brain, misperceptions during a sleep state, and/or a psychological disorder, rather than the existence of a co-existing alternate reality. It is important to remember that history is filled with unrealistic ideas which eventually became fact. At this stage in our embryonic technological development, there exists a staggering amount of yet-to-be-discovered scientific laws and principles, and the related technologies controlled by them. After all, it took only 66 years from the time Wilbur and Orville flew at Kitty Hawk to when Neil and Buzz walked on the moon. What will the next 66 years, let alone a few more centuries and generations reveal? The same foresight and wisdom, cultivated and integrated using both traditional and newly discovered scientific principles, will eventually lend itself toward understanding modern accounts of the "unexplained." Who knows, the answers may be provided once the hard drive crashes and the screen fades to black upon your demise.[53]

John Lennon nailed it when he sang "Love is the Answer," and maybe "death" itself will also provide the "answer" to the greatest mystery of all. If all the answers that future generations will come to realize were announced on major news channels this evening, humanity would be shocked to the core—the residue of changes in personal, philosophical, and religious/spiritual ways seem too dramatic and complex to just even contemplate.

Given our current limited understanding of the universe, and that roundish thing above your shoulders, we are not yet in the position, either scientifically or psychologically, either to logically explain or emotionally handle the potential, incomprehensible implications of PE on both a personal and societal level. The magnitude of emotion you felt on September 11, 2001, or when you looked in the eyes of your newborn child for the first time, may very well be on par with the magnitude of reverence felt when the answers to the many complex issues addressed in this book are proven without a shadow of doubt. It is indeed a very slow and evolving process that must be integrated in a stepwise fashion to integrate successfully—personally, spiritually, and culturally.

Conclusion

The limited research performed to date leaves open many questions concerning the nature and associated reason why some people have a PE. I can't help but wonder, for instance, if a PE represents the evolution of our species toward the next stage of higher consciousness by unlocking dormant human potentials. This highly speculative and unanswerable question must be asked since studies show that PEs transform people from their pre-PE personalities into more loving and compassionate individuals—a symptomatic behavioral outcome inconsistent with psychotic disorders. So, whatever the cause may be, keep it coming! A Noble Prize likely awaits the one who successfully bottles it for world consumption.

The question, what is consciousness? and the popular statement that "consciousness creates reality" raise numerous questions. Does this mean we as individuals can shape and create whatever reality we'd like for ourselves? Does it mean we can manifest a certain lifestyle, and attract certain experiences? If so, how do we do it? Although science is unable to answer these questions with certainty, we do know there is a relationship between consciousness and our physical material world and that it must have some degree of significance yet-to-be-fully-realized. Although the PE seems implausible by any stretch of the imagination, there exists sufficient scientific evidence in the form of anecdotal (subjective) and physiological (objective) evidence to support the validity of ESP. Combined with scientific theories, the pieces of the puzzle suggest that we now possess appropriate preliminary evidence to tentatively support the validity of the PE phenomenon. While it is important to keep in mind that the surface toward explaining the PE is just being scratched, the pieces are connecting in the right direction for experiencers to believe their PE to indeed be real. At the very least, theories in QM strongly hint this may indeed be the case.

The existence of nonlocal perception, or ESP, must be acknowledged by mainstream science. But science is unwilling to do so since the phenomena violates established physical laws. Despite this biased limitation, however, it is still difficult to accept how science continues to completely ignore the overwhelming body of evidence to support ESP. This includes meta-analyses of ESP results using statistical approaches from more than 200 studies conducted by different researchers with more than 6,000 participants and replicated numerous times by independent investigators. This convincing outcome, which is not marginal nor impossible to replicate, provides more than enough evidence to suggest that the human mind may have undiscovered properties and capabilities—that is, perceptual abilities extending beyond the space and time constraints of sensory organs.

It appears quite clear, therefore, that the overall results of experimentation are indicative of an anomalous process of information transfer. Despite this fact, the investigation of psychic phenomena has not produced a useful, reliable finding, or experimental evidence that, at least to most hardcore materialist scientists, is convincing. People with dispositions that are attracted to science naturally tend to debunk such phenomena. Skepticism is healthy and encouraged but debunking is appalling. It prevents scientific progress toward understanding the essence of such phenomena and represents a personal assault against those who experience a PE.

This persuasive evidence has yet to motivate science to take non-physical phenomena research to the next level of significant discovery along with its associated significant implications. The evolution of mind is simply impeded by too many closed-minded, inside-the-box egotistical thinkers. Science, and the world at large, is in dire need of more outside-the-box scholars bold enough to buck the conventional trend of academia and established concrete scientific principles. Once successful, if ever, we may then realize the emphatic conclusion of renowned scientist Nikola Tesla, who stated: "The day science begins to study non-physical phenomena, it will make more progress in one decade than in all the previous centuries of its existence."[54]

You may have experienced a sense of frustration by your inability to form conclusive answers to life's many perplexing questions, such as: am "I" my brain; what is consciousness; is there life after death, and are spiritual, mystical, and extraordinary experiences valid? Seeking answers to these and other questions raised by the PE may have crossed your mind at least once in your life and are a normal part of human existence; a personal characteristic that may be programmed by your innate tendencies. Despite these elusive questions, there exists only a few answers to the PE phenomenon. That is, the PE occurs often, it is real to those who experience it, and it cannot be explained by established scientific principles. In recent times, however, many well-respected scientists are informing us that the brain may behave as a hologram and that reality may be holographic in nature. What is especially intriguing and hard to ignore is that fact that the holographic concept appears consistent with many subjective characteristics of the PE.

Interestingly, one of the most significant implications of the PE and its associated symptom of nonlocal perception, is that it may represent the ideal behavioral model to determine if an aspect of consciousness exists beyond the brain. This notion will remain just a passing thought until science accepts the fact that enough evidence suggests this is a distinct possibility. That is, you may not be just a brain. If proven true, once apart from the brain, you may be free from its limiting influence. You may be capable of experiencing alternate realms of existence as conscious "eternal aspects of waves."

Since evidence to support this yet-to-be-realized assumption may very well be available in the form of the PE, it is imperative for science to recognize the possible connection between existing theories, experimental evidence in non-physical phenomena, and the subjective nature and personal impact of the PE on those who experience it. This connection may very well provide an answer but only if the specific pieces to the PE puzzle are addressed with fierce determination by unbiased outside-the-box, truth-seeking minds.

Many generations after your body is among the 150,000 people who die each day, sufficient principles applied in a creative way will eventually provide humankind with answers to many unresolved significant questions about the meaning and purpose of life and reality. But at this time, when we are only just beginning to understand the quantum world, the infinite cosmos, and the 100 billion neurons inside your skull, I can only offer a few "connecting dots" that may, in some small but meaningful way, wake us up to the significance of it all. This realization alone may help pave the direction and focus of attention for others to explain one of life's most perplexing experiences that leaves one yearning, with fierce resolve, for an answer. But don't waste your time waiting for science to find answers to the many questions in this book. Science will likely never find the answers to consciousness, the PE, or human existence any time soon. The answers are likely within you. And if you happen to have the answers, you know where to find me.

END NOTES

Introduction

1. "Collection of Quotes, May 12, 2018," https://rezamusic. yolasite.com/reza-ganjavi-collection-of-quotes.php.

2. R. Musil, *Precision and Soul. Essays and Addresses* (Chicago: University of Chicago Press; 1990).

3. G. Santoro et al., "The Anatomic Location of the Soul from the Heart, Through the Brain, To the Whole Body, and Beyond: A Journey through Western History, Science, and Philosophy," *Neurosurgery* 65, (2009): 633–643.

4. S. Greenfield, *The Human Brain. A Guided Tour* (London: Weidenfeld and Nicolson, 1997).

5. Greenfield, *The Human Brain: A Guided Tour.*

6. O. Rank, *Psychology and the Soul. A Study of the Origin, Conceptual Evolution, and Nature of the Soul* (Baltimore: Johns Hopkins University Press, 2002).

7. S. Pandya, "Understanding Brain, Mind and Soul: Contributions from Neurology and Neurosurgery," *Mens Sana Monograph* 9, (2011): 129–149.

8. Mario Beauregard, *Brain Wars* (New York, N.Y: Harper One, 2013).

9. R. Griffiths, A. Richards, M. Johnson, U. McCann and R. Jesse, "Mystical-type experiences occasioned by psilocybin mediate the attribution of personal meaning and spiritual

significance 14 months later," *Journal of Psychopharmacology* 22, (2008): 621–632.

10. D. B. Yaden, D. Khoa, L. Nguyen, and M. Kern, "The Noetic Quality: A Multimethod Exploratory Study Psychology of Consciousness: Theory, Research, and Practice," *Journal of Abnormal Psychology* 4, (2017): 526–535.

11. H. Koenig, D. King, and V. B. Carson, V. B, *Handbook of Religion and Health* (New York, N.Y: Oxford University Press, 2012).

12. J. Waldron, "The timeless moment: A study of transcendent experience through a focus on the nature and integration of the noetic quality of the experience," *NESS The Journal of Transpersonal Psychology* 30, (1998).

13. D. B. Yaden, J. Iwry, K. Slack and A. B. Newberg, "The overview effect: Awe and self-transcendent experience in space flight," *Psychology of Consciousness: Theory, Research, and Practice* 3, (2016): 1–11.

14. A. Maslow, "Religions, Values, and Peak Experiences," June 14, 2012, http://www.bahaistudies.net/asma/peak_experiences.pdf.

15. A. Maslow, "Religions, Values, and Peak Experiences."

16. A. Maslow, *The Farther Reaches of Human Nature* (New York, N.Y: Penguin Books, 1971).

17. W. Stace, *Mysticism and Philosophy* (New York: The MacMillan Press, 1960).

18. Edgar D. Mitchell and Robert Staretz, "The Quantum Hologram and the Nature of Consciousness," *Journal of Cosmology* 14, (2011): 84.

19. J.P., personal communication.

20. Bruce G. Charlton, "Peak Experiences, Creativity and the Colonel Flastratus Phenomenon," *Abraxas* 14, (1998): 10-19 https://www.hedweb.com/bgcharlton/peak.html.

21. Eugene W. Mathes, "Peak Experience Tendencies Scale Development and Theory Testing," *Journal of Humanistic Psychology* 22, (1982): 92-108.

22. A. Maslow, *The Farther Reaches of Human Nature*.

23. The Harris Poll, "The Religious and Other Beliefs of Americans," Feb 26, 2013, http://wiki.creation.org/ Public_Opinion.

24. R. M. Fewkes, Carl Sagan's Cosmos," Dec 7, 1997, https:// www.firstparishnorwell.org/sermons/cosmos.htm.

25. C. Agrillo, "Near-death Experience: Out-of-Body and Out-of-Brain," *Rev. Gen. Psychology* 15, (2011). 1–10.

26. "Physicists Claim that Consciousness Lives in Quantum State after Death," July 10, 2016, https://www.outerplaces.com/ science/item/4518-physicists-claim-that-consciousness-lives-in-quantum-state-after-death?qs=2&utm_expid=68243097-1.LutSYZjjRsmSMx2YZefKRA.2&utm_referrer=https%3A%2F%2Fwww.google.com%2F.

27. G. Schwartz, *The Afterlife Experiments: Breakthrough Scientific Evidence of Life after Death* (New York, N.Y: Atria Books, 2002).

28. I. Stevenson, C. Tart and M. Grosso, "The Possible Nature of Past Life Memory Case Studies: A Discussion," *Journal of the American Society for Psychical Research* 74, (1980): 413.

29. B. Greyson, "Dissociation in People who Have Near-Death Experiences: Out of their Bodies or Out of Their Minds?" *Lancet* 355, (2000): 460.

30. "Out-of-Body Experiences and Survival After Death." May 20, 2016, www.survivalafterdeath.info/articles/braude/obe.htm.

31. FBI Records: The Vault. August 23, 2018, https://vault.fbi.gov/Project%20Blue%20Book%20%28UFO%29%20.

32. R. Strassman, *DMT – The Spirit Molecule*. Vermont: Park Street Press, 2001.

33. B. Guggenheim and J. Guggenheim, *Hello from Heaven* (New York, N.Y: 1997).

34. I. Barušs, and J. Mossbridge, *Transcendent mind: Rethinking the science of consciousness* (Washington, DC: American Psychological Association, 2017).

Chapter 1:
The Peak Experience: Encounters with an Unseen Realm

1. A. Newberg and J. Iversen, "The neural basis of the complex mental task of meditation: neurotransmitter and neurochemical considerations," *Med Hypotheses* 61, (2003):282–291.

2. R. Hood, "Chemically assisted mysticism and the question of veridicality," in *Seeking the Sacred with Psychoactive Substances: Chemical Paths to Spirituality and God. Vol. I: History and Practices,* ed. J. H. Ellens (Santa Barbara, CA: Praeger, 2014), 395-410.

3. R. Griffiths, A. Richards, M. Johnson, U. McCann and R. Jesse, "Mystical-type experiences occasioned by psilocybin mediate the attribution of personal meaning and spiritual significance 14 months later," *Journal of Psychopharmacology* 22, (2008): 621–632.

4. R. Hernandez, R. Davis, R. Scalpone, and R. Schild, "A Study on Reported Unidentified Aerial Phenomena and Associated Contact with Non-Human Intelligence," *Journal of Scientific Exploration* 32, (2018): 298–348.

5. D. B. Yaden, D. Khoa, L. Nguyen and M. Kern, "The Noetic Quality: A Multimethod Exploratory Study Psychology of Consciousness: Theory, Research, and Practice," *Journal of Abnormal Psychology* 4, (2017): 526–535.

6. D. B. Yaden, D. Anderson, M. Mattar and A. B. Newberg, "Pyschoactive stimulation and psychoactive substances: Conceptual and ethical considerations," in *The Psychedelic Policy Quagmire: Health, Law, Freedom, and Society,* ed. J. H. Ellens and T. B. Roberts (Santa Barbara, CA: Praeger, 2016), 219-236.

7. P.W., personal communication.

8. L.G., personal communication.

9. P. S., personal communication.

10. L. P., personal communication.

11. G. S., personal communication.

12. R. D., personal communication.

13. R. Hood, P. Hill, and B. Spilka, *The Psychology of Religion* (New York, N.Y: Guilford Press, 2009).

14. C. Alvarado, "Out-of-Body Experiences," in *Varieties of anomalous experience: Examining the scientific evidence*: ed. by E. Cardeña, S. J. Lynn and S. Krippner. (Washington, DC: Charles C. Thomas, 2000).

15. R. A. Moody and P. Perry, *Glimpses of Eternity* (New York, NY: Guideposts, 2010).

16. B. Greyson, "The Incidence of Near-Death Experiences," *Med Psychiatry* 92, (1998): 392-399.

17. R. Hood, *The Psychology of Religion*.

18. E. G. D'Aquili and A. B. Newberg, "The Neuropsychology of Aesthetic, Spiritual, and Mystical States," *Zygon* 35, (2000): 39-51.

19. The Nobel Prize: Werner Karl Heisenberg, https://www.nobelprize.org/prizes/physics/1932/heisenberg/facts/

20. D. Bohm, and B. Hiley, *The Undivided Universe* (New York, NY: Routledge, 1993).

21. E. Mitchell, and D. Williams, *The Way of the Explorer* (New York, N.Y: Putnam, 1996).

22. L. Miller, personal communication.

23. R. Griffiths, et al. "Mystical-type experiences occasioned by psilocybin mediate the attribution of personal meaning and spiritual significance 14 months later."

24. R. Hood, *The Psychology of Religion.*

25. H. Irwin, *An Introduction to Parapsychology* (Jefferson, NC: McFarlend and Company, 2003).

26. G. Gabbard and S. Twemlow, "Do "near-death experiences" occur only near death?-revisited," *Journal of Near-Death Studies* 10, (1991): 41-47.

27. L. Miller, personal communication.

28. J. Miller. "Mystical Experiences, Neuroscience, and the Nature of Reality," https://etd.ohiolink.edu/rws_etd/document/get/bgsu1174405835/inline.

29. J. Waldron, "The timeless moment: A study of 'transcendent experience through a focus on the nature and integration of the noetic quality of the experience," *The Journal of Transpersonal Psychology* 30, (1998), 145-156.

30. L. Miller, personal communication.

31. K. Ring, "Precognitive and Prophetic Visions in Near-Death Experiences," *Anabiosis* 2, (1982): 47.

32. W. Buhlman, *Adventures in the Afterlife* (CreateSpace Independent Publishing Platform, 2013).

33. Ring, K. *The Omega Project: Near-Death Experiences, UFO Encounters, and Mind at Large.* (New York, NY: William Morrow, 1992).

34. G. Groth-Marnat and R. Summers, "Altered Beliefs, Attitudes, and Behaviors Following Near-Death," *Experiences Journal of Humanistic Psychology* 38, (1998):110-125.

35. S. R., personal communication.

36. D. B. Yaden, "The Noetic Quality: A Multimethod Exploratory Study Psychology of Consciousness: Theory, Research, and Practice."

37. D. B. Yaden, "The Noetic Quality: A Multimethod Exploratory Study Psychology of Consciousness: Theory, Research, and Practice."

38. G. Gabbard, and S. Twemlow, *With the Eyes of the Mind: An Empirical Analysis of Out-of-Body States* (New York, N.Y: Praeger Scientific, 1984).

39. P. van Lommel, "Near-Death Experiences," Annals NY Academy of Sciences, *Near-Death Studies* 29, (2010): 362-376.

40. P. van Lommel, "Near-Death Experiences."

41. P. van Lommel, *Consciousness Beyond Life. The Science of the Near-Death Experience* (New York, NY: Harper Collins, 2010).

42. C. Sutherland, *Transformed by the Light: Life after Near-Death Experiences* (Sydney, AS: Bantam Books, 1992).

43. P. van Lommel, R. Wees, V. Meyers and I. Elfferich, "Near-Death Experience in Survivors of Cardiac Arrest: A prospective Study in the Netherlands," *Lancet* 358, (2001): 2039.

44. R. Hernandez, R. Davis, R. Scalpone, and R. Schild, "A Study on Reported Unidentified Aerial Phenomena and Associated Contact with Non-Human Intelligence."

45. R. Hernandez, R. Davis, R. Scalpone, and R. Schild, "A Study on Reported Unidentified Aerial Phenomena and Associated Contact with Non-Human Intelligence."

46. Ring, K. *The Omega Project: Near-Death Experiences, UFO Encounters, and Mind at Large.*

47. K. Marden, "The MUFON Experiencer Survey: What it Tells us about Contact and the Implications for Humanities Future." Unpublished.

48. K. Marden, "The MUFON Experiencer Survey: What it Tells us about Contact and the Implications for Humanities Future."

49. K. Marden, "The MUFON Experiencer Survey: What it Tells us about Contact and the Implications for Humanities Future."

50. J. Mack, *Passport to the cosmos: Human transformation and alien encounters* (New York, NY: Crown Publishers, 1999).

51. J. Mack, *Passport to the cosmos: Human transformation and alien encounters.*

52. C. Grob et al., "Pilot study of psilocybin treatment for anxiety in patients with advanced-stage cancer," *Arch. Gen. Psychiatry* 68, (2011): 71–78.

53. M. Forstmann, and C. Sagioglou, "Lifetime experience with (classic) psychedelics predicts pro-environmental behavior through an increase in nature relatedness," *J. Psychopharmacology* 31, (2017): 975–988.

54. F. Palhano-Fontes et al., "Rapid antidepressant effects of the psychedelic ayahuasca in treatment-resistant depression: a randomized placebo-controlled trial," *Psychol. Med* (2018): 1–9.

55. M. Bogenschutz, "Psilocybin-assisted treatment for alcohol dependence: a proof-of-concept study," *J. Psychopharmacol* 29, (2016): 289–299.

56. R. Carhart-Harris, "Psilocybin with psychological support for treatment-resistant depression: an open-label feasibility study," *Lancet Psychiatry* 3, (2016): 619–627.

57. S. R., personal communication.

58. P. van Lommel, R. Van Wees, and V. Meyers, "Near-death experience in survivors of cardiac arrest: a prospective study in the Netherlands," *Lancet* 358, (2001): 2039-2045.

59. L. M., personal communication.

60. PMH Atwater, *From Beyond the Light* (New York, N.Y: Avon Books 1994).

61. N. Nour, L. Evans, L. and R. Carhart-Harris, "Psychedelics," *J. Psychoactive Drugs* 49, (2017): 182–191.

62. W. Stace, *Mysticism and Philosophy* (Philadelphia, PA: Lippincott 1960).

63. A. Maslow, (1959), "Cognition of being in the peak experiences," *J. Genet. Psychol* 94, (1959): 43–66.

64. C. Timmermann et al., "DMT Models the Near-Death Experience," *Front. Psychology* 15, (2018).

65. J. Waldron, "The timeless moment: A study of transcendent experience through a focus on the nature and integration of the noetic quality of the experience," *NESS The Journal of Transpersonal Psychology* 30, (1998).

66. A. Maslow, "Cognition of being in the peak experiences."

67. D. B. Yaden, J. Iwry, K. Slack and A. B. Newberg, "The overview effect: Awe and self-transcendent experience in space flight," *Psychology of Consciousness: Theory, Research, and Practice* 3, (2016): 1–11.

68. D. B. Yaden, "The overview effect: Awe and self-transcendent experience in space flight."

69. E. Mitchell and R. Staretz, "The Quantum Hologram and the Nature of Consciousness," *Journal of Cosmology* 14, (2011): 84.

70. C. White, and C. Smith, "Bringing the Overview Effect Down to Earth," (1987), https://libraryofprofessionalcoaching. com/wp-app/wp-content/uploads/2013/04/Bringing-the-Overview-Effect-Down-to-Earth1.pdf.

71. "Savikalpa Samadhi," (2016), https://www.yogapedia. com/definition/8524/savikalpa-samadhi.

72. D. Radin, "Institute of Noetic Sciences," http://noetic. org/about/overview.

73. F. White, and C. Smith, "Bringing the Overview Effect Down to Earth," 1987, https://libraryofprofessionalcoaching.com/ wp-app/wp-content/uploads/2013/04/Bringing-the-Overview-Effect-Down-to-Earth1.pdf.

74. F. White, "Bringing the Overview Effect Down to Earth."

75. C. Grof, and S. Grof, *The Stormy Search for the Self* (New York, N.Y.: Jeremy P. Tarcher, 1992).

76. C. Grof, and S. Grof, *The Stormy Search for the Self.*

77. C. Grof, and S. Grof, *The Stormy Search for the Self.*

78. S. Robbin, personal communication.

79. PMH Atwater, "Common Elements Are Found in Near-Death Experiences," 2017, http://pmhatwater.com/resource/articles/html.

80. PMH Atwater, *From Beyond the Light.*

81. B. Greyson, "Near-Death Experiences: Clinical Implications," *Archives of Clinical Psychiatry* 12 (2007).

82. PMH Atwater, "Common Elements Are Found in Near-Death Experiences."

83. PMH Atwater, "Common Elements Are Found in Near-Death Experiences."

84. PMH Atwater, *From Beyond the Light.*

85. PMH Atwater, "Common Elements Are Found in Near-Death Experiences."

Chapter 2:
Consciousness, the Mind-Brain, and You

1. D. Masci, "What do scientists think about religion?," November 24, 2009, http://articles.latimes.com/2009/nov/24/opinion/la-oe-masci24-2009nov24.

2. F. Crick, *The Astonishing Hypothesis* (New York, NY: Simon & Schuster, 1994).

3. B. Baars, *A Cognitive Theory of Consciousness* (Cambridge, MA: Cambridge University, 1988).

4. F. Crick and C. Koch, "Towards a neurobiological theory of consciousness," *Seminars Neuroscience* 2, (1990): 263–275.

5. G. Edelman and G.Tononi G, *A Universe of Consciousness: How Matter Becomes Imagination* (London: Allen Lane, 2000).

6. E. Wigner, "Remarks on the mind-body question," in *The Scientist Speculates*, ed. Good I. J., editor; (London: Heinemann), in *Quantum Theory and Measurement*, ed. J. Wheeler, W. Zurek (Princeton, N.J: Princeton University Press). Reprinted in Wigner, E. (1967), *Symmetries and Reflections*, (Bloomington, IN: Indiana University Press 1961).

7. E. Schrödinger, "Die gegenwärtige situation in der Quantenmechanik," (The present situation in quantum mechanics), *Naturwissenschaften* 23, (1935): 807–812. (Translation by J. T. Trimmer in *Proc. Amer. Phil. Soc* 124, 1980: 323–338).

8. J. Eccles, "Evolution of consciousness," *Proc. Natl. Acad. Sci* 89, (1992): 7320–7324.

9. D. Bohm, *The Undivided Universe* (New York, NY: Routledge, 1993).

10. G. Tononi, "An information integration theory of consciousness," *Trends Cogn. Sci* 5, (2004): 472–478.

11. Tononi, "An information integration theory of consciousness."

12. C. Koch, "Is Consciousness Universal?" January 1, 2014, https://www.scientificamerican.com/article/is-consciousness-universal/.

13. E. Laszlo, *Science and the Akashic Field. An Integral Theory of Everything* (Rochester, VT: Inner Traditions International, 2004).

14. P.W., personal communication.

15. E. Laszlo, *Science and the Akashic Field. An Integral Theory of Everything.*

16. P. van Lommel, "Near-death experience, consciousness, and the brain: a new concept about the continuity of our consciousness based on recent scientific research on near-death experience in survivors of cardiac arrest," World Futures 62, (2006): 134–151.

17. P. van Lommel, *Consciousness Beyond Life. The Science of the Near-Death Experience* (New York, NY: Harper Collins, 2010).

18. E. Laszlo, *Science and the Akashic Field. An Integral Theory of Everything.*

19. S. Pandya, "Understanding Brain, Mind and Soul: Contributions from Neurology and Neurosurgery," *Mens Sana Monogr* 9, (2011): 129–149.

20. S. Pandya, "Understanding Brain, Mind and Soul: Contributions from Neurology and Neurosurgery."

21. S. Pinker, *The Blank Slate. The modern denial of human nature* (New York: N.Y: Penguin, 2003).

22. J. Brown, *Aphasia; Apraxia and Agnosia; Clinical and theoretical aspects* (Springfield, IL. Charles C. Thomas, Publisher, 1972).

23. R. Carter, *Mapping the Mind* (Berkeley, CA: University of California Press; 1998).

24. Pinker S, *The Blank Slate. The modern denial of human nature.*

25. S. Pandya, "Understanding Brain, Mind and Soul: Contributions from Neurology and Neurosurgery."

26. W. Penfield, "Damage to discrete areas within the brain can thus produce a variety of disorders of the mind," *Neurosurgery* 41, (1997): 314–318.

27. S. Pandya, "Understanding Brain, Mind and Soul: Contributions from Neurology and Neurosurgery."

28. R. Sperry, "Nobel Lecture," December 8, 1981, https://www.nobelprize.org/prizes/medicine/1981/sperry/25059-roger-w-sperry-nobel-lecture-1981/.

29. R. Carter, *Mapping the Mind.*

30. R. Sperry, Nobel Lecture.

31. R. Sperry, Nobel Lecture.

32. R. Carter, *Mapping the Mind.*

33. R. Carter, *Mapping the Mind.*

34. S. Pandya, "Understanding Brain, Mind and Soul: Contributions from Neurology and Neurosurgery."

35. E. Krishnamoorthy, "When your mind and soul meet," *The Hindu Magazine* 30 (2009).

36. R. Meares R. "The contribution of Hughlings Jackson to an understanding of dissociation," *Am J Psychiatry* 156, (1999): 1850–1855.

37. D. Chalmers, *The Conscious Mind - in Search of a Fundamental Theory* (New York, NY: Oxford University Press, 1996).

38. F. Crick, *The Astonishing Hypothesis.*

39. F. Crick, *The Astonishing Hypothesis.*

40. S. Belbase, "A Unified Theory of Mind-Brain Relationship: Is It Possible?" *Open Journal of Philosophy* 3, (2013): 443-450.

41. I. Miller, "Synchronicity: When Cosmos Mirrors Inner Events," March 2012, https://www.researchgate.net/publication/277161877_Synchronicity_When_Cosmos_Mirrors_Inner_Events.

42. V. Limar, "Synchronicity Phenomena by C.G. Jung: Perspectives of Study and Possible Psychophysiological Substantiation," *NeuroQuantology* 3, (2010): 354-358.

43. V. Limar, "Synchronicity Phenomena by C.G. Jung: Perspectives of Study and Possible Psychophysiological Substantiation."

44. K. Surprise, *"Synchronicity: The Art of Coincidence, Choice, and Unlocking Your Mind,"* Dr. Kirby Surprise – The Science Behind Synchronicity. https://futurethinkers.org/kirby-surprise-synchronicity/

45. D. Novack et al., "Psychosomatic medicine: the scientific foundation of the biopsychosocial model," *Acad Psychiatry* 31, (2007): 388-401.

46. C. Nemeroff, "Paradise lost: the neurobiological and clinical consequences of child abuse and neglect," *Neuron* 89, (2016): 892-909.

47. M. Currier, and C. Nemeroff, "Depression as a risk factor for cancer," *Annu Rev Med* 65, (2014): 203-221.

48. C. Nemeroff, and P. Goldschmidt-Clermont, "Heartache and heartbreak - the link between depression and cardiovascular disease," *Nat Rev Cardiol* 9, (2012): 526-539.

49. B. Schöttker et al., "Associations of metabolic, inflammatory and oxidative stress markers with total morbidity and multi-morbidity in a large cohort of older German adults," *Age Ageing* 45 (2016): 127-135.

50. S. Pressman, and S. Cohen, "Does positive affect influence health?" *Psychol Bull* 131, (2005): :925-971.

51. C. Ryff, "Psychological well-being revisited: advances in the science and practice of Eudaimonia," *Psychother Psychosom* 83, (2014):10-28.

52. Frederickson et al., "Psychological well-being and the human conserved transcriptional response to adversity," *PLoS One* 10, (2015).

53. G. Fava, "Current Psychosomatic Practice," *Psychother Psychosom* 86, (2017): 13-30.

54. G. Fava, "Current Psychosomatic Practice."

55. S. Thrane, and S. Cohen, "Effect of Reiki Therapy on Pain and Anxiety in Adults: An In-Depth Literature Review of Randomized Trials with Effect Size Calculations," *Pain Management Nursing* 15, (2014): 897–908.

56. C. Streeter et al., "Effects of yoga on the autonomic nervous system, gamma-aminobutyric-acid, and allostasis in epilepsy, depression, and post-traumatic stress disorder." *Med Hypotheses* 78, (2012): 571–579.

57. C. Streeter et al., "Effects of yoga versus walking on mood, anxiety, and brain. GABA levels: a randomized controlled MRS study," *J Altern Complement Medi*cine 16, (2010):1145–1152.

58. L. Colloca L, and F. Benedetti, "Placebos and painkillers: is mind as real as matter?" *Nature Reviews Neuroscience* 6, (2005): 545–552.

59. F. Eippert et al., "Activation of the Opioidergic Descending Pain Control System Underlies Placebo Analgesia," *Neuron* 63, (2009): 533-543.

60. K. Hall et al., "Catechol-O-Methyltransferase val158met Polymorphism Predicts Placebo Effect in Irritable Bowel Syndrome," *PLOSOne* (2012): https://doi.org/10.1371/journal.pone.0048135.

61. J. Howick et al., "Are treatments more effective than placebos? A systematic review and meta-analysis," *PLOSOne* 8, (2013).

62. *Harvard Men's Health Watch*, "The power of the placebo effect," May, 2017, https://www.health.harvard.edu/mental-health/the-power-of-the-placebo-effect.

63. *Harvard Men's Health Watch*, "The power of the placebo effect."

64. A. Walia, "This Is How Powerful The Mind-Body Connection Really Is," January 6, 2017, https://www.collective-evolution.com/2017/01/06/this-is-how-powerful-the-mind-body-connection-really-is/.

65. B. Lipton, *The Biology of Belief* (New York, N.Y: Hay House, Inc, 2005).

66. A. Walia, "This Is How Powerful The Mind-Body Connection Really Is."

67. A. Walia, "This Is How Powerful The Mind-Body Connection Really Is."

68. K. Pribram, *Brain and Perception* (Hillsdale, NJ: Lawrence Erlbaum, 1961).

69. S. Hameroff, "The "conscious pilot" - dendritic synchrony moves through the brain to mediate consciousness," *J. Biol. Physics* 36, 2010: 71–93.

70. S. Hameroff, "The Penrose-Hameroff "Orch OR" model of consciousness," *Philos. Trans. R. Society* 356, (2001): 1869–1896.

71. R. Penrose, and S. Hameroff, "Consciousness in the universe: neuroscience, quantum space-time geometry and Orch OR theory," *J. Cosmology* (2011): http://journalofcosmology.com/Consciousness160.html.

72. S. Hameroff, "The Penrose-Hameroff Orch OR model of consciousness."

73. C. Powell, "Could the Universe Be Conscious?" NBC Universal Media, LLC, June 16, 2017, https://futurism.com/could-universe-conscious/.

74. S. Hameroff, "The Penrose-Hameroff Orch OR model of consciousness."

75. R. Penrose, and S. Hameroff, "Consciousness in the universe: neuroscience, quantum space-time geometry and Orch OR theory."

76. S. Hameroff, "The Penrose-Hameroff Orch OR model of consciousness."

77. C. Swanson, *The Synchronized Universe: New Science of the Paranormal* (New York, N.Y: Poseidia Press, 2003).

78. A. Tiller, *Science and Human Transformation* (California, Pavoir Publishing, 1997).

79. H. Romijn, "About the origin of consciousness. A new, multidisciplinary perspective on the relationship between brain and mind," *Proc Kon Ned Akad v Wetensch* 100, (1997): 181-267.

80. H. Romijn, "Are Virtual Photons the Elementary Carriers of Consciousness?" *Journal of Consciousness Studies* 9, (2002): 61-81.

81. N. Bohr, *Atomic Theory and the Description of Nature, Reprinted as The Philosophical Writings of Niels Bohr, Vol. I,* (Woodbridge, NJ: Ox Bow Press, 1934/1987)

82. The Veterans Administration, 2018, https://www.ptsd. va.gov/public/materials/apps/mobileapp_mindfulness_ coach.asp.

83. Sciencedaily, "Mindfulness meditation training changes brain structure in eight weeks," January 21, 2011, https://www. sciencedaily.com/releases/2011/01/110121144007.htm.

84. Sciencedaily, "Mindfulness meditation training changes brain structure in eight weeks."

Chapter 3:
Interactions with Non-Human Entities

1. A. P. Elkin, *Aboriginal Men of High Degree: Initiation and Sorcery in the World's Oldest Tradition* (New York, N.Y: Inner Traditions, 1993).

2. A. P. Elkin, *Aboriginal Men of High Degree: Initiation and Sorcery in the World's Oldest Tradition.*

3. J. Mack, *Passport to the cosmos: Human transformation and alien encounters* (New York, NY: Crown Publishers, 1994).

4. C.G. Jung, "Archetypes and quantum physics and psychology," *NeuroQuantology|* 9, (2011): 563-571.

5. C.G. Jung, "Archetypes and quantum physics and psychology."

6. S. Adamski, "Archetypes and the Collective Unconscious of Carl G. Jung in the Light of Quantum Psychology," NeuroQuantology 9, (2011): 563-571, https://www.researchgate.net/publication/289172420.

7. C.G. Jung, *Modern man in search of a soul* (New York: Grove Press Inc, 1941).

8. C.G. Jung, *Flying Saucers: A Modern Myth of Things Seen in the Skies* (Princeton, N.J: Trans. R.F.C. Hull 1964).

9. C.G. Jung, *Flying Saucers: A Modern Myth of Things Seen in the Skies.*

10. S. Adamski, "Archetypes and the Collective Unconscious of Carl G. Jung in the Light of Quantum Psychology."

11. B. Raynes, *Visitors from Hidden Realms* (Memphis, TN: Eagle Wing Books, 2004).

12. J. Vallee, *Challenge to Science: The UFO Enigma* (New York, NY: Ballantine Books, 1977).

13. J. Vallee, *Challenge to Science: The UFO Enigma.*

14. L. Minero, *Demystifying the Out-of-Body Experience: A Practical Manual for Exploration and Personal Evolution* (Woodbury, MN. Llewellyn Publications, 2012).

15. R. Monroe, *Journeys Out of the Body* (New York, NY: Doubleday, 1977).

16. J. Long, *Evidence of the Afterlife* (New York, NY: HarperCollins, 2011).

17. C. Adams, and D. Luke, *Breaking Convention: Essays on Psychedelic Consciousness* (Berkeley, CA: North Atlantic Books, 2013).

18. R. Targ, *The Reality of ESP: A Physicist's Proof of Psychic Abilities* (Wheaton, IL: Theosophical Publishing House, 2012).

19. C. Adams, and D. Luke, *Breaking Convention: Essays on Psychedelic Consciousness.*

20. R. Strassman, *DMT: The Spirit Molecule* (South Paris, ME: Park St Press, 2001).

21. J. Mack, *Passport to the cosmos: Human transformation and alien encounters.*

22. J. Vallee, J. *Messengers of Deception: UFO Contacts and Cults,* (Internet Library Archive. Daily Grail Publishing, 2008).

23. Eaves, et al., 2017). "Jacob's Dream," William Blake Archive. September 25, 2013, http://listverse.com/2017/07/26/10-bible-accounts-that-could-be-interpreted-as-ufos-or-aliens/.

24. "Moses and the Burning Bush," http://listverse. com/2017/07/26/10-bible-accounts-that-could-be-interpreted-as-ufos-or-aliens/, https://www.biblegateway. com/passage/?search=Exodus+3&version=NI.

25. "Moses and the Burning Bush."

26. "Bible accounts that could be interpreted as ufos or aliens," https://www.biblegateway.com/passage/? search=Exodus+3&version=NIV. http://listverse. com/2017/07/26/10-bible-accounts-that-could-be-interpreted-as-ufos-or-aliens/.

27. Gaia, "Was Ezekiel Describing Extraterrestrial Visitors in the Bible?" *September 4th, 2017,* https://www.gaia.com/ lp/content/is-ezekiels-vision-of-the-wheel-evidence-of-ufos-in-the-bible/ https://www.biblegateway.com/ passage/?search=Exodus+3&version=NIV.

28. Gaia, "Was Ezekiel Describing Extraterrestrial Visitors in the Bible?"

29. Bible accounts that could be interpreted as ufos or aliens.

30. Bible accounts that could be interpreted as ufos or aliens.

31. M. Talbot, *The Holographic Universe: The Revolutionary Theory of Reality* (New York, N.Y: Harper Perennial, 2011).

32. B. Steiger, "Angel Miracles," Interview by Brent Raynes - *Alternate Perceptions Magazine*," December 2015, http:// www.apmagazine.info/index.php?option=com_ content&view=article&id=747&Itemid=53

33. B. Steiger, Angel Miracles.

34. J. Vallee, J. *Messengers of Deception: UFO Contacts and Cults.*

35. A. Hynek, *The UFO Experience: A Scientific Enquiry* (New York, NY: Ballantine Books, 1972).

36. A. Hynek, United Nations committee to research and investigate global UFO reports. July 14, 1978.

37. J. Keel, *Operation Trojan Horse: The Classic Breakthrough Study of UFOs* (New York: Anomalist Books 2013).

38. J. Keel, *Operation Trojan Horse: The Classic Breakthrough Study of UFOs.*

39. R. Davis, *The UFO Phenomena: Should I Believe?* (Atglen, PA: Schiffer Publishing, 2015).

40. C. Kelleher and G. Knapp, *Hunt for the Skinwalker: Science Confronts the Unexplained at a Remote Ranch in Utah* (Paraview Pocket Books, 2005).

41. R. Davis, *The UFO Phenomena: Should I Believe?*

42. R. Davis, *The UFO Phenomena: Should I Believe?*

43. J. Caravaca, "The Distortion Theory," 2018, http:// caravaca102.blogspot.com/.

44. J. Vallee, *UFOs: The Psychic Solution* (E.P. Dutton and Company Inc 1975) Under the title of The Invisible College.

45. K. Marden, and D. Stoner, *The Alien Abduction Files* (Pompton Plains, NJ: New Page Books, 2013).

46. B. Hopkins, D. Jacobs, and R. Westrum, *Unusual Personal Experiences: An Analysis of the Data from Three Major Surveys* (Las Vegas, NV: Bigelow Holding Corporation, 1992).

47. R. Hernandez, R. Davis, R. Scalpone, and R. Schild, "A Study on Reported Unidentified Aerial Phenomena and Associated Contact with Non-Human Intelligence," *Journal of Scientific Exploration* 32, (2018): 298–348.

48. D. Luke, "Discarnate Entities and DMT: Psycho-pharmacology, phenomenology, and Ontology," *Journal of the Society for Psychical Research* 75, (2011).

49. R. Strassman, *DMT: The Spirit Molecule.*

50. E. Gouzoulis-Mayfrank, "Psychological Effects of (S)-Ketamine and N,N-Dimethyltryptamine (DMT): a double-blind," *Pharmacopsychiatry* 38, (2005): 301–311.

51. R. Strassman, "The varieties of the DMT experience," In Strassman, R., Wojtowicz, S., Luna, L. E. and Frecska, E, *Inner Paths to Outer Space: Journeys to Alien Worlds Through Psychedelics and Other Spiritual Technologies*, 51-80 (Rochester, VT: Park Street Press, 2008).

52. S. Beyer, *Singing to the Plants: A Guide to Mestizo Shamanism in the Upper Amazon* (Albuquerque, NM: University of New Mexico Press, 2009).

53. D. Luke, "Discarnate Entities and DMT: Psychopharmacology, phenomenology, and Ontology."

54. R. Meyer, "Apparent communication with discarnate entities induced by dimethyltryptamine (DMT)," In Lytell, *Psychedelics*, 161-203 (New York: Barricade Books, 1994).

55. D. Luke, "Discarnate Entities and DMT: Psychopharmacology, phenomenology, and Ontology.

56. R. Strassman, *DMT: The Spirit Molecule*.

57. C. Cott, and A. Rock, "Phenomenology of N, N-Dimethyltryptamine use: a thematic analysis," *Journal of Scientific Exploration* 22, (2008): 359-370.

58. D. Luke, "Discarnate Entities and DMT: Psychopharmacology, phenomenology, and Ontology."

59. D. Luke, "Discarnate Entities and DMT: Psychopharmacology, phenomenology, and Ontology."

60. L. Shanon, *The Antipodes of the Mind: Charting the Phenomena of the Ayahuasca Experience* (Oxford: Oxford University Press, 2002).

61. D. Luke, "Disembodied Eyes Revisited. An Investigation into the Ontology of Entheogenic Entity Encounters," *Entheogen Review* 17, (2008): 38–40.

62. R. Strassman, *DMT: The Spirit Molecule*.

63. P. Meyer, "Apparent Communication with Discarnate Entities Related to DMT," In *Psychedelic Monographs and Essays*, ed. Thomas Lyttle, 29–69. Boynton Beach, FL: PM and E Publishing, "340 DMT Trip Reports," http://www.serendipity.li/dmt/340_dmt_trip_reports. htm#66, December, 2017.

64. G. St. John, "The Breakthrough Experience: DMT Hyperspace and its Liminal Aesthetics," *Anthropology of Consciousness*, March 2018, https://anthrosource.onlinelibrary.wiley.com/.

65. L. Tramacchi, "Vapours and Visions: Religious Dimensions of DMT Use," PhD thesis, School of History, Philosophy, Religion and Classics, (2006): University of Queensland.

66. R. Strassman, *DMT: The Spirit Molecule.*

67. A. Gallimore, and D. Luke. 2015, "DMT Research from 1956 to the End of Time." In *Neurotransmissions: Essays on Psychedelics From Breaking Convention*, ed. D. King, D. Luke, B. Sessa, C. Adams and A. Tollen, (London: Strange Attractor, 2015): 291–316.

68. D. Luke, and D. Terhune. 2013. "The Induction of Synaesthesia with Chemical Agents: A Systematic Review," *Frontiers in Psychology* 4, (2013): 753.

69. C. Cott, and A. Rock, "Phenomenology of N, N-Dimethyltryptamine Use: A Thematic Analysis," *Journal of Scientific Exploration* 22, (2008): 359–70.

70. C. Cott, and A. Rock, "Phenomenology of N, N-Dimethyltryptamine Analysis."

71. P. Meyer, "Apparent Communication with Discarnate Entities Related to DMT."

72. D. Handon, "Hierarchies of Hyperspace, A Collection" by Erowid 10 Powerful DMT Journeys—From Ego Deaths

To Unconditional Love, February 24, 2015, http://reset. me/story/powerful-dmt-journeys-ego-deaths-dancing-aliens/.

73. D. Handon, "Hierarchies of Hyperspace, A Collection by Erowid 10 Powerful DMT Journeys — From Ego Deaths To Unconditional Love."

74. D. Handon, "Infinity of the Now" by Erowid, February 24, 2015, http://reset.me/story/powerful-dmt-journeys-ego-deaths-dancing-aliens/.

75. D. Handon, "The Realization of Love" by Erowid. February 24, 2015, 10 Powerful DMT Journeys - From Ego Deaths To Unconditional Love. http://reset.me/story/powerful-dmt-journeys-ego-deaths-dancing-aliens.

76. D. Handon, "Homecoming Raised to the DMT Power" by Erowid10 Powerful DMT Journeys — From Ego Deaths To Unconditional Love, February 24, 2015, http://reset. me/story/powerful-dmt-journeys-ego-deaths-dancing-aliens/.

77. R. Strassman, *DMT: The Spirit Molecule.*

78. G. St. John, "The Breakthrough Experience: DMT Hyperspace and its Liminal Aesthetics."

79. C. Cott, and A. Rock, "Phenomenology of N, N-Dimethyltryptamine Analysis."

80. R. Strassman, *DMT: The Spirit Molecule.*

81. D. Luke, "Discarnate Entities and DMT: Psychopharmacology, phenomenology, and Ontology."

82. J. Mack, *Passport to the cosmos: Human transformation and alien encounters.*

83. K. Marden, *Psychological Studies on Abduction Experiencers.*

84. R. Hernandez, R. Davis, R. Scalpone, and R. Schild, "A Study on Reported Unidentified Aerial Phenomena and Associated Contact with Non-Human Intelligence."

85. R. Strassman, "The varieties of the DMT experience."

86. R. Strassman, "The varieties of the DMT experience."

87. R. Strassman, *DMT: The Spirit Molecule.*

88. D. Luke, "Discarnate Entities and DMT: Psycho-pharmacology, phenomenology, and Ontology."

89. D. Hill, and M. Persinger, "Application of transcerebral, weak (1 mi-croT) complex magnetic fields and mystical experiences: Are they generated by field-induced dimethyltryptamine release from the pineal organ?" *Perceptual and Motor Skills* 97, (2003): 1049–1050.

90. C. Timmermann, et al., "DMT Models the Near-Death Experience," *Front. Psychology* 15, (2018): 34-56.

91. C. Cott, and A. Rock, "Phenomenology of N, N-Dimethyltryptamine Analysis."

92. D. Luke, "Discarnate Entities and DMT: Psycho-pharmacology, Phenomenology, and Ontology."

93. R. Strassman, "The varieties of the DMT experience."

94. C. Timmermann, et al., "DMT Models the Near-Death Experience."

95. C. Timmermann, et al., "DMT Models the Near-Death Experience."

96. H. Carhart-Harris et al., "Psychedelics and the essential importance of context," *J. Psychopharmacol* 32, (2018): 725–731.

97. D. Luke, "Discarnate entities and dimethyltryptamine (DMT)," *Journal for the Society for Psychical Research* 75, (2011): 26–42.

98. S. Harvey-Wilson, "Shamanism and alien abductions: a comparative study," *Australian Journal of Parapsychology* 1, (2001): 103-116.

99. K. Ring, "Near-death and UFO encounters as shamanic initiations: some conceptual and evolutionary implications," *ReVision* 11, (1989): 14-22.

100. J. Kent, *Psychedelic Information Theory* (Seattle, WA: PIT Press, 2010).

101. P. Meyer, "Apparent Communication with Discarnate Entities Related to DMT."

102. B. Severi, "Sciamani e psichedelia, [Shamans and psychedelics]," *Quaderni de Parapsychologia* 34 (2003):

103. G. Hancock, *Supernatural: Meetings with the Ancient Teachers of Mankind* (London: Century, 2005).

104. R. Strassman, "The varieties of the DMT experience."

105. B. Severi, "Sciamani e psichedelia, [Shamans and psychedelics].

106. R. Strassman, "The varieties of the DMT experience."

107. G. Hancock, *Supernatural: Meetings with the Ancient Teachers of Mankind.*

108. P. Meyer, "Apparent Communication with Discarnate Entities Related to DMT."

109. J. Kent, *Psychedelic Information Theory.*

110. D. Turner, "Exploring hyperspace: Entheogen Review," *The Journal of Unauthorized Research on Visionary Plants and Drugs* 4, (1995): 4-6.

111. P. Meyer, "Apparent Communication with Discarnate Entities Related to DMT."

112. D. Luke, "Discarnate entities and dimethyltryptamine (DMT)."

113. D. Luke, "Disembodied Eyes Revisited. An Investigation into the Ontology of Entheogenic Entity Encounters."

114. R. Strassman, *DMT: The Spirit Molecule*.

115. C. Jung, *Archetypes and quantum physics and psychology*.

116. C. Jung, *Archetypes and quantum physics and psychology*.

117. R. Ellen Guiley, and P. Imbrogno, *The Vengeful Djinn: Unveiling the Hidden Agenda of Genies, and The Djinn Connection* (New York: Llewellyn 2014).

118. B. Raynes, *Visitors from Hidden Realms*.

119. D. Perkins, "Tangling with the Trickster," January 2003, http://magoniamagazine.blogspot.com/2014/01/trickster.html?m=1.

120. R. Ellen Guiley, *The Djinn Connection* (New Milford, CT: Visionary Living, 2013).

121. R. Ellen Guiley, *The Djinn Connection*.

122. R. Ellen Guiley, *The Djinn Connection*.

123. R. Scalpone, personal communication.

124. R. Scalpone, personal communication.

125. R. Davis, *The UFO Phenomenon: Should I Believe?*

126. K. Marden, *Psychological Studies on Abduction Experiencers*.

127. R. Hernandez, R. Davis, R. Scalpone, and R. Schild, A Study on Reported Unidentified Aerial Phenomena and Associated Contact with Non-Human Intelligence.

128. K. Ring, "Near-death and UFO encounters as shamanic initiations: some conceptual and evolutionary implications."

129. R. Davis, *The UFO Phenomenon: Should I Believe?*

130. R. Davis, *The UFO Phenomenon: Should I Believe?*

131. E. Mitchell, and D. Williams, *The Way of the Explorer* (New York, N.Y: Putnam, 1996).

132. R. Davis, *The UFO Phenomenon: Should I Believe?*

133. R. Davis, *The UFO Phenomenon: Should I Believe?*

134. S. Hawking, *The Grand Design* (New York, N.Y: Bantam, 2012).

135. S. Hawking, *The Grand Design.*

136. B. Green, "About Brian Green," https://www.briangreene.org/.

137. B. Green, "About Brian Green."

138. J. Mack, *Passport to the Cosmos: Human Transformation and Alien Encounters.*

139. J. Vallee, *Challenge to Science: The UFO Enigma.*

Chapter 4:
Communicating with the Deceased

1. M. Lawrence, and E. Repede, "The incidence of deathbed communications and their impact on the dying process," *American Journal of Hospice and Palliative Care* 30, (2013): 632-639.

2. D. Arcangel, *Afterlife Encounters* (Charlottesville, VA: Hampton Roads, 2005).

3. J. Assante, *The Last Frontier: Exploring the Afterlife and Transforming Our Fear of Death* (Novato, CA: New World Library 2012).

4. L. Nahm, "Reflections on the context of near-death experiences," *Journal of Scientific Exploration 25*, (2011): 453-478.

5. A. Mazzarino-Willett, "Deathbed phenomena: Its role in peaceful death & terminal restlessness," *American Journal of Hospice & Palliative Medicine 27*, (2010):127-133.

6. D. Kessler, "Visions, trips, & crowded rooms: Five common deathbed experiences," October 14, 2011, http://www.examiner.com/trasitions-grief-in-naitonal/visions-trips-c.

7. M. Callanan, and P. Kelley, *Final Gifts: Understanding the Special Awareness, Needs, and Communications of the Dying* (New York, N.Y: Simon & Schuster 2012).

8. P. Kircher, and M. Callanan, IANDS "NDEs and Nearing Death Awareness in the Terminally Ill," December 14, 2017, https://iands.org/resources/support/seriously-or-terminally-ill/ndes-and-ndas.html.

9. M. Callanan, and P. Kelley, *Final Gifts: Understanding the Special Awareness, Needs, and Communications of the Dying.*

10. T. Morita, et al., "Nationwide Japanese Survey About Deathbed Visions: My Deceased Mother Took Me to Heaven," *Symptom Manage* (2016).

11. A. Mazzarino-Willett, "Deathbed phenomena: Its role in peaceful death & terminal restlessness," *American Journal of Hospice and Palliative Medicine* 27, (2010): 127-133.

12. J. Lerma, *Learning From the Light: Pre-death Experiences, Prophecies, and Angelic Messages of Hope* (New York: New Page Books, 2009).

13. W. Barrett, *Deathbed Visions* (New York: White Crow Books, 2011).

14. W. Barrett, *Deathbed Visions.*

15. A. Mazzarino-Willett, "Deathbed phenomena: Its role in peaceful death & terminal restlessness."

16. J. Lerma, *Learning From the Light: Pre-death Experiences, Prophecies, and Angelic Messages of Hope.*

17. J. Lerma, *Learning From the Light: Pre-death Experiences, Prophecies, and Angelic Messages of Hope.*

18. J. Lerma, *Learning From the Light: Pre-death Experiences, Prophecies, and Angelic Messages of Hope.*

19. W. Barrett, *Deathbed Visions.*

20. M. Lawrence, and E. Repede, The incidence of deathbed communications and their impact on the dying process.

21. M. Lawrence, and E. Repede, "The incidence of deathbed communications and their impact on the dying process.

22. C. Wills-Brandon, "The Trigger of Deathbed Visions' Research," https://www.near-death.com/experiences/triggers/deathbed-visions.html.

23. C. Wills-Brandon, *One Last Hug Before I Go: The Mystery and Meaning of Deathbed Visions* (New York: HCI, 2000).

24. C. Wills-Brandon, "The Trigger of Deathbed Visions' Research."

25. P. Fenwick, H. Lovelace, and S. Brayne, "Comfort for the dying: Five year retrospective and one year prospective studies of end of life experiences," *Archives of Gerontology and Geriatrics* 51, (2009):173-179.

26. P. Fenwick, H. Lovelace, and S. Brayne, "Comfort for the dying: Five year retrospective and one year prospective studies of end of life experiences."

27. P. Fenwick, H. Lovelace, and S. Brayne, "Comfort for the dying: Five year retrospective and one year prospective studies of end of life experiences."

28. Out-of Body Research Foundation, "Nearing End of Life Events & Death Bed Visions," http://www.oberf.org/dbv.htm.

29. Out-of Body Research Foundation, "Nearing End of Life Events & Death Bed Visions."

30. B. Guggenheim, and J. Guggenheim, *Hello from Heaven* (New York, N.Y: Bantam Books, 1995).

31. B. Guggenheim, and J. Guggenheim, *Hello from Heaven.*

32. B. Guggenheim, and J. Guggenheim, *Hello from Heaven.*

33. C. Alvarado, "Ernesto Bozzano on the Phenomena of Bilocation," Survival After Death, https://www.survivalafterdeath.info/articles/alvarado/bozzano.htm.

34. B. Guggenheim, and J. Guggenheim, *Hello from Heaven.*

35. C. Wills-Brandon, *One Last Hug Before I Go: The Mystery and Meaning of Deathbed Visions.*

36. C. Wills-Brandon, "The Trigger of Deathbed Visions' Research."

37. S. Brayne, H. Lovelace, and P. Fenwick, "End-of-life experiences and the dying process in a Gloucestershire nursing home as reported by nurses and care assistants," *American Journal of Hospice & Palliative Medicine* 25, (2008):195-206.

38. K. Osis, and E. Haraldsson, *At the Hour of Death* (New York: Avon, 1997).

39. M. Callanan, and P. Kelley, *Final gifts. Deathbed Visions: Social Workers' Experiences, Perspectives, Therapeutic Responses, and Direction for Practice.*

40. "Deathbed Visions," October 10, 2015, rdeath.com.

41. M. Lawrence, and E. Repede, The incidence of deathbed communications and their impact on the dying process.

42. B. Greyson, "Seeing Dead People Not Known to Have Died: "Peak in Darien" Experiences," *Anthropology and Humanism* 35, (2010): 159–171.

43. B. Greyson, "Seeing Dead People Not Known to Have Died: "Peak in Darien" Experiences.

44. R. Crookall, *The Study and Practice of Astral Projection* (New Hyde Park, NY: University Books, 1960).

45. K. Osis, and E. Haraldsson, *At the Hour of Death.*

46. K. Ring, *Life at Death: A Scientific Investigation of the Near-Death Experience* (New York: Coward, McCann and Geoghegan, 1980).

47. P. Sartori, *The Near-Death Experiences of Hospitalized Intensive Care Patients: A Five Year Clinical Study* (Lewiston U.K: Edwin Mellen, 2008).

48. M. Rawlings, *Beyond Death's Door* (Nashville, TN: Thomas Nelson, 1978).

49. M. Morse, and P. Perry, *Closer to the Light: Learning from the Near-Death Experiences of Children* (New York: Villard, 1990).

50. P. van Lommel, "About the Continuity of Our Consciousness," *Advances in Experimental Medicine and Biology* 550, (2004): 115–132.

51. B. Greyson, "Seeing Dead People Not Known to Have Died: 'Peak in Darien' Experiences."

52. I. Stevenson, "The Uncomfortable Facts About Extrasensory Perception," *Harper's Magazine* 219, (1959): 19–25.

53. B. Greyson, "Seeing Dead People Not Known to Have Died: 'Peak in Darien' Experiences."

54. E. Kübler-Ross, *On Children and Death* (New York: Macmillan, 1983).

55. B. Greyson, "Seeing Dead People Not Known to Have Died: 'Peak in Darien' Experiences."

56. R. Moody, and P. Perry, *The Light Beyond* (New York: Bantam, 1988).

57. B. Greyson, "Seeing Dead People Not Known to Have Died: 'Peak in Darien' Experiences."

58. B. Steiger, and S. Steiger, *Children of the Light: The Startling and Inspiring Truth About Children's Near-Death Experiences and How They Illuminate the Beyond* (New York: Signet Penguin, 1995).

59. B. Greyson, "Seeing Dead People Not Known to Have Died: 'Peak in Darien' Experiences."

60. E. Alexander, *Proof of Heaven: A Neurosurgeon's Journey into the Afterlife* (New York: Simon and Schuster, 2012).

61. E. Alexander, *Proof of Heaven: A Neurosurgeon's Journey into the Afterlife.*

62. E. Alexander, *Proof of Heaven: A Neurosurgeon's Journey into the Afterlife.*

63. E. Alexander, *Proof of Heaven: A Neurosurgeon's Journey into the Afterlife.*

64. B. Greyson, "Seeing Dead People Not Known to Have Died: 'Peak in Darien' Experiences."

65. B. Greyson, "Seeing Dead People Not Known to Have Died: 'Peak in Darien' Experiences."

66. R. Moody, *Glimpses of Eternity: An Investigation into Shared Death Experiences* (New York: Guideposts; Book Club Edition, 2010).

67. Universal Life Church Monastary, "The Mystery of Empathic and Shared Death Experiences," January 5, 2012, https://www.themonastery.org/blog/2012/01/the-mystery-of-empathic-and-shared-death-experiences/#5w Mt7eGTCak11Ywr.99.

68. Out-of Body Research Foundation, "Nearing End of Life Events and Death Bed Visions."

69. Out-of Body Research Foundation, "Nearing End of Life Events and Death Bed Visions."

70. Out-of Body Research Foundation, "Nearing End of Life Events and Death Bed Visions."

71. E. Roxburgh and C. Roe, "A Survey of Dissociation, Boundary-Thinness, and Psychological Well-Being in Spiritualist Mental Mediumship," *Journal of Parapsychology* 75, (2011): 279.

72. R. Davis, *Life after Death: An Analysis of the Evidence* (Atglen, PA: Schiffer Publishing, 2017).

73. R. Davis, *Life after Death: An Analysis of the Evidence.*

74. R. Davis, *Life after Death: An Analysis of the Evidence.*

75. G. Schwartz, *The Afterlife Experiments: Breakthrough Scientific Evidence of Life After Death* (New York, N.Y: Atria Books. 2002).

76. A. Roy and T. Robertson, "Results of the Application of the Robertson-Roy Protocol to a Series of Experiments with Mediums and Participants," *Journal Society Psychical Research* 68, (2004): 161.

77. J. Beischel, "Anomalous Information Reception by Research Mediums Under Blinded Conditions II: Replication and Extension," *Explore*, 2015.

78. C. O'Keeffe and R. Wiseman, "Testing Alleged Mediumship: Methods and Results," *British Journal of Psychology* 96, (2005): 165.

79. Emily Kelly and D. Arcangel, "An Investigation of Mediums who Claim to Give Information about Deceased Persons," *Journal Nervous Mental Disorders* 199, (2011): 11.

80. J. Beischel and G. Schwartz, "Anomalous Information Reception by Research Mediums Demonstrated Using a Novel Triple-Blind Protocol," *Explore* 3, (2007): 23.

81. C. Jensen, and A. Cardeña, "A controlled long-distance test of a professional medium," *Eur. J. Parapsychology* 24, (2009): 53–67.

82. J. Beischel, "Contemporary Methods Used in Laboratory-Based Mediumship Research," *Journal of Parapsychology* 71, (2007): 37–68.

83. J. Beischel, "Contemporary Methods Used in Laboratory-Based Mediumship Research."

84. A. Roy and T. Robertson, "Results of the Application of the Robertson-Roy Protocol to a Series of Experiments with Mediums and Participants."

85. J. Beischel, "Contemporary Methods Used in Laboratory-Based Mediumship Research."

86. R. Davis, *Life after Death: An Analysis of the Evidence.*

87. J. Beischel, "Contemporary Methods Used in Laboratory-Based Mediumship Research."

88. D. Radin, *Entangled Minds* (New York: Simon & Schuster; 2006).

89. R. Davis, *Life after Death: An Analysis of the Evidence.*

90. G. Schwartz, L. Russek, L. A. Nelson, and C. Barentsen, "Accuracy and Replicability of Anomalous After-Death Communication across Highly Skilled Mediums," *Journal of the Society for Psychical Research* 65, (2001): 1.

91. M. Sudduth, "Super-Psi and the Survivalist Interpretation of Mediumship," *Journal of Scientific Exploration* 23, (2009): 167.

92. M. Sudduth, "Super-Psi and the Survivalist Interpretation of Mediumship."

93. M. Sudduth, "Super-Psi and the Survivalist Interpretation of Mediumship."

94. R. Davis, *Life after Death: An Analysis of the Evidence.*

95. R. Davis, *Life after Death: An Analysis of the Evidence.*

96. "Nearly Half of Americans Believe in Ghosts," January, 14th, 2016, http://disinfo.com/2013/02/nearly-half-of-americans-believe-in-ghosts/.

97. R. Davis, *Life after Death: An Analysis of the Evidence.*

98. R. Davis, *Life after Death: An Analysis of the Evidence.*

99. R. Davis, *Life after Death: An Analysis of the Evidence.*

100. J. Assante, *The Last Frontier: Exploring the Afterlife and Transforming Our Fear of Death.*

101. C. Green and C. McCreery, *Apparitions* (London, U.K: Hamish Hamilton, 1975).

102. A. Gauld. "Discarnate Survival," in *Handbook of Parapsychology*: ed. B. B Wolman (New York, NY: Van Nostrand Reinhold, 1977).

103. H. J. Irwin, *An Introduction to Parapsychology* (London, UK: McFarland and Company, 2003).

104. H. J. Irwin, *An Introduction to Parapsychology.*

105. H. J. Irwin, *An Introduction to Parapsychology.*

106. R. Davis, *Life after Death: An Analysis of the Evidence.*

107. J. Assante, *The Last Frontier: Exploring the Afterlife and Transforming Our Fear of Death.*

108. R. Davis, *Life after Death: An Analysis of the Evidence.*

109. P. Granqvist, "Sensed Presence and Mystical Experiences are Predicted by Suggestibility, Not by the Application of Transcranial Weak Complex Magnetic Fields, Randomized Controlled Trial," *Neuroscience Letters* (2005): 23.

110. L. Gearhart and M. A. Persinger, "Geophysical Variables and Behavior: Onsets of Historical and Contemporary Poltergeist Episodes Occurred with Sudden Increases in Geomagnetic Activity," *Perceptual and Motor Skills* 62, (1986): 440.

111. R. Davis, *Life after Death: An Analysis of the Evidence.*

112. R. Davis, *Life after Death: An Analysis of the Evidence.*

113. R. Davis, *Life after Death: An Analysis of the Evidence.*

114. R. Davis, *Life after Death: An Analysis of the Evidence.*

Chapter 5:
Unseen Forces and the Spiritual Brain

1. R. Hood, "Psychological strength and the report of intense religious experience," *Journal of the Scientific Study of Religion* 57, (2005): 29-41.

2. C. Alvarado, "Out-of-Body Experiences," in *Varieties of anomalous experience: Examining the scientific evidence*: ed E. Cardeña, S. J. Lynn and S. Krippner (Washington, DC: Charles C. Thomas, 2000).

3. R. A. Moody and P. Perry, *Glimpses of Eternity* (New York, NY: Guideposts, 2010).

4. B. Greyson, "The Incidence of Near-Death Experiences," *Med Psychiatry* 4, (1998): 92-102.

5. S. Pinker, "The Evolutionary Psychology of Religion Freethought Today," 22, (2005), https://ffrf.org/outreach/item/13184-the-evolutionary-psychology-of-religion.

6. E. Kelly, *Beyond Physicalism: Toward a Reconciliation of Science and Spirituality* (Lanham, MD: Rowman & Littlefield, 2015).

7. F. Capra, "Transliminality as the mediating factor," *Journal of Parapsychology* 74, (1999): 359-381).

8. A. Winseman, "Religious Tolerance Score Edged Up in 2004," March 15, 2005, https://news.gallup.com/poll/15253/religious-tolerance-score-edged-2004.aspx.

9. P. Boyer, *Religion Explained: The Evolutionary Origins of Religious Thought* (New York: Basic Books, 2001).

10. J. Bering, and D. Bjorklund, "Intuitive conceptions of dead agents' minds: The natural foundations of afterlife beliefs as phonomenological boundary," *Journal of Cognition and Culture* 2, (2004): 263-308.

11. N. Postman, *Technopoly: The Surrender of Culture to Technology* (New York: Vintage Books, 1992).

12. J. Barrett, et al., "When seeing is not believing: Children's understanding of humans' and nonhumans' use of background knowledge in interpreting visual displays," *Journal of Cognition and Culture* 3, (2003): 91–108.

13. J. Barrett, et al., "When seeing is not believing: Children's understanding of humans' and nonhumans' use of background knowledge in interpreting visual displays."

14. R. Hood, "Psychological strength and the report of intense religious experience."

15. R. Trigg, "Oxford study," Nov 25; 2016, 6:376   https:// www.telegraph.co.uk/news/politics/8510711/Belief-in-God-is-part-of-human-nature-Oxford-study.html.

16. T. Adams, "Spirituality, Religion, and Science," 2001, http:// easternhealingarts.com/Articles/SpititualityReligion. html.

17. S. Gibbens, "Are We Born Fearing Spiders and Snakes?" October 26, 2017 https://news.nationalgeographic. com/2017/10/infant-fear-phobia-science-snakes-video-spd/?user.testname=none.

18. S. Novella, "Hyperactive Agency Detection," March 2010, https://theness.com/neurologicablog/index.php/ hyperactive-agency-detection/.

19. E. Palermo, "The Origins of Religion: How Supernatural Beliefs Evolved," October 5, 2015, Live Science, https:// www.yahoo.com/news/origins-religion-supernatural-beliefs-evolved-173454622.html.

20. A. Spiegel, "Is Believing In God Evolutionarily Advantageous?" February 11, 2011, https://www.npr.org/ people/90889243/alix-spiegel/archive?date=2-28-2011.

21. K. Munoz, "Epigenetics: Will It Change the Way We Treat Disease?" August 16, 2017, https://draxe.com/epigenetics/.

22. M. Pember, "Trauma May Be Woven Into DNA of Native Americans," May 28, 2015, http://indiancountrytodaymedianetwork.com/trauma-may-be-woven-dna-native-americans-160508.

23. N. Vincent, et al., "Historical trauma as public narrative: A conceptual review of how history impacts present-day health," *Social Science & Medicine* 106 (2014): 128-136.

24. M. Marcello, "Historical Trauma and PTSD: The "Existential" versus the "Clinical," Psychiatry On-Line, POL.IT, (2002), http://www.psychiatryonline.it/ital/fromstates2e.htm.

25. M. Szyf and M. Meaney, "Epigenetics, DNA methylation, and chromatin modifying drugs," *Annu Rev Pharmacol Toxicol* 49, (2009):243-63.

26. T.Bottner,"It'sintheDNA:EpigeneticsandIntergenerational Trauma," 2017, https://wholebeinginstitute.com/dna-epigenetics-intergenerational/.

27. A. K. Willard, and A. Norenzayan, "The long-term psychological consequences of the Holocaust on survivors and their offspring," in R.L. Braham, ed. *The psychological perspective of the Holocaust and of its aftermath* (New York: Columbia University Press, 2017).

28. M. Marcello, "Historical Trauma and PTSD: The 'Existential' versus the 'Clinical'."

29. Dias, et al., "Epigenetic mechanisms underlying learning and the inheritance of learned behaviors," *Trends Neuroscience* 38, (2015): 96–107.

30. H. Brown, "What Really Happens In Our Brains When We Have Spiritual Experiences?" Dec 6, 2017, https://www.huffingtonpost.com/entry/science-behind-spiritual-experiences_n_4078519.

31. P. Urgesi, et al., "The spiritual brain: selective cortical lesions modulate human self-transcendence," Neuron 65, (2010): 309–319.

32. S. Harris, et al., "The neural correlates of religious and nonreligious belief," PLoS ONE 4, (2009).

33. B. Johnstonea, et al., "Right Parietal Lobe-Related "Selflessness" as the Neuropsychological Basis of Spiritual Transcendence," *International Journal of the Psychology of Religion,* 2012: https://www.sciencedaily.com/releases/2012/04/120419091223.htm.

34. L. Miller, et al., "Neural Correlates of Personalized Spiritual Experiences," *Cerebral Cortex* 102, (2018).

35. D. Newberg, and D'Aquili, *Neuroscience and Religion: Surveying the Field* (Macmillan Reference Gale, Cengage Learning, 2017) 200-210.

36. D. Newberg, and D'Aquili, *Neuroscience and Religion: Surveying the Field.*

37. D. Newberg, and D'Aquili, *Neuroscience and Religion: Surveying the Field.*

38. J. Taylor, *My Stroke of Insight* (New York, N.Y: Penquin Group, 2006).

39. J. Taylor, *My Stroke of Insight.*

40. H. Brown, "What Really Happens In Our Brains When We Have Spiritual Experiences?

41. M. A. Persinger, "The Neuropsychiatry of Paranormal Experiences," *Journal of Neuropsychiatry and Clinical Neuroscience* 13, (2001): 515.

42. D. Newberg, and D'Aquili, *Neuroscience and Religion: Surveying the Field.*

Chapter 6:
The Science of Unseen Forces

1. M. Beauregard, *Brain Wars* (New York, N.Y: Harper One, 2013).

2. D. Radin, *Entangled Minds*: *Extrasensory Experiences in a Quantum Reality* (New York, NY: Paraview, 2006).

3. D. Radin, "Exploring relationships between random physical events and mass human attention: Asking for whom the bell tolls," *Journal of Scientific Exploration* 16, (2002): 533-567.

4. D. Radin, "Testing nonlocal observation as a source of intuitive knowledge." (New York, NY: Jan-Feb. Explore, 2008).

5. A. Walia, "Why Nikola Tesla Was A Spiritual Mystic and Told The World To Study Non-Physical Phenomena," June 2, 2018, https://www.collective-evolution.com/2018/06/02/why-nikola-tesla-was-a-spiritual-mystic-told-the-world-to-study-non-physical-phenomena/.

6. F. Popp, "Principles of complementary medicine in terms of a suggested scientific basis," *Indian Journal of Experimental Biology* 46 (2008): 378-383.

7. F. Popp, Principles of complementary medicine in terms of a suggested scientific basis.

8. C. Swanson, *The Synchronized Universe: New Science of the Paranormal* (New York, N.Y: Poseidia Press, 2003).

9. C. Swanson, *The Synchronized Universe: New Science of the Paranormal*.

10. B. Payne, "The Spin Force a Collection of Articles and Experiments," February 2016, http://www. growingempowered.org/wp-content/uploads/2016/02/ The-Spin-Force-A-Collection-ofArticles-and-Experiments-2nd-Edition.pdf.

11. D.G. Yurth, "Torsion Field Mechanics," June 2017, www. clayandiron.com/news.jhtml?method=view&news. id=1509.

12. B. Payne, "The Biofield: A Different Type of Magnetism?" Nexus 15 (2008).

13. B. Payne, The Spin Force a Collection of Articles and Experiments.

14. C. Swanson, The Synchronized Universe: New Science of the Paranormal.

15. Gaia, "Dr. Nikolai Kozyrev and the Mystery of Torsion Fields," Dec 22, 2016 https://www.gaia.com/article/ mystery-of-torsion-fields.

16. C. Swanson, "The Torsion Field and the Aura," Subtle Energies and Energy Medicine Journal Archives 19, (2012). http://journals.sfu.ca/seemj/index.php/seemj/article/ view/425.

17. C. Swanson, "The Torsion Field and the Aura."

18. B. Murphy, "A Brief Overview of Torsion: The Key to a Theory of Everything - Including Consciousness?" March 5, 2012, http://blog.world-mysteries.com/science/ torsion-the-key-to-theory-of-everything/.

19. C. Swanson, "The Torsion Field and the Aura."

20. Gaia, "Dr. Nikolai Kozyrev and the Mystery of Torsion Fields."

21. M. Talbot, *The Holographic Universe* (London, UK: Harper Collins, 1991).

22. D. Yurth, "Torsion Field Mechanics."

23. B.T. Dotta, K.S.Saroka, and M.A.Persinger, "Support for Bókkon's biophoton hypothesis," *Neuroscience Letters* In press.

24. K. Kiser, "Torsion as a Force of the Universe - What's in it for Us? January, 12, 2012, https://fmbr.org/torsion-as-a-force-of-the-universe-kiser-jan12.

25. K. Kiser, "Torsion as a Force of the Universe - What's in it for Us?"

26. B. Payne, "The Biofield: A Different Type of Magnetism?" *Nexus* 15, (2008).

27. B. Payne, "The Spin Force A Collection of Articles and Experiments," February 2016, http://www. growingempowered.org/wp-content/uploads/2016/02/ The-Spin-Force-A-Collection-of-Articles-and-Experiments-2nd-Edition.pdf.

28. B. Rubik, "Biofield Science and Healing: History, Terminology, and Concepts," *Global advances in health and medicine,* 2015, https://www.semanticscholar. org/paper/Biofield-Science-and-Healing%3A-History%2C-Terminology%2C-Rubik-Muehsam/ b6f66c968cb2126be8d032a836519a8ab702a544.

29. J. Mossbridge, and D. Radin, "Psychology of Consciousness: Theory, Research, and Practice," *American Psychological Association* 5, (2018): 28.

30. The Rhine Institute, "What is Parapsychology," https:// www.rhine.org/what-we-do/parapsychology/what-is-parapsychology.html.

31. J. Klimo, "The Anomalous: A New Category of Diversity for Those with Non-Ordinary Experiences: The Care and Preservation of Private Experience and Beliefs," (1998): 345-356.

32. L. Dossey, "7 Billion Minds, or One?" October 24, 2013, https://www.huffingtonpost.com/dr-larry-dossey/one-mind_b_4158463.html 10/24/2013.

33. L. Dossey, *Healing words: the power of prayer and the practice of medicine* (San Francisco, Calif: Harper, 1993).

34. L. McTaggart, *The Field: The Quest for the Secret Force of the Universe* New York, N.Y.: (Harper Perennial, 2008).

35. L. Standish, et al., "Evidence of correlated functional MRI signals between distant human brains," *Altern Ther Health Med* 9, (2003):122-128.

36. K. Hearne, "Visually evoked responses and ESP," *J Soc Psychical Res* 49, (1977): 648-657.

37. E. Kelly, and J. Lenz, "EEG changes correlated with a remote stroboscopic stimulus: A preliminary study," in J. Morris, and W. Roll, *Research in Parapsychology* (NJ: Scarecrow Press; 1975).

38. D. Lloyd, "Objective events in the brain correlating with psychic phenomena," *New Horizons* 1, (1973): 69-758.

39. J. Millay, *Multidimensional Mind: Remote Viewing in Hyperspace* (Berkeley, CA: North Atlantic Books, 2000).

40. D, Orme-Johnson, M. Dillbeck, and R. Wallace, "Intersubject EEG coherence: is consciousness a field?" *Int J Neurosci* 16, (1982): 203-209.

41. J. Wackermann et al., "Correlations between brain electrical activities of two spatially separated human subjects," *Neurosci Letters* 336, (2003): 60-64.

42. L. Hendricks, W. Bengston, and J. Gunkelman, "The Healing Connection: EEG Harmonics, Entrainment, and Schumann's Resonances," *Journal of Scientific Exploration* 24, (2010): 655.

43. D. Radin, "Event-Related EEG Correlations between Isolated Human Subjects," *Journal of Alternative and Complementary Medicine* 10, (2004): 315.

44. D. Radin, "Unconscious Perception of Future Emotions: An Experiment in Presentiment," *Journal Scientific Exploration* 11, (1997): 163.

45. D. Radin, "Testing Nonlocal Observation as a Source of Intuitive Knowledge," *Explore* (2008): Jan-Feb.

46. R. Davis, *Life after Death: An Analysis of the Evidence* (Atglen, PA: Schiffer Publishing, 2017).

47. R. Dobrin, et al., "Experimental measurements of the human energy field," in *Psychoenergetic Systems: The Interface of Consciousness, Energy and Matter*, ed. S. Krippner (New York: Gordon and Breach, 1979) 227–230.

48. R. Dobrin, et al., Experimental measurements of the human energy field.

49. Applied Behavioral Analysis, "What is an Autistic Savant," https://www.appliedbehavioranalysisedu.org/what-is-an-autistic-savant/.

50. Daily Grail, "New Research Suggests Autistic Savants May Have Enhanced Telepathic Abilities," August 20, 2014, http://dailygrail.com/Mind-Mysteries/2014/8/.

51. Daily Grail, "New Research Suggests Autistic Savants May Have Enhanced Telepathic Abilities."

52. D. Powel, "The ESP Enigma: A Scientific Case for Understanding Psychic Phenomena," 2008, http://dianehennacypowell.com/evidence-telepathy-nonverbal-autistic-child/.

53. D. Powel, "The ESP Enigma: A Scientific Case for Understanding Psychic Phenomena."

54. K. Surprise, *Synchronicity: The Art of Coincidence, Choice, and Unlocking Your Mind* https://futurethinkers.org/kirby-surprise-synchronicity/.

55. K. Surprise, *Synchronicity: The Art of Coincidence, Choice, and Unlocking Your Mind.*

56. C.G. Jung, *Synchronicity an Acausal Connecting Principle* (Princeton, New Jersey: Bollingen Foundation-Princeton, 1969).

57. J. Ironmonger, *Coincidence: A Novel* (Harper Perennial, 2014).

58. C. Hardy, "Multilevel Webs Stretched Across Time," *Systems Research and Behavioral Science* 20, (2003): 201-215.

59. J. Butterfield, "The end of time?" *British Journal for the Philosophy of Science* 53, (2002): 289-330.

60. G. Musser, "Why Space and Time Might Be an Illusion," Dec 6, 2017 https://www.huffingtonpost.com/george-musser/space-time illusion_b_9703656.html04/26/2016.

61. J. Butterfield, "The end of time?"

62. G. Musser, "Why Space and Time Might Be an Illusion."

63. S. Paulson, "On reconciling atheism and meaning in the universe," *The Atlantic* (2012).

64. I. Barušs, "Meaning Fields: Meaning Beyond the Human as a Resolution of Boundary Problems Introduced by Nonlocality," *Edge Science* 35, (2018).

65. I. Barušs, "Meaning Fields: Meaning Beyond the Human as a Resolution of Boundary Problems Introduced by Nonlocality."

66. J. Butterfield, "The end of time?"

67. S. Olchover, "The End of Time New Quantum Theory Could Explain the Flow of Time," April 25, 2014, https://www.researchgate.net/publication/36443520 https://www.wired.com/2014/04/quantum-theory-flow-time/ 04.25.14.

68. H. Irwin, *An Introduction to Parapsychology* (Jefferson, NC: McFarlend and Company, 2003).

69. K. Murch, *Journal Physical Review Letters* 114, (2015): 403.

70. D. Bem, "Feeling the future: Experimental evidence for anomalous retroactive influences on cognition and affect," *Journal of Personality and Social Psychology* 100, (2011): 407–425.

71. D. Bem, "Feeling the future: Experimental evidence for anomalous retroactive influences on cognition and affect."

72. D. Radin, "Unconscious perception of future emotions: An experiment in presentiment," *J Sci Exploration* 11, (1997): 163–180.

73. D. Bierman, and D. Radin, "Anomalous anticipatory response on randomized future conditions," *Percept Mot Skills* 84, (1997): 689–690.

74. T. MacIsaac, "Neuroscientist discusses precognition—or 'mental time travel," https://nexusnewsfeed.com/article/consciousness/neuroscientist-discusses-precognition-or-mental-time-travel/.

75. D. Radin, "Unconscious perception of future emotions: An experiment in presentiment."

76. D. Radin, "Unconscious perception of future emotions: An experiment in presentiment."

77. D. Radin, "Predicting the unpredictable: 75 years of experimental evidence," *AIP Conference Proceedings* 1408, (2011): 204.

78. D. Radin, and A. Borges, "Intuition through time: What does the seer see?" *The Journal of Science and Healing* 5, (2009): 200 –211.

79. D. Radin, and A. Pierce, "Psi and psychophysiology," in E. Cardeña, J. Palmer, and D. Marcusson-Clavertz (Eds.), *Parapsychology: A handbook for the 21st century* (Jefferson, NC: McFarland, 2015).

80. M. Beauregard, *Brain Wars* (New York, N.Y.: HarperOne, 2012).

81. D. Bierman, and D. Radin, "Anomalous anticipatory response on randomized future conditions."

82. B. Libert, "Unconscious Cerebral Initiative and the Role of Conscious Will in Voluntary Action," *Behavioral and Brain Sciences* 8, (1985): 529.

83. R. Davis, *Life after Death: An Analysis of the Evidence.*

84. R. Davis, *Life after Death: An Analysis of the Evidence.*

85. J. Mossbridge et al., "Predictive physiological anticipation preceding seemingly unpredictable stimuli: A meta-analysis," *Frontiers in Psychology* 3, (2012): 390.

86. L. Dossey, "One Mind: How Are Individual Mind is a Part of a Greater Consciousness and Why it Matters," http://www.dosseydossey.com/larry/Larry_One_Mind_Twenty_Questions.pdf.

87. L. Hewitt, "Genius and the Akashic Records," June 7, 2015, https://www.historicmysteries.com/akashic-records/ Genius and the Akashic Records.

88. L. Hewitt, "Genius and the Akashic Records."

89. R. Smith, and J. Kounios, "Sudden insight: All-or-none processing revealed by speed-accuracy decomposition," Journal of Experimental Psychology: Learning, Memory, and Cognition 22, (1996): 1443–1462.

90. R. Smith, and J. Kounios, "Sudden insight: All-or-none processing revealed by speed-accuracy decomposition."

91. M. Beauregard, *Brain Wars*.

92. R. G. Jahn, "Correlations of Random Binary Sequences with Pre-stated Operator Intention: A Review of a 12-Year Program," Explore NY (2007): May-Jun.

93. D. Radin, "Predicting the unpredictable: 75 years of experimental evidence."

94. D. Radin, "Unconscious perception of future emotions: An experiment in presentiment."

95. D. Radin, "Predicting the unpredictable: 75 years of experimental evidence."

96. D. Radin, and A. Borges, "Intuition through time: What does the seer see?" *The Journal of Science and Healing* 5, (2009): 200 –211.

97. D. Bem, "Feeling the future: Experimental evidence for anomalous retroactive influences on cognition and affect."

98. R. G. Jahn, "Correlations of Random Binary Sequences with Pre-stated Operator Intention: A Review of a 12-Year Program."

99. J. Klimo, "The Anomalous: A New Category of Diversity for Those with Non-Ordinary Experiences: The Care and Preservation of Private Experience and Beliefs."

100. D. Radin, *The conscious universe: The scientific truth of psychic phenomena* (New York, NY: Harper, 1997).

101. A. Walia, "CIA Document Confirms Reality Of Humans With 'Special Abilities' Able To Do 'Impossible' Things," November 11, 2016, https://www.collective-evolution. com/2016/11/11/cia-document-confirms-reality-of-humans-with-special-abilities-able-to-do-impossible-things/.

102. E. Lazlo, "Science and Spirituality," *Syntropy* 3, (2005): 69-84, www.sintropia.it.

103. D. Radin, "Predicting the unpredictable: 75 years of experimental evidence."

104. R. G. Jahn, "Correlations of Random Binary Sequences with Pre-stated Operator Intention: A Review of a 12-Year Program."

105. R. Davis, *Life after Death: An Analysis of the Evidence.*

106. R. Davis, *Life after Death: An Analysis of the Evidence.*

107. P. van Lommel, "Non-local Consciousness A Concept Based on Scientific Research on Near-Death Experiences During Cardiac Arrest," *Journal of Consciousness Studies* 20, (2013): 1-2.

108. R. Davis, *Life after Death: An Analysis of the Evidence.*

109. R. Davis, *Life after Death: An Analysis of the Evidence.*

110. R. Davis, *Life after Death: An Analysis of the Evidence.*

111. R. Schild, and D. Leiter, "Black hole or MECO?: Decided by a Thin Luminous Ring Structure Deep within Quasar," *Journal of Cosmology* 6, (2010): 1400.

112. R. Davis, *Life after Death: An Analysis of the Evidence.*

113. Nelson, R. "Is the Global Mind Real?" Edge Science 1, (2009), 8.

Chapter 7
The Peak Experience: Another Reality, Psychopathology, or a Physiological Disorder?

1. World Health Organization, "Investing in Mental Health," 2003, http://www.who.int/mental_health/media/investing_mnh.pdf.

2. R. Pechey, and P. Halligan, "The prevalence of delusion-like beliefs relative to sociocultural beliefs in the general population," *Psychopathology* (2011): 106-115.

3. A. Newberg, et al., "The measurement of regional cerebral blood flow during the complex cognitive task of meditation: A preliminary SPECT study," *Psychiatry Research: Neuroimaging* 106, (2001):113–122.

4. A. Newberg, and J. Iversen, "The neural basis of the complex mental task of meditation: neurotransmitter and neurochemical considerations," *Med Hypotheses* 61, (2003): 282–291.

5. M. Alper, *The "God" part of the brain: Scientific interpretation of human spirituality and Go* (New York, NY: Rogue, 2001).

6. E. D'Aquili, and A. Newberg, *The mystical mind: Probing the biology of religious experience* (Minneapolis: Fortress Press, 1999).

7. E. D'Aquili, and A. Newberg, "The neuropsychology of aesthetic, spiritual, and mystical states," *Zygon* 35, (2000): 39-52.

8. E. Facco, and C. Agrillo, "Near-death experiences between science and prejudice," *Frontiers in Human Neuroscience* 4, (2012).

9. R. Urgesi, et al., "The spiritual brain: selective cortical lesions modulate human self-transcendence," *Neuron* 65, (2010): 309–319.

10. E. Facco, and C. Agrillo, "Near-death experiences between science and prejudice."

11. R. Siegel, "The psychology of life after death," *American Psychologist* 35, (1980): 911-931.

12. B. Spivak, et al., "Acute transient stress-induced hallucinations in soldiers," *British Journal of Psychology* 160, (1992): 412-414.

13. A. Grimby, "Bereavement among elderly people," *Acta Psychiatrica Scandinavia* 87, (1993): 72-80.

14. W. Reese, "The hallucinations of widowhood," *British Medical Journal* 210, (1971): 37-41.

15. H. Hecaen, and M. Albert, *Human Neuropsychology* (New York: John Wiley, 1978).

16. R. Joseph, *Neuropsychiatry, Neuropsychology, Clinical Neuroscience,* (Baltimore: Williams & Wilkins, 1996).

17. D'Acquili, and A. Newberg, *The Mystical Mind* (Minneapolis, MN: Fortress Press, 1999).

18. D'Acquili, and A. Newberg, "Religious and Mystical States: A Neuropsychological Model," *Zygon* 28, (1993): 251-266.

19. D'Acquili, and A. Newberg, "Religious and Mystical States: A Neuropsychological Model."

20. S. Harris, et al., "The neural correlates of religious and nonreligious belief," *PLoS ONE* 4, (2009).

21. E. Facco, and C. Agrillo, "Near-death experiences between science and prejudice."

22. S. Blackmore, "Near-death experiences," *J. R. Soc. Med* 89, (1996): 73–76.

23. R. Davis, *Life after Death: An Analysis of the Evidence* (Atglen, PA: Schiffer Publishing, 2017).

24. R. Davis, *Life after Death: An Analysis of the Evidence.*

25. R. Davis, *Life after Death: An Analysis of the Evidence.*

26. R. Davis, *Life after Death: An Analysis of the Evidence.*

27. M. Thonnard et al., "Characteristics of near-death experiences memories as compared to real and imagined events memories," PLoS ONE 8 (2013).

28. R. Davis, *Life after Death: An Analysis of the Evidence.*

29. R. Davis, *Life after Death: An Analysis of the Evidence.*

30. R. Davis, *Life after Death: An Analysis of the Evidence.*

31. M. Thonnard et al., "Characteristics of near-death experiences memories as compared to real and imagined events memories."

32. J. Borjigin, et al., "Surge of neurophysiological coherence and connectivity in the dying brain," *Proc. Natl. Acad. Sci.* 10, (2013): 14432–14437.

33. J. Braithwaite, "Towards a cognitive neuroscience of the dying brain," *Skeptic* 21, (2008): 16.

34. A. Bardy, "Near death experiences (commentary)," *Lancet* 359, (2002): 2116.

35. M. Thonnard et al., "Characteristics of near-death experiences memories as compared to real and imagined events memories."

36. C. Agrillo, "Near-death experience: out-of-body and out-of-brain?" *Rev. Gen. Psychol.* 15, (2011): 1–10.

37. C. Nosek, "End-of-life dreams and visions: a qualitative perspective from hospice patients," *Am. J. Hosp. Palliat. Care* (2014).

38. P. van Lommel. *Consciousness Beyond Life. The Science of the Near-Death Experience* (New York, NY: Harper Collins, 2010).

39. P. van Lommel, "Near-Death Experiences: The Experience of the Self as Real and Not As An Illusion," *Ann. N.Y. Acad. Sci* 19 (2011).

40. E. F. Kelly, *Irreducible Mind: Toward a Psychology for the 21st Century* (Lanham, MD: Rowman & Littlefield, 2007).

41. S. Parnia, and P. Fenwick, "Near Death Experiences in Cardiac Arrest," *Resuscitation* 52, (2002): 5.

42. E. Facco, and C. Agrillo, "Near-death experiences between science and prejudice."

43. E. Facco, and C. Agrillo, "Near-death experiences between science and prejudice."

44. C. Martial, et al., "Fantasy proneness correlates with the intensity of near-death experience," *Front. Psychiatry* 9, (2018): 190.

45. E. Studerus, et al., "Prediction of psilocybin response in healthy volunteers," *PLoS One* 7, (2012).

46. R. Carhart-Harris, "The entropic brain – Revisited," *Neuropharmacology* 10, (2018): 1016.

47. T. Carbonaro et al., "Survey study of challenging experiences after ingesting psilocybin mushrooms: Acute and enduring positive and negative consequences," *J Psychopharmacology* 12, (2016):1268-1278.

48. R. Carhart-Harris, The entropic brain – Revisited.

49. B. Greyson, "Incidence and correlates of near-death experiences in a cardiac care unit," *Gen. Hosp. Psychiatry* 25, (2003): 269–276.

50. R. Carhart-Harris, "The entropic brain – Revisited."

51. A. Kellehear, "Culture, biology, and the near-death experience. A reappraisal," *J. Nerv. Ment. Disorders* 181, (1993): 148–156.

52. A. Kellehear, et al., "The absence of tunnel sensations in near-death experiences from India" *J. Near Death Studies* 13, (1994): 109–113.

53. R. Joseph, "The Limbic System and the Soul," *Zygon* 66, (2003): 105.

54. R. Joseph, "The Limbic System and the Soul."

55. R. Joseph, "Quantum physics and the Multiplicity of Mind," *Journal of Cosmology* 6, (2009): 641.

56. R. Saxe, "People thinking about thinking people. The role of the temporo-parietal junction in "theory of mind," *Neuroimage* 19, (2003): 1835-42.

57. M. Persinger, *Neurophysiological Bases of God Beliefs* (Westport, CT. Praeger, 1987).

58. R. Joseph, "Frontal lobe psychopathology: Mania, depression, aphasia, confabulation, catatonia, perseveration, obsessive compulsions, schizophrenia," *Journal of Psychiatry* 62, (1999): 138-172.

59. H. Irwin, *Flight of Mind: A Psychological Study of the Out-Of-Body Experience* (Metuchen, NJ: Scarecrow Press, 1985).

60. J. Sellers, "Out-of-Body Experience: Review and a Case Study," *Journal of Consciousness Exploration and Research.* 8, (2017): 686-708.

61. O. Blanke, et al., "Out-of-body experience and autoscopy of neurological origin," *Brain* 127, (2004): 243–258.

62. W. Penfield, *The Mystery of the Mind: a Critical Study of Consciousness and the Human Brain* (Princeton, NJ: Princeton University Press, 1975).

63. W. Penfield, *The Mystery of the Mind: a Critical Study of Consciousness and the Human Brain.*

64. P. MacLean, *The Evolution of the Triune Brain* (New York: Plenum, 1990).

65. D. Bear, "Temporal lobe epilepsy: A sydnrome of sensory-limbic hyperconnexion," *Cortex* 15, (1979): 357-384.

66. P. Gloor, *The Temporal Lobes and Limbic System* (Oxford University Press. New York. Horowitz, 1997).

67. M. J., Adams, and B. Rutkin, "Visual imagery on brain stimulation." *Archives of General Psychiatry* 19, (1968): 469-486.

68. P. MacLean, *The Evolution of the Triune Brain* (New York, Plenum, 1990).

69. W. Penfield, and P. Perot, "The brains record of auditory and visual experience," *Brain* 86, (1963): 595-695.

70. M. Trimble, *The psychoses of epilepsy* (New York, Raven Press, 1991).

71. S. Weingarten, et al., "The relationship of hallucinations to depth structures of the temporal lobe," *Acta Neurochirugica* 24, (1977): 199-216.

72. O. Devinsky, and G. Lai, "Spirituality and religion in epilepsy," *Epilepsy Behavior* 12, (2008): 636-43.

73. R. Carhart-Harris, "The entropic brain – Revisited."

74. J. Sellers, "Out-of-Body Experience: Review and a Case Study."

75. J. Sellers, "Out-of-Body Experience: Review and a Case Study."

76. J. Braithwaite, et al., "Cognitive correlates of the spontaneous out-of-body experience (OBE) in the psychologically normal population: evidence for an increased role of temporal-lobe instability, body-distortion processing, and impairments in own-body transformations," *Cortex* 47, (2011): 839-53 Epub 2010 May 21.

77. J. Sellers, "Out-of-Body Experience: Review and a Case Study."

78. K. Nelson, "Are Out-of-Body Experiences Always Spiritual? How we interpret our out-of-body experiences," Nov 03, 2010, https://www.psychologytoday.com/us/blog/the-spiritual-doorway-in-the-brain/201011/are-out-body-experiences-always-spiritual.

79. F. Waters, and C. Fernyhough, "Hallucinations: A Systematic Review of Points of Similarity and Difference Across Diagnostic Classes," *Schizophr Bull.* 43, (2016): 32–43.

80. J. Sellers, "Out-of-Body Experience: Review and a Case Study."

81. F. Waters, and C. Fernyhough, "Hallucinations: A Systematic Review of Points of Similarity and Difference Across Diagnostic Classes."

82. F. Waters et al., "Mind and spirit: hypnagogia and religious experience," *Science Daily*, April 5, 2018. https://www.sciencedaily.com/releases/2018/06/180601170056.htm.

83. A. Salleh, "What happens in our brains when we hallucinate?" March 2016, https://www.abc.net.au/news/science/2016-03-14/what-happens-in-our-brains-when-we-hallucinate/6939874.

84. K. Nelson, "Are Out-of-Body Experiences Always Spiritual? How we interpret our out-of-body experiences," Nov 03, 2010 K. Nelson, "Are Out-of-Body Experiences Always Spiritual? How we interpret our out-of-body experiences.

85. K. Nelson, "Are Out-of-Body Experiences Always Spiritual? How we interpret our out-of-body experiences."

86. K. Nelson, "Are Out-of-Body Experiences Always Spiritual? How we interpret our out-of-body experiences."

87. https://www.psychologytoday.com/us/blog/the-spiritual-doorway-in-the-brain/201011/are-out-body-experiences-always-spiritual.

88. K. Nelson, "Are Out-of-Body Experiences Always Spiritual? How we interpret our out-of-body experiences."

89. K. Nelson, "Are Out-of-Body Experiences Always Spiritual? How we interpret our out-of-body experiences."

90. K. Nelson, et al., "Does the arousal system contribute to near death experience?" *Neurology* 66, (2006): 1003–9.

91. K. Nelson, Are Out-of-Body Experiences Always Spiritual? How we interpret our out-of-body experiences.

92. J. Cheyne, S. Rueffer and I. Newby-Clark, "Hypnagogic and Hypnopompic Hallucinations during Sleep Paralysis: Neurological and Cultural Construction of the Night-Mare," *Conscious Cognition* 8, (1999): 319.

93. Science Daily, "People With Near Death Experiences Can Differ In Sleep-Wake Control," www.sciencedaily.com/releases/2006/04/060417110256.htm.

94. American Psychiatric Association, *Diagnostic and Statistical Manual of Mental Disorders (DSM-5), Fifth Edition* (2013).

95. S. Grof and C. Grof, *Spiritual Emergency: When Personal Transformation Becomes a Crisis* (New York, N.Y.: TarcherPerigee, 1989).

96. American Psychiatric Association, *Diagnostic and Statistical Manual of Mental Disorders (DSM-5), Fifth Edition.*

97. American Psychiatric Association, *Diagnostic and Statistical Manual of Mental Disorders (DSM-5), Fifth Edition.*

98. American Psychiatric Association, *Diagnostic and Statistical Manual of Mental Disorders (DSM-5), Fifth Edition.*

99. J. Goll, *Hearing God* (Ventura, CA: Regal Pub, 2008).

100. J. Goll, *Hearing God.*

101. J. Goll, *Hearing God.*

102. D'Acquili, and A. Newberg, "Religious and Mystical States: A Neuropsychological Model."

Chapter 8:
Connecting the Dots: A New Paradigm Shift

1. F. Crick, and C. Koch, "The Hidden Mind," *Scientific American* 2002, http://people.brandeis.edu/~teuber/theproblem.pdf.

2. The Human Radio, "Wholeness and the implicate order," November 28, 2016, https://www.thehumanradio.org/blog/wholeness-and-the-implicate-order.

3. B. Doctrine, "*The Basics of Philosophy*," https://www.philosophybasics.com/branch_instrumentalism.html.

4. B. Doctrine, *The Basics of Philosophy*.

5. M. Woollacott, *Infinite Awareness: The Awakening of a Scientific Mind* (New York, N.Y.: Rowman & Littlefield Publishers, 2015).

6. M. Woollacott, *Infinite Awareness: The Awakening of a Scientific Mind*.

7. J. Taylor, *My Stroke of Insight* (New York, N.Y.: Penguin Publishing, 2006).

8. J. Taylor, *My Stroke of Insight*.

9. J. Taylor, *My Stroke of Insight*.

10. PSI Encyclopedia, "Terminal Lucidity," https://psi-encyclopedia.spr.ac.uk/articles/terminal-lucidity.

11. M. Nahm, "Terminal lucidity in people with mental illness and other mental disability: An overview and implications for possible explanatory models," *Journal of Near-Death Studies* 28, (2009): 87-106.

12. M. Nahm, "Reflections on the context of near-death experiences," *Journal of Scientific Exploration* 25, (2011): 453-478.

13. M. Nahm, et al., "Terminal lucidity: A review and a case collection," *Archives of Gerontology and Geriatrics* 55, (2012): 138-142.

14. M. Woollacott, *Infinite Awareness: The Awakening of a Scientific Mind.*

15. J. Taylor, *My Stroke of Insight.*

16. M. Woollacott, *Infinite Awareness: The Awakening of a Scientific Mind.*

17. M. Planck, "Science Quotes by Max Planck," https://todayinsci.com/P/Planck_Max/PlanckMax-Quotations.htm.

18. The Human Radio, "Wholeness and the implicate order."

19. D. Bohm, *The Undivided Universe* (New York, N.Y.: Routledge 1993).

20. D. Bohm, *The Undivided Universe.*

21. Science Daily, "Dark Matter And Dark Energy Make Up 95 Percent Of Universe, Detailed Measurements Reveal," November 3, 2009, https://www.sciencedaily.com/releases/2009/11/091102121644.htm.

22. Omni Magazine, "Candace Pert on Molecules of Emotion," October 12, 2017, http://omnimagazine.com/interview-candace-pert-molecules-emotion/.

23. C. Swanson, *The Synchronized Universe: New Science of the Paranormal* (New York, N.Y: Poseidia Press, 2003).

24. C. Swanson, *The Synchronized Universe: New Science of the Paranormal.*

25. Quanta Magazine, "Quantum Phenomena of Biological Systems as Documented by Biophotonics," http://quantmag.ppole.ru/Articles/Quo_Vadis_Quantum_Mechanics.pdf#.

26. F. Popp, and Y. Yan, "Delayed luminescence of biological systems in terms of coherent states," *Phys. Letters* 293, (2002): 93.

27. F. Popp, "Principles of complementary medicine in terms of a suggested scientific basis," *Indian Journal of Experimental Biology* 46, (2008): 378-383.

28. L. Smolin, *Time reborn: From the crisis in physics to the future of the universe* (Toronto: Alfred A. Knopf Canada, 2013).

29. I. Baruss, "Meaning Fields: Meaning Beyond the Human as a Resolution of Boundary Problems Introduced by Nonlocality," *Edge Science* 35, (2018).

30. C. Swanson, *The Synchronized Universe: New Science of the Paranormal*.

31. E. Laszlo, *The Connectivity Hypothesis. Foundations of an Integral Science of Quantum, Cosmos, Life, and Consciousness* (Albany, New York: SUNY Press, 2003).

32. E. Laszlo, *Science and the Akashic Field. An integral theory of everything* (Rochester, VT: Inner Traditions International, 2004).

33. D. Bohm, *Wholeness and the implicate order* (Boston, MA: Routledge, 1980).

34. The Human Radio, "Wholeness and the implicate order."

35. R. Davis, Life after Death: *An Analysis of the Evidence* (Atglen, PA: Schiffer Publishing, 2017).

36. R. Davis, *The UFO Phenomena: Should I Believe?* (Atglen, PA: Schiffer Publishing, 2015).

37. W. Broad, "Even in death Carl sagan's influence is still cosmic," New York Times, December 2012, https://www.nytimes.com/1998/12/01/science/even-in-death-carl-sagan-s-influence-is-still-cosmic.html.

38. R. Hernandez, R. Davis, R. Scalpone, and R. Schild, "A Study on Reported Unidentified Aerial Phenomena and Associated Contact with Non-Human Intelligence," *Journal of Scientific Exploration* 32, (2018): 298–348.

39. R. Hernandez, R. Davis, R. Scalpone, and R. Schild, "A Study on Reported Unidentified Aerial Phenomena and Associated Contact with Non-Human Intelligence."

40. R. Hernandez, R. Davis, R. Scalpone, and R. Schild, "A Study on Reported Unidentified Aerial Phenomena and Associated Contact with Non-Human Intelligence."

41. G. Eghigian, "How UFO reports change with technology," Zócalo Public Square smithsonian.com, February 1, 2018 https://www.smithsonianmag.com/history/how-ufo-reports-change-with-technology-times-180968011/#7pFF pOjfyHgZG8C4.99.

42. S. Novella, "UFOs: The Psychocultural Hypothesis," October 2000, https://theness.com/index.php/ufos-the-psychocultural-hypothesis/.

43. C. French, "Close encounters of the psychological kind," The Psychologist, October 2015, https://thepsychologist. bps.org.uk/volume-28/october-2015/close-encounters-psychological-kind.

44. G. Eghigian, "How UFO reports change with technology."

45. C. French, "Close encounters of the psychological kind."

46. C. French, "Close encounters of the psychological kind."

47. J. Caravaca, "The Distortion Theory," 2018, http://caravaca102.blogspot.com/.

48. J. Caravaca, "The Distortion Theory."

49. J. Caravaca, "The Distortion Theory."

50. R. Davis, *Life after Death: An Analysis of the Evidence.*

51. R. Davis, *The UFO Phenomena: Should I Believe?*

52. R. Davis, *The UFO Phenomena: Should I Believe?*

53. R. Davis, *Life after Death: An Analysis of the Evidence.*

54. P. Tressoldi, "Extraordinary claims require extraordinary evidence: the case of non-local perception, a classical and Bayesian review of evidences," *Frontiers in Psychology* June 2011, https://www.goodreads.com/quotes/139502-the-day-science-begins-to-study-non-physical-phenomena-it-will.

55. F. DePasquale, personal communication.

ABOUT THE AUTHOR

Dr. Robert Davis is an internationally recognized scientist in his field. He graduated with a PhD in sensory neuroscience from the Ohio State University and served as a professor at the State University of New York for over 30 years. Davis has published over 60 articles in scholarly journals, lectured at numerous national and international conferences, and was awarded major grants by scientific organizations to fund research in the neurosciences.

He is the author of two popular books: *The UFO Phenomenon: Should I Believe?* and *Life after Death: An Analysis of the Evidence.* He has discussed his work at conferences throughout the world and has appeared on many podcast and radio shows.

His website is www.Bobdavisspeaks.com.

Made in the USA
Middletown, DE
15 June 2023

32592680R00189